Scaling Enterprise Solutions with Large Language Models

Comprehensive End-to-End Generative AI Solutions for Production-Grade Enterprise Solutions

Arindam Ganguly

Scaling Enterprise Solutions with Large Language Models: Comprehensive End-to-End Generative AI Solutions for Production-Grade Enterprise Solutions

Arindam Ganguly
Howrah, West Bengal, India

ISBN-13 (pbk): 979-8-8688-1153-1 ISBN-13 (electronic): 979-8-8688-1154-8
https://doi.org/10.1007/979-8-8688-1154-8

Managing Director, Apress Media LLC: Welmoed Spahr
Acquisitions Editor: Aditee Mirashi
Desk Editor: James Markham
Editorial Project Manager: Jacob Shmulewitz
Copy Editor: Kezia Endsley

Distributed to the book trade worldwide by Springer Science+Business Media New York, 1 New York Plaza, New York, NY 10004. Phone 1-800-SPRINGER, fax (201) 348-4505, e-mail orders-ny@springer-sbm.com, or visit www.springeronline.com. Apress Media, LLC is a Delaware LLC and the sole member (owner) is Springer Science + Business Media Finance Inc (SSBM Finance Inc). SSBM Finance Inc is a **Delaware** corporation.

For information on translations, please e-mail booktranslations@springernature.com; for reprint, paperback, or audio rights, please e-mail bookpermissions@springernature.com.

Apress titles may be purchased in bulk for academic, corporate, or promotional use. eBook versions and licenses are also available for most titles. For more information, reference our Print and eBook Bulk Sales web page at http://www.apress.com/bulk-sales.

Any source code or other supplementary material referenced by the author in this book is available to readers on GitHub. For more detailed information, please visit https://www.apress.com/gp/services/source-code.

If disposing of this product, please recycle the paper

*Dedicated to my better half, Sugandha Ghosh,
and to my mother*

Table of Contents

About the Author

Arindam Ganguly is an experienced data scientist at a leading multi-national software service firm, where he is responsible for developing and designing intelligent solutions by leveraging his expertise in AI and data analytics. He has over nine years of experience delivering enterprise products and applications and has proven skillsets in developing and managing a number of software products with various technical stacks.

Arindam also is well-versed in developing automation and hyper-automation solutions that leverage automated workflow engines and integrating them with AI. Additionally, he is the author of *Build and Deploy Machine Learning Solutions Using IBM Watson*, which teaches readers how to build AI applications using the popular IBM Watson toolkit.

About the Technical Reviewer

 **Varunsaagar Saravanan** is an experienced AI/ML engineer specializing in Generative AI, Large Language Models, and NLP. With over six years of experience, he has contributed to groundbreaking AI solutions across the media, entertainment, and e-governance sectors. Recognized for award-winning innovations like the *ePaarvai AI Cataract Application* and his leadership in AI-driven local news broadcasting, Varunsaagar has published research and mentored teams in AI strategy. His work integrates cutting-edge AI techniques into impactful, scalable products, driving transformation and innovation.

Acknowledgments

This book would not be possible without the constant support of my partner, Sugandha Ghosh. There were many times when she pushed me to complete the book when I thought it was not within me to do so. A big hug and a thanks to my mother, Moli Ganguly, for always putting up with me when I'm too busy working and writing and not being able to give her the time she deserves. It would not be just if I didn't mention my childhood pal, Dipanjan Bosu, for being on my side when I needed motivation.

A lot of this book is derived from public documentation available on various frameworks, including LangChain and LangGraph. The Scikit-Learn and OpenAI documentation are worth mentioning here, as most of the book relies on them.

Last, but not the least, a big thanks to the team at Apress, especially Aditee and Shobana, for helping me during the project.

Introduction

It will not be long before the world adapts AI into daily life for even the simple things. The information industry will be overwhelmed with the demands of consumers. Many AI enthusiasts and self-proclaimed experts have good knowledge of certain parts of AI, but they usually fail when attempting to put all these concepts together.

I had been a long-term enthusiast when AI was still a buzzword and the information age was gearing up for Big Data. I have seen my colleagues and seniors struggle to manage large datasets, let alone analyze and play around with them.

After Big Data was sorted with technologies such as Hadoop and Spark, and machine learning was established using Scikit-Learn, anticipation ran wild with the kinds of opportunities it could bring to the market. Developers soon realized that, although these AI techniques are good tools for solving smaller isolated problems, there was no way to marry them together to create a large enterprise application. Soon interest dropped, and AI became dormant in areas dealing with large scale applications.

I have seen some of the biggest players throw away machine learning just because it couldn't address these real-world datasets.

There are two types of people working with AI—the scientists who give their heart and soul in bettering the algorithms and the practitioners who try to use these algorithms in the real world. Although it was going good for the scientists, the constant setbacks of the practitioners led the AI industry to a halt—that is, until the introduction of the Transformers architecture. The world quickly saw the inception of Generative AI and LLMs. Suddenly, there was an overwhelming demand for embedding AI into these applications. But again, practitioners realized the struggles of infusing Generative AI into large-scale enterprise applications.

During some very tough months, the AI practitioner community came up with techniques to use the best of ML and Generative AI in real-world, large-scale applications and data. This is when I realized the necessity to author a book to spread the word that MLOps, Gen AI, and data engineering can carefully coexist and create wonderful additions to non-intelligent large-scale enterprise applications.

This book follows a structured approach, where a practitioner can relate to the struggle and an enthusiast who has perfected their AI skills is introduced to the real-world struggle of putting their skills into place for large applications and datasets. This book introduces AI and Generative AI concepts and explains ways to infuse them into applications to run them in production. I hope this book will be a revelation into the tricks and techniques needed to set you apart in the world of AI.

CHAPTER 1

Machine Learning Primer

The world has gone through a lot of revolutions since the dawn of time. For example, during the stone age, humans invented powerful tools for basic survival (such as the wheel). With the advent of city life, humans started embedding structures into all forms of work, and this lead to the industrial revolution. One of the biggest revolutions taking place now is called the artificial intelligence (AI) revolution.

Although it may seem intuitive from a 30,000-foot level, the current advancements are products of multiple waves of AI inventions, starting from the first Turing machine concept. To give you a better understanding of machine learning (ML), this chapter provides an overview of the subject.

The Origins of Machine Learning

According to Wikipedia, "The term machine learning was coined in 1959 by Arthur Samuel, an IBM employee and pioneer in the field of computer gaming and artificial intelligence. The synonym self-teaching computers was also used in this time period." To understand this, consider the difference between traditional problem solving and machine learning (see Figure 1-1).

© Arindam Ganguly 2025
A. Ganguly, *Scaling Enterprise Solutions with Large Language Models*,
https://doi.org/10.1007/979-8-8688-1154-8_1

Problem solving has been an inherent human skill since the beginning of time. Problem-solving methods were put into structures in the form of algorithms. With the advent of computers, algorithms could be programmed into computers and solve complex problems flawlessly. These algorithms can be structured into computers as procedural or functional programming. Procedural programming takes each step one by one and uses iterations and conditions in a monolithic structure. On the other hand, functional programming uses the concept of mathematical functions to break a problem down into smaller problems and arrive at a final solution. With the advancement of time, more problem-solving skills have come to existence, but the basic theory remains the same. Given a set of data as the input and a set of rules, the outcome is a set of outputs.

These problem-solving methods work best when there is a predefined set of rules or a known set or path to follow. When the ruleset is not known but the desired output is known, the input and output is used to create a set of rules. In other words, the machine tries to learn a rule (or pattern), in order to produce the known output as accurately as possible.

Machine learning is an application of statistics. In other words, it is the study of statistical inference. Hence, all the machine learning algorithms are derived from various statistical inference techniques.

The following sections look at some of the popular machine learning algorithms.

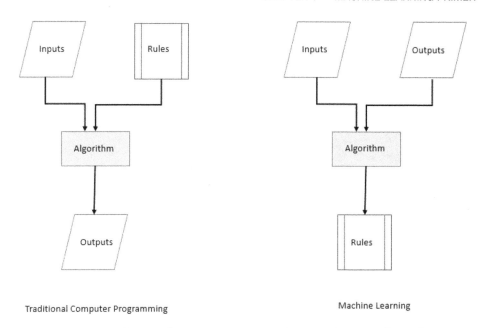

Figure 1-1. *Traditional computer programming vs machine learning*

Linear Regression

Linear regression (see Figure 1-2) is one of the most popular and intuitive machine learning algorithms. It assumes that the dataset is linearly shaped and hence tries to use a linear line equation on the dataset.

$$Y = WX + b$$

3

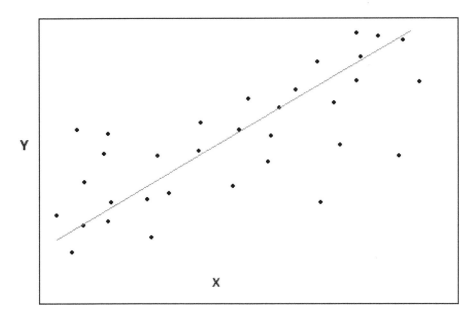

Figure 1-2. *Linear regression*

The task of the machine learning algorithm is to figure out W and b, given X is the set of inputs and Y is the set of outputs. Since there is no fixed rule, the algorithm iterates with some initial values of W and b, producing new values of Y (say Y') and X (say X') until the differences between Y and Y' and X and X' are so small that they can be ignored.

Although this might seem easy, the detailed math behind it is very complex. But developers need not worry so much about the mathematical intricacies, because Python many packages to abstract all the complexities behind single lines of code.

Python is the most popular language choice for data scientists and machine learning engineers. The most popular package for traditional machine learning algorithms is Scikit-Learn (see `https://scikit-learn.org`).

Scikit-Learn can help you develop a simple linear regression with just four lines of code:

```
from sklearn import datasets, linear_model

X, y = datasets.load_diabetes(return_X_y=True)

X = X[:,8].reshape(-1,1)

lr = linear_model.LinearRegression()

lr.fit( X, y )
```

This code uses the diabetes dataset available in the Scikit-Learn datasets.

Note the line X = X[:,8].reshape(-1,1).

It works in two steps:

1. It takes only the eighth column of data. If you want to see other columns instead, you can run the following Python code and include the name of those columns:

```
db = datasets.load_diabetes()
print(db.feature_names)
```

2. The second step is reshaping the datasets. Since you are only taking one column out of the complete matrix, it is just one row. Hence the X matrix becomes a one-dimensional array. But linear regression expects data in two-dimensional format. Hence it is necessary to convert an array of type [a1,a2,a3,...] to [[a1],[a2],[a3],...]. Reshaping to (-1,1) does this trick. -1 in reshape tells Python to keep the length as it is. Hence reshaping from (n) to (-1,1) means reshaping from (n) to (n,1).

Once the regression is complete, you can generate sample predictions using the following code:

```
sample_preds = lr.predict( X )
```

The linear regression algorithm uses gradient descent, which uses a loss function to iteratively check how close the real output is to the predicted output. It does this using derivatives of the weights and biases (the W in the linear regression and b, respectively).

The code is in the GitHub repository for the book SimpleLR.ipynb.

Although the code for linear regression is just a single line, machine learning mostly comprises a lot of phases apart from these algorithms, which I discuss separately in consecutive chapters.

Let's look at some of the other algorithms and see how their Scikit-Learn implementations look.

Decision Tree

There are a lot of complex techniques to track what is going on inside the algorithms. Among all of the machine learning algorithms, decision tree is one of the most intuitive. Some machine learning algorithms, such as the deep learning algorithms, are black boxes in terms of interpretability.

A decision tree works by breaking down the features and their values into a tree so it can reach a decision on the value of the outcome. As with other algorithms, Scikit-Learn helps you use this algorithm in just a few lines of code:

```
from sklearn.datasets import load_iris
from sklearn.tree import DecisionTreeClassifier

iris = load_iris()
X, y = iris.data, iris.target
clf = DecisionTreeClassifier()
clf = clf.fit(X, y)
```

The dataset used is the Iris dataset, which uses Sepal Length, Sepal Width, Petal Length, and Petal Width to predict the type of iris—Setosa, Versicolor, or Virginica.

To see how the decision tree fits on the dataset, you can use this code:

```
from sklearn import tree
tree.plot_tree(clf)
```

The output is shown in Figure 1-3.

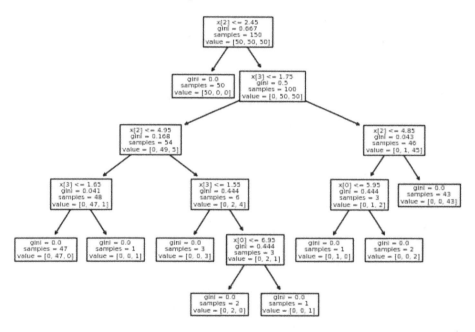

Figure 1-3. *Decision tree classifier on the Iris dataset*

Using this visualization, you can clearly see how the algorithm fits the dataset in the form of a tree. The algorithm to form the tree lies in the algorithm it uses to break down a node. There has been a lot of research into coming up with ways to form the tree. One such way is CART (Classification And Regression Tree), which uses a concept known as impurity or more technically, Gini impurity.

A Gini impurity is calculated from the number of elements of each category that exists in a node versus the total number of elements in the node. For instance, in Figure 1-3, if you focus on the topmost node in the figure, Gini=0.667 and the number of samples is [50,50,50], all the categories are of equal length, this is how we set the dataset to begin training so as to start with a balanced dataset. The formula to calculate Gini is as follows

$$\text{Gini} = 1 - \sum(\text{cat}_i/\text{total number of samples})^2$$

where cat_i is the number of data samples in the ith category.

Assume that the decision tree algorithm wants to split the node into two based on a certain column and condition. The [column j]<=x value, which leads to m_left items in the left node after the split and m_right items in the right node after the split. The CART algorithm starts calculating a cost using this formula:

$$\frac{m\_left}{m}Gini(left) + \frac{m\_right}{m}Gini(right)$$

where m is the total number of elements, *Gini(left)* is the Gini impurity of the left node, and Gini(right) is the Gini impurity at the right node. The CART algorithm will then employ its optimization technique so that it can find a split condition with most minimum cost.

It does this recursively until either the Gini impurity is zero or it reaches the maximum depth of the tree. The maximum depth can be specified by the hyperparameter called max_depth, which you can pass in the DecisionTreeClassifier constructor as follows:

```
clf = DecisionTreeClassifier(max_depth=5)
```

This line of code ensures that the number of levels of the tree does not cross 5.

Other hyperparameters you can use are min_samples_leaf and min_samples_split, which restrict the tree to split only into a certain number of nodes.

You can also recursively tune and test these hyperparameters to find your best fit by using grid search, which I discuss in an upcoming chapter.

There are also techniques—such as ID3 and C4.5—which you can check out.

Although CART is a good enough algorithm to use, you can further optimize it using hyperparameters such as the following:

```
max_depth : max_depth resi
```

There are numerous algorithms that are used by developers, some of the most popular ones are:

K-Nearest Neighbors

Support Vector Machines

PCA

Discussing all of them is out of the scope of this book. Scikit-Learn's official website is a wonderful place to start digging.

Ensemble Methods

There has been continuous innovation in the field of data science and with data scientists developing various machine learning algorithms with every passing day, there is a new machine learning algorithm or a new technique involving them just to make predictions better. It is similar to finding a new software developer everyday just to make your organization work a little better. But what if you could combine the best of the lot to get more accurate predictions, surpassing the individual algorithms!

Ensemble learning deals with taking one or multiple such algorithms and combining them to get a better result than the individual ones. The idea behind ensemble learning is to leverage the idea behind the "wisdom of the crowd," which says that collective opinion is more accurate than any one individual.

There are various ensemble learning techniques in which ensemble learning can be achieved that this section briefly touches on.

The Case of the Late Night Burglar

Assume for this example that your home was burgled and the police have two suspects. Your neighbors claim to have seen a man in your premises and they have been called in for identification.

If you try to map this analogy using machine learning, the task is a classification task and it chooses between two classes—the two suspects. Your neighbors are your machine learning algorithms trying to match the suspects with the burglar they spotted from far in the dark on the basis of body height and structure (which are the features that your algorithms will consume).

Your neighbors may have been from various age groups and staying at various locations around your house. Some of your neighbors were in front of your house, whereas others were a bit farther away. These factors determine the accuracy of the neighbors in determining who is the real perpetrator.

Voting Classifier

One of the best ways to discern with certain precision who the real burglar is is to let the neighbors predict it and ask them to score their confidence levels. Suppose you get the following table from the neighbors' guesses, as shown in Figure 1-4.

Neighbor	Prediction	Confidence Score (out of 100)	House Location
Neighbor 1	Suspect 1	78	next building to the left
Neighbor 2	Suspect 2	46	next building to the right
Neighbor 3	Suspect 2	90	next to next building to the left
Neighbor 4	Suspect 1	83	right in front of your building
Neighbor 5	Suspect 1	51	diagonal to your house

Figure 1-4. *Neighbor's predictions*

You can employ a private detective to analyze the situation or you can employ your data science skill and try to arrive at a solution using the voting classifier technique.

To use a voting classifier, you take an aggregate of the scores for each suspect, as shown here:

Score for Suspect 1 = (78+83+51)/3 = 70.67

Score for Suspect 2 = (46+90)/2 = 68

Using this technique, Suspect 1 seems to be the legit perpetrator.

The voting classifier uses multiple predictors (ML algorithms such as decision tree, SVM, and so on) to draw predictions and then uses the scores of those predictions to aggregate and determine the class based on the scores, exactly as was done in the burglar scenario.

This technique is known as *soft voting*. If you had counted the number of times your algorithms predicted one class and compared it to the other class, and you make a decision based on that difference, it is known as *hard voting*.

In Python, you can leverage `VotingClassifier` from `sklearn. ensemble`, as shown in this code snippet:

```
voting_clf = VotingClassifier(
    estimators=[
        ('lr', LogisticRegression(random_state=42)),
        ('rf', RandomForestClassifier(random_state=42)),
```

```
        ('svc', SVC(random_state=42))
    ]
)
voting_clf.fit(X_train, y_train)
```

As you can see, the code snippet uses multiple predictors—such as logistic regression, random forest classifier, and SVM-to get their scores and aggregate to get the best voted class.

Bagging and Pasting

Let's return to the late night burglar crime scene. In the previous technique, the cops called the neighbors of all the neighboring houses. But since some of the houses were farther away, it was obvious that their confidence scores would be smaller than the neighbor's score of the house right in front of yours (the crime scene). You can instead ask the cops to ask only the neighbors of that house.

To correlate this to the machine learning ensemble technique, you can think of the family in the house in front as one single ML algorithm. For example, if you chose a decision tree as the algorithm, you can take multiple instances of the decision tree and sample the training data for each instance of the decision tree. You can then employ the voting classifier for all these instances, similar to the technique you used earlier. This technique is known as *bagging*. See Figure 1-5.

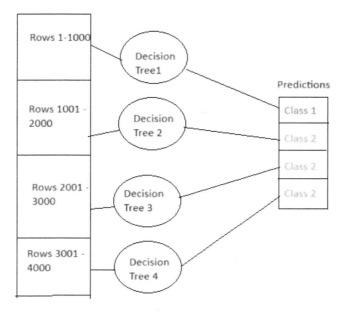

Figure 1-5. *Simple voting classifier*

In bagging, the number of training instances is divided and spread among the instances of the decision tree. Each instance has different samples of the training data. If there are overlaps in the samples, bagging turns into pasting. In the *pasting* technique, each time a sample of the training dataset is drawn, it is replaced and a fresh sample is drawn. This is as opposed to bagging, where each sampling is done without replacing anything. Hence there are no overlaps in bagging, as the sampling excludes the samples drawn for the previous instance. See Figure 1-6.

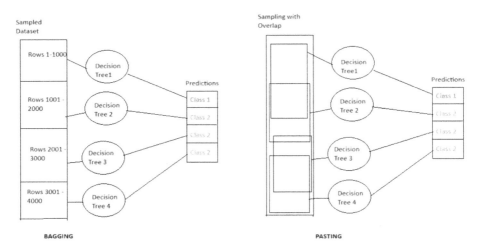

Figure 1-6. *Bagging and pasting*

Pasting and bagging may seem counterintuitive as opposed to the voting classifier, since it's using the same algorithm every time. But it uses the law of large numbers to increase the confidence of the predictions by taking multiple instances of the same algorithm.

Pasting takes more CPU power, since it uses redundancy to bulk up the confidence and hence arrives with less bias than bagging. But bagging remains the favorite among industries due to its lightweight nature.

Scikit-Learn has an encapsulation for this as well and you can use bagging as follows:

```
from sklearn.ensemble import BaggingClassifier
from sklearn.tree import DecisionTreeClassifier

bag_clf = BaggingClassifier(DecisionTreeClassifier(), n_
estimators=500, max_samples=100, n_jobs=-1, random_state=42)
bag_clf.fit(X_train, y_train)
```

n_estimators tells the bagging classifier to use 500 instances of the decision tree classifier and max_samples tells the bagging classifier to take 100 training data records for each sample. You can add bootstrap=False if you want to perform pasting instead of bagging.

Random Forest

The bagging classifier also has two parameters to sample features along with training records—max_features and bootstrap_features. They work similar to max_samples and bootstrap, but for features instead of training data records. So, if you have max_features set to something less than 1, it will sample the feature set and should take that fraction of features (training data columns) for each instance and sample. Similarly, bootstrap_features will ensure that there are no overlaps on feature sampling if it is set to False. If bootstrap_features is True, it means pasting but with feature sampling.

If you allow the bagging classifier to take 100 percent of the training dataset records but sample only on features and keep the bootstrap_ feature set to True (i.e. ensuring bagging instead of pasting), you have a random forest classifier.

This is one of the most popular and widely used techniques, and Scikit-Learn offers the random forest classifier as a separate module to be imported and used.

```
from sklearn.ensemble import RandomForestClassifier
clf = RandomForestClassifier()
clf.fit(X, y)
```

Boosting

Another popular ensemble class is boosting, where you can take several weak training instances and boost them so they fit well the next time. This section takes you through two popular boosting techniques.

Ada Boost

Let's break down the bagging classifier for a moment and suppose that you record the scores for each training sample instance. Now you take the ones that are low according to a preset threshold and decide on a weight that you are going to add the next time you process the algorithm again. For the same samples, having low scores or a true value that doesn't match the predicted one, i.e. the misclassified instances. If you iterate like this until you get a decent score and keep on updating the weight every time, you have resorted to the Ada boost technique.

Mathematically, in Ada boost you calculate the error rate for each ith instance as $r_i = \sum w^{(i)}_j$ for all j rows in the ith sample, where true y_i is not equal to predicted y_i. You can consider an initial weight for all samples and all rows.

Now, you calculate the predictor weight as $\alpha_i = (1-r_i)/r_i$

η is your learning rate.

Finally, every time the true y_i value is not equal to the predicted y_i value, you update the weight of that training instance sample as $w^{(i)}\exp(\alpha_i)$.

You can keep on iterating as long as the true y_i value is not equal to the predicted y_i value.

You can invoke Ada boost from Scikit-Learn as follows:

```
from sklearn.ensemble import AdaBoostClassifier

adaclf = AdaBoostClassifier(DecisionTreeClassifier(),
n_estimators=30, learning_rate=0.5)
```

The next variation of boosting is more popularly used.

Gradient Boosting

To understand gradient boosting, you should understand what residual errors are. A residual error is the difference between the true and the predicted value. Ada boost corrects the weights for each misclassified instance. In gradient boosting, you set up a new algorithm instance (i.e., a predictor) for the residual error and combine the prediction scores of the residuals with the predicted scores on the training instances.

For example, you calculate a predicted y value using an ML algorithm such as this:

```
y_pred =  ML_algo(y)
```

Your next step is to calculate residual as y_res1 = y-y_pred.

You use the same ML_algo to calculate a new prediction as follows:

```
y_res_pred1 = ML_algo(y_res1)
```

Let's calculate another level of residual as y_res2 = y_res_pred1-y_res1 and allow ML_algo to calculate another level of prediction as follows:

```
y_res_pred2 = ML_algo(y_res2)
```

Now you take y_pred, y_res_pred1 and y_res_pred2 and you can use an aggregator function such as sum or average to get the final score. Gradient boosting is widely used; to implement it in Python, use sklearn.ensemble.GradientBoostingClassifier.

Stacking

The final ensemble technique I want to talk about is Stacking. Stacking is an interesting concept where you divide the training set into certain layers. The number of layers determines the number of blenders in your stacking method. Consider a single layer of blenders. Hence, your training data is divided into two layers.

You use the first layer to make predictions using the algorithms you selected, similar to a voting classifier. Now, instead of using an aggregate function to combine the prediction scores, if you can note down these predictions and allow another training algorithm to train on these predictions to arrive at a final score, what you have is a *blender*. The final output of your blender is the result of your stacking method (see Figure 1-7).

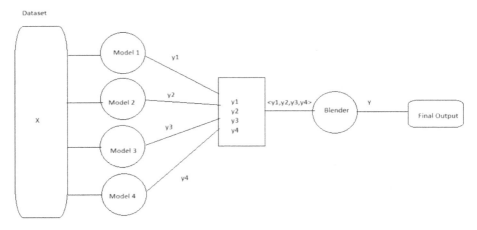

Figure 1-7. *Stacking*

As mentioned, you can stack multiple layers of blenders by dividing the training set into those many datasets.

Stacking has been adopted by contestants appearing in competitions hosted in platforms such as Kaggle.

Although fitting an algorithm to a dataset is the primary concern, you also need to know how the algorithm is performing. You need some evaluation metrics to understand which algorithm is better. The following section discusses some of the popular metrics used to evaluate machine learning models.

Metrics

The popular metrics discussed in this section are applicable to most machine learning algorithms.

Before moving on to metrics, make sure that you know the popular classification of machine learning algorithms according to the problem statement. Machine learning algorithms can be broadly classified into two types of tasks:

- Classification

- Regression

A *classification* task is a problem where you are given a set of categories for the output and the algorithm is supposed to map its output to one or many of these categories or classes. For example, predicting whether an email is spam or not is a classification task; the output must be either spam or not spam. Some classification task might also be multi-label classification problem, where the output can map to multiple, nonexclusive categories. For example, the task of predicting the genre of a movie can have the algorithm outputting multiple genre classes for a single movie. For instance, the famous Hollywood movie *Citizen Kane* could be identified as a drama and a mystery (as you can see on IMDB and in Figure 1-8).

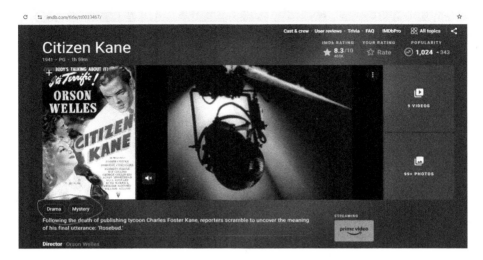

Figure 1-8. *The IMDB website*

A regression task, on the other hand, predicts simple values. For example, the task of predicting the temperature should output the temperature (such as 23 degrees) and not categorize data into classes.

Accuracy

Whenever we talk of predictions, we generally say that a prediction is accurate to a certain degree. Accuracy is a metric that can be defined mathematically. Consider a classification task where you have a training dataset containing 100 samples of class A and 100 samples of class B (i.e. a total of 200 samples). After training using some model, if you get an accuracy of 90 percent (or a score of 0.90), you can safely say that the model has recognized 180 samples correctly and 20 samples incorrectly.

If you modify the dataset a bit so that you have 150 samples of class A and 50 samples of class B, and the same model gives the same amount of accuracy, can you say that the sample has recognized 90 percent of 150 samples (i.e., 135 samples) of class A correctly and 45 samples (90 percent of 50) of class B correctly? Since the total accuracy of the model is

90 percent, it is possible that it classified all samples of class B as class B but correctly classified only 80 percent of 150 samples (120 samples) of class A correctly (90+10 percent of class B and 90-10 percent of class B, which comes to 90 percent of the total sample). The reason for this is that the dataset is skewed.

In such cases, you have to resort to other metrics.

Precision

Before understanding precision, you need to know a few concepts. For any classification problem, you have the actual dataset that is used as training data and the predicted dataset. Suppose you have to predict whether a set of data belongs to class A or not:

- True Positives (TP) are when the model predicts that the dataset belongs to class A and the actual dataset also says that it belongs to class A.

- True Negatives (TN) are when the model predicts that the dataset does not belong to class A and the actual dataset also says that it doesn't belong to class A.

- False Positives (FP) are when the model predicts that the dataset belongs to class A but the actual dataset says that it doesn't belong to class A.

- False Negatives (FN) are when the model predicts that the dataset does not belong to class A but the actual dataset says that it does belong to class A.

Precision is mathematically defined as $\dfrac{TP}{TP + FP}$

You now see how this resolves problems with skewed data using the same example as before. Considering that it classified all samples of class B as class B (i.e., 50 samples), but correctly classified only 80 percent of 150 samples (120 samples) of class A correctly, the number of True Positives are 50+120, or 170 and False Positives are 30. Thus the precision is $\frac{170}{170+30}$, or 85 percent, which makes better sense than simple accuracy.

Recall

Another useful matric is Recall, which is mathematically defined as $\frac{TP}{TP+FN}$. This metric is used in problems where the system is allowed to tolerate a few False Positives, but the True Positives must not be missed. For instance, with a system that catches identified convicts from facial recognition in real time in an airport, the security guards can afford a few false alarms, but the recall must be high.

There is often a tradeoff that a data scientist must consider when building a prediction system, but a balanced system is in general considered the best approach to start with. To get a system with balanced precision and recall, you can use the harmonic mean of precision and recall as a metric, which is popularly known as an F1 score.

Confusion Matrix

You can leverage something known as a confusion matrix to visually check at a glance how your algorithm is performing now that you understand precision and recall. A confusion matrix shows you visually the amount of True Positives, True Negatives, False Positives, and False Negatives achieved by the system.

Consider the classification task discussed earlier to predict whether the genre of the movie is drama or not (mystery or others). This is a simple binary classification task and you can employ a simple model.

Once you are done with the model building and have a holdout set for testing, you have true and predicted values and you can create a confusion matrix from them.

In Python, you can simply use the `confusion_matrix` class from `sklearn.metrics` as follows:

```
cm = confusion_matrix(y,y_preds)
```

where y are your true values and y_preds are your predicted values.

If there were 5,500 samples being classified, your confusion matrix would look like the following:

```
array([ 5000,1500,
        1500, 4000])
```

Since this is a simple binary classification, it is pretty easy to check the various quadrants of your confusion matrix.

The first quadrant gives you the number of True Positives where the actual genre was drama and so was the predicted ones. The one below, on the other hand, mentions the False Positives, where your system predicts that the genre was drama but it was not. The one beside the False Positive quadrant is the True Negative count and one the one above it is the False Negative count.

Your requirement should determine the kind of confusion matrix you need to see.

The best use of a confusion matrix is when you are building a multi-class classification model. For example, say your task was expanded to predict the following genres:

```
[Drama, Mystery, Horror, Romance, Comedy]
```

To visually determine the performance of your model, you can calculate the confusion matrix and then see it through a heatmap as follows:

```
import seaborn as sns
import matplotlib.pyplot as plt

sns.heatmap(cm)
plt.ylabel('Actual', fontsize=13)
plt.title('Confusion Matrix', fontsize=17, pad=20)
plt.gca().xaxis.set_label_position('top')
plt.xlabel('Prediction', fontsize=13)
plt.show()
```

Then you may have a confusion matrix resembling Figure 1-9.

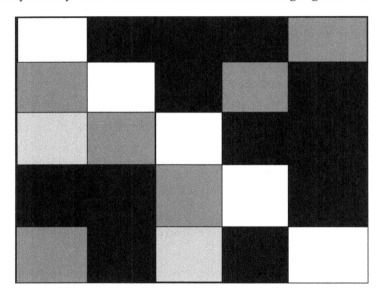

Figure 1-9. *Confusion matrix*

As you may already realize, the diagonal ones should have 100 percent of the number of elements of that class (i.e., the number in diagonal cells equals the number of rows of that class in the test dataset), indicating perfect match for a best model. The rest of the cells indicate the number of predicted values out of true values. For instance, the first cell in the second row tells you how many drama movies it classified out of mystery movies. A perfect model should have all these cells as 0.

This visual gives you an overview of how your model performs and which of the classes should be weighted more than the others to tune your model.

ROC AUC

Before showing how these metrics can be converted to Python code, a final metric cannot be overlooked, which is Receiver Operating Curve (ROC). ROC is the ratio of the True Positive rate (another name for recall) to the False Positive rate. The False Positive rate is 1-the True Negative rate. The True Negative rate is the ratio of negative instances that are correctly classified as negative (called *specificity*). When the ROC is plotted with the True Positive rate and the False Positive rate on the axes, the area of the curve plotted is called Area Under Curve (or AUC). AUC is desired to be close to 1 for a model to give a balanced score.

Mean Squared Error

All the previous metrics are particularly designed for classification problems. Regression problems are simpler to evaluate and one such popular metric is Mean Square Error (MSE). Considering true values from training dataset values (Y) and predicted values (Y') from a dataset of n samples, MSE is calculated as:

$$MSE = \frac{1}{n} \Sigma \ (Y\text{-}Y')$$

Scikit-Learn again comes to the rescue. As mentioned, Scikit-Learn can make this happen with a few lines of code.

But before that, you need to divide the dataset into train and test datasets using the following Scikit-Learn code:

```
from sklearn.model_selection import train_test_split
X_train, X_test, y_train, y_test = train_test_split(X, y, test_size=0.33, random_state=42)
```

Here, X and y are the features and output columns respectively, and the function is dividing the dataset into a training dataset (X_train, y_train) and testing dataset (X_test, y_test), with 33 percent of the dataset reserved for training instances and the rest for testing instances.

Coming back to the evaluation metrics, you first need to import the functions pertaining to each of the metrics before using them, and thankfully all of them fall under the same module. Considering the predictions are stored as y_test_predictions, the following code should make it clear:

```
from sklearn.metrics import accuracy_score, precision_score, recall_score, f1_score, roc_curve, auc
y_test_predictions = model.predict(y_test)
accuracy = accuracy_score(y_test, y_test_predictions)
precision = precision_score(y_test, y_test_predictions)
recall = recall_score(y_test, y_test_predictions)
f1score = f1_score(y_test, y_test_predictions)
fpr, tpr, thresholds = roc_curve(test_y, y_test_predictions)
auc = auc(fpr,tpr)
```

Although these algorithms form the foundation of machine learning, they don't closely relate to how a human brain works. It was not very long ago that computers could simulate how human brains function through understanding neurons (one of the basic building blocks of the human brain). This led to an important discipline in data science known as deep learning.

Deep Learning

Deep learning started with scientists trying to figure out how the human brain works. The started in the 1800s, when Joseph von Gerlach first proposed that the nervous system works as a single network of discrete cells, to the 1890s when Santiago Ramon y Cajal proposed that the nervous system was made up of discrete individual cells forming a network. It was during the era of big scientific achievements around 1950 when the electron microscope was invented that scientists confirmed that the nervous system is indeed a system of interconnected individual nerve cells, which they called *neurons*.

During that time, the first version of the neuron model was devised by McCulloch and Pitts, which is popularly known as the McCulloch and Pitts Neuron. The McCulloh and Pitts Neuron (see Figure 1-10) has an aggregation function g(x), which aggregates the inputs and an activation function f(g(x)), which further calculates the probabilities as predictions. For example, you can consider a threshold, say Θ, such that

$$f(g(x)) = 1 \text{ if } f(g(x)) > \Theta, \text{ and}$$
$$f(g(x)) = 0 \text{ if } f(g(x)) <= \Theta$$

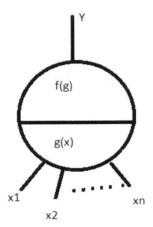

Figure 1-10. *McCulloch Pitts Neuron*

A modified version of the McCulloh and Pitts Neuron was later derived, and is currently present in present Python modules. This is the *perceptron,* which uses weights during the initial input aggregation.

$g(x) = \sum x$ for McCulloh and Pitts neuron, which is modified to $g(x) = \sum(wx)$ for Perceptron.

With a threshold function, you can have a mathematical model that can prepare a boundary for separation of one class from the other. Correlating weights and biases of a neuron with a slope and intercept, you can also graphically visualize and concur on how your threshold function prepares a linear boundary for separation of the classes.

But in real-world scenarios, most of the problems you encounter will be nonlinear and hence it would be difficult to propose a single neuron with activation functions to tackle such tasks.

In such cases, you have to resort to using a multilayer perceptron. A multilayer perceptron uses a middle layer to consider all possible inputs through permutation of multiple neurons, as shown in Figure 1-11, so that any combination of input activates a certain neuron and hence doesn't fail to accommodate any combination of input and output, whether it is linearly separable or not.

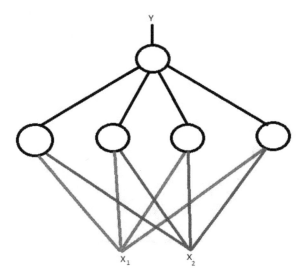

Figure 1-11. *Multilayer perceptron*

As mentioned, each layer of the MLP has a set of weights that the neuron calculates on top of. According to the image, as there are four red and four blue lines connecting to the first layer of neurons from the inputs. There are eight weights and in the second layer there are four weights. For such a network of neurons, there are a total of 12 weights that are calibrated and adjusted to get the desired output. Such networks are also known as neural networks.

Sigmoid Neuron

Now, as you may have already picked up, the main building block of the neural networks is the neuron, similar to the human brain. One way to model these neurons artificially is using the aggregation function and the threshold function. But one problem with such neurons is the threshold function. The threshold function fails in situations where the values might be fuzzy. In such cases, the function switches its output suddenly when a certain value (threshold value) is reached. The threshold function, when plotted, looks like Figure 1-12.

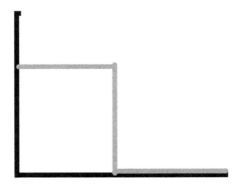

Figure 1-12. *Threshold function*

Instead of this, a more suitable function modeling the real world problems should be smooth. A sigmoid is a class of function that forms variations of the following function:

$$S(x) = \frac{1}{1+e^{-x}}$$

The function, when plotted, looks like Figure 1-13.

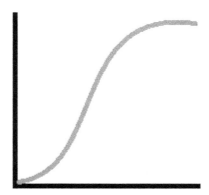

Figure 1-13. *Sigmoid function*

The sigmoid function has several variations that are used in neural networks.

Problems with Sigmoid Neuron

While sigmoid identifies the first activation neuron, it suffers from two major problems—the vanishing gradient problem and the non-zero center problem. Vanishing gradient is a conundrum the activation functions face when the input and eventually the derivatives from the inputs reach near zero. I discuss this briefly in upcoming sections. The non-zero center problem, on the other hand, prevents the neuron from capturing strongly negative, neutral, and positive values. This problem can be mitigated by using the Tanh activation function.

Tanh

The Tanh activation function models a neuron based on this equation:

$$\tanh(x) = \frac{2}{1+e^{-2x}} - 1$$

The function, when plotted, looks like Figure 1-14.

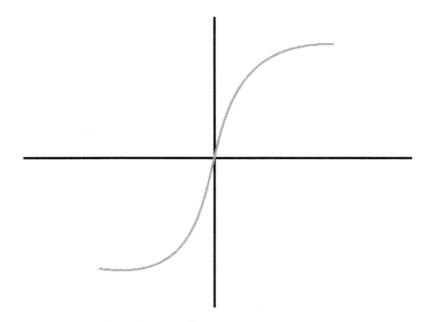

Figure 1-14. *Tanh activation function*

Although this activation function mitigates the zero center problem, it still suffers from the vanishing gradient problem. The following section explores the vanishing gradient problem in detail before explaining how to mitigate it.

Vanishing Gradient Problem

Consider a sequence modelling problem in which you are trying to predict the next part of the sequence from the previous parts (such as a stock prediction algorithm or a sentence completion algorithm). In such cases, by the time you reach the *nth* part of the sequence (where $n>>1$), the neuron has applied the derivative of the first input n times. This derivative will reach near zero if the input value of the first input is a very small value or is itself near or less than zero. In such cases, the neuron fails to retain that information and a large n can drop the values down significantly.

This in turn can lead the weights to drop down to zero and hence training with such weights and biases will not lead to convergence. You will see later how this can be mitigated through recurrent neural network variants, but for now you'll learn how to improve on the activation function to constrain this problem as much as possible.

ReLU

A very naive way to prevent the vanishing gradient problem from ever occurring is to arrive at a constant as soon as the value falls below zero. ReLU sets the value to zero for any values less than or equal to zero. Hence, the ReLU activation function uses the following equation:

$$relu(x) = max(x,0)$$

As you can see, this is a very naive way that data scientists conjured up to prevent the derivatives from reaching near zero. The ReLU function looks like Figure 1-15.

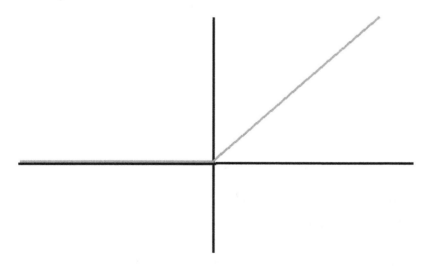

Figure 1-15. *ReLU activation function*

One issue with this activation function is that, although it blocks any value less than or equal to zero, it doesn't account for those values even if they are important for the use case. What if your business case requires you to model a solution for values that are mainly negative? In that case, you can use Leaky ReLU.

Leaky ReLU

The Leaky ReLU function is as follows:

$$leaky\_relu(x) = max(0.01x, x)$$

The activation function resembles Figure 1-16.

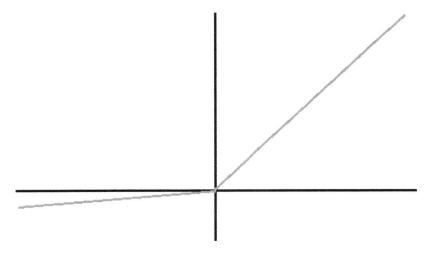

Figure 1-16. *Leaky ReLU activation function*

As you can see, to ensure that the negative values are accounted for, the leaky ReLU function can add a small weight to the input value so that it doesn't turn to zero.

But with all these activation functions in mind, how do you select the best one?

Start with sigmoid or tanh for any kind of classification problems and see how your training proceeds. Or, you can start with ReLU, as it is the most popular one. But all of them can fall prey to the dead neuron problem. To detect dead neurons, you should monitor for slow convergence and the loss coming equal to *nan*. If your loss is *nan,* you have a dead neuron problem. In such cases, change your activation function to leaky ReLU.

Problems in the current market scenario does not comprise a single layer of neurons like in MLP, but a multilayer of neurons interacting with each other and producing a set of outputs. The aggregation function from the final layer of neurons is called the *output function,* as it is the one that produces the final predictions. Also, instead of the threshold function, a function similar to sigmoid is used, which is called the *activation function.* Another function measures the difference between the actual output and the predicted output during training, called the *loss function.*

Now, using all these functions, the algorithm to train a system using training data runs in two main steps in a neural network:

- Feedforward

- Backpropagation

During the feedforward step, the neurons in each step calculate the values of each neuron, until reaching the output neurons. It is also noteworthy that each connection between the neurons consists of weights similar to MLP. The values in the output neurons are then passed to the loss function along with actual output values. In the backpropagation step, based on the loss function value, the weights are adjusted for each layer and each connection based on the gradient function, as follows:

W' = W − ∇W, where W' is the new weight, W is the previous weight

and $\nabla W = \dfrac{\delta L}{\delta W}$

L is the loss function value.

These two steps are performed several times (each iteration is termed an epoch), until the loss function value is as small as can be tolerated.

As discussed previously, any machine learning model addresses either of two types of problems—classification or regression. The output function for classification produces probability scores and the output function for the regression function produces real number values.

The output function to produce a probability score can be a softmax function. A softmax function is a variant of a sigmoid function and any linear function can be used as the output function to produce a real number.

Similarly, to compare probability scores, cross entropy is a common loss function. Here is the cross entropy function:

Cross entropy(p,q) = $\Sigma q(x) log p(x)$, where q is the true probability values from the training dataset and p is the predicted probability values.

To compare real number values, MSE (mean square error), described in the previous section, can be used as a loss function.

TensorFlow and Keras

Just like Scikit-Learn, which is used to develop machine learning applications by leveraging their powerful abstractions, TensorFlow and Keras are used to develop deep learning algorithms. Keras is a Python library that uses TensorFlow as backend to provide almost all the functions used in deep learning algorithms, starting from all kinds of activation functions to all kinds of loss functions and many more.

This section dives into the Python code directly instead of covering the theory. You are going to implement a very interesting use case to identify numbers from images, similar to how Google Lens works.

The first step is to gather data. The MNIST database consists of a large volume of images annotated properly to their corresponding number representations. MNIST is open source and is also available in the Keras dataset.

Now that you know where the data is, you can start by writing the code. As the first step, you need to include the tensorflow and keras packages into your script.

```
import tensorflow as tf
from tensorflow import keras
```

You also need two important packages (numpy and pandas), which are extensively used for numerical calculations and data analysis, respectively.

```
import numpy as np
import pandas as pd
```

Next, you need to load the dataset. The dataset consists of images tagged to the numbers they represent. Each image can be considered a matrix of 28x28 pixel values.

```
mnist = keras.datasets.mnist
(x_train_full, y_train_full), (x_test, y_test) = mnist.
load_data()
X_train_full = x_train_full/255.0
X_test_full = x_test_full/255.0
```

As you can see, Keras divides the dataset into train and test sets.

You can check the shape of the train set by using x_train_full.shape.

The values in x_train_full and x_test_full are not normalized; that is, they fall under the gap of 0 to 255, which can cause the neuron values to explode or vanish (which I discuss later when adding optimizers). Hence, it's better to normalize the values, as shown in the last two lines of the code.

Now you can start building the algorithm:

```
model = keras.models.Sequential()
model.add(keras.layers.Flatten(input_shape=[28,28]))
```

```
model.add(keras.layers.Dense(300, activation="relu"))
model.add(keras.layers.Dense(100, activation="relu"))
model.add(keras.layers.Dense(10, activation="softmax"))
```

This code initializes the model as a sequential model in the beginning. A sequential model executes each layer one step at a time. After that, you start defining the layers. In the first layer, you flatten the matrix from a (28,28) dimension to a 748 dimension vector. Then you start building the subsequent layers by defining the activation function and the number of neurons in each layer. The second layer has 300 neurons with the ReLU activation function and the third one has 100 neurons of the ReLU function. ReLU is a popular function used by most data scientists, as its performance is optimal. In the final output layer, as the problem is a classification problem (since you are predicting digits from images and there are ten digits or ten classes), you need to get probability score, and as discussed previously, softmax is the best output activation.

Finally, you have to compile this model by providing the loss function to be used (cross entropy as discussed), the metric to see how well the model is performing (accuracy should suffice as of now), and an optimizer.

Optimizers

Optimizers take care of how the weights are updated.

SGD

One of the basic ways to update weights is as follows:

$$w_{t+1} = w_t + \eta \Delta w_t$$

where η is the learning rate.

This is the Stochastic Gradient Descent (SGD) optimizer and you can leverage the optimizers class to import and use it with this code `keras.optimizers.SGD(learning_rate=0.01)`.

Momentum-based SGD

Simple SGD can be very slow, in which case you can add a momentum resembling this equation:

$$\text{update}_t = \Upsilon * \text{update}_{t-1} + \eta \Delta w_t$$

$$\text{update}_{t+1} = w_t + \text{update}_t$$

where Υ is the momentum.

To use it in Keras, add the momentum parameter as follows:

```
keras.optimizers.SGD(learning_rate=0.01, momentum=0.1)
```

Sometimes momentums can lead your training to loop round and round near the convergence but never reach it (see Figure 1-17).

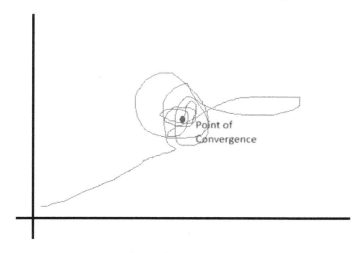

Figure 1-17. *Momentum-based SGD missing point of convergence*

The missed point of convergence depends not only on the momentum parameter, but also on the input values. For example, for the same optimizer, some feature values might be very sparse (mostly zero) and some not. For the non-sparse ones, the optimizer will work best but for the features that are very sparse, the zero values will lead the optimizer to miss the convergence more frequently than the non-sparse ones.

One way to mitigate this is to figure out a way to change the learning rate depending on the frequency of the feature values.

Adagrad

Adagrad can decay the learning rate based on previous input values. If there are mostly zero values, it will decay the learning rate and increment it when a non-zero value is encountered.

$$v(t) = v(t-1) + (\Delta w_t)^2$$

$$w_{t+1} = w_t + \text{update}$$

$$\text{update} = \Delta w_t{}^* \, (\eta / v(t)_{+\epsilon})$$

where $_\epsilon$ is a small value to prevent zero division.

In Keras, you can use the Adagrad class as follows:

```
keras.optimizers.Aadgrad(learning_rate=0.01, epsilon=1e-07)
```

Although Adagrad was originally a promising optimizer, it suffered from aggressive decays, mainly when the denominator of the update parameter increased significantly.

RMSPorp

As mentioned previously, Adagrad suffers from aggressive decay. To prevent that, you have to prevent denominator growth. Consider the following equations:

$$v(t) = \beta v(t-1) + (1-\beta)(\Delta w_t)^2$$

$$w_{t+1} = w_t + \text{update}$$

$$\text{update} = \Delta w_t{}^* \, (\eta / v(t)_{+\epsilon})$$

where the parameter β is added to tune the $v(t)$ and hence reduce the denominator.

Adam

Adam, a popular optimizer, should be your go-to. Adam introduces another parameter to tune the denominator as well.

$$m(t) = \beta_1 m(t-1) + (1-\beta_1)\Delta w_t$$
$$v(t) = \beta_2 v(t-1) + (1-\beta_2)(\Delta w_t)^2$$
$$M(t) = m(t)/1 - \beta_1$$
$$V(t) = v(t)/1 - \beta_2$$
$$w_{t+1} = w_t + \text{update}$$
$$\text{update} = M(t) * (\eta/V(t)_{+\epsilon})$$

As you can see here, instead of one parameter (β), Adam introduces two parameters (β_1 and β_2) to decay the weight update and the denominator.

Keras allows you to add this optimizer using the Adam class as follows:

```
keras.optimizers.Adam(learning_rate=0.001, beta_1=0.9,
beta_2=0.999, epsilon=1e-07)
```

The following example uses Adam. If you don't want to mess with the parameters and let the default values do the magic, you can simply express the optimizer algorithm as a string, such as "sgd", "rmsprop" and "adam".

```
model.compile(loss="sparse_categorical_crossentropy",
optimizer="adam", metrics=["accuracy"])
```

Otherwise, you can use the optimizer class from Keras.

```
model.compile(loss="sparse_categorical_crossentropy",
optimizer=keras.optimizers.Adam() metrics=["accuracy"])
```

Now that the model is compiled, you can fit it to your dataset and train.

```
history = model.fit(x_train_full, y_train_full, epochs=30)
```

You will see each epoch running and giving the loss and accuracy at each epoch.

After training, you can see how the model performed by evaluating it. The model evaluation will be done based on the validation set that you set.

```
print(model.evaluate(x_test, y_test))
```

This will give an idea of how well the model has performed.

But if you want to specifically check out the evaluation metrics, you can start with accumulating the predictions:

```
y_pred = model.predict(x_test)
y_pred_classes = np.argmax(y_pred, axis=1)
```

The second line allows you to gather the class labels from the prediction values by selecting the maximum probability class using argmax.

Now you are ready to calculate the precision:

```
from sklearn.metrics import precision_score
precision = precision_score(y_test, y_pred_classes)
print(precision)
```

You can also calculate recall as follows:

```
from sklearn.metrics import recall_score
recall = recall_score(y_test, y_pred_classes)
print(recall)
```

As discussed previously, you have to ensure a proper tradeoff based on your use case. Otherwise, you can try to ensure a good F1 score as follows:

```
from sklearn.metrics import f1_score
f1 = f1_score(y_test, y_pred_classes)
print(f1)
```

Unsupervised Learning

Up until now you have used a historical dataset to train on. When the model is decided and trained, the model is prepared to predict on some part of the true dataset and is compared to the predicted dataset to see how the model is performing.

But what if you don't have the luxury of gathering proper data annotated with proper labels? This happens when you have past data of the predictors but don't have the labels or the true outputs tagged. For instance, say you need to predict churn reduction for a retail chain. You have to predict the customer category (such as adults, teenagers, senior citizens, or kids) based on the shop data inventory category (such as grocery items, fashion products, medicines, or toys) to determine which products attract which category of customer. With the human eye, it's easy to map the shop product categories with the customer categories, as we know such patterns from our experiences. But it's going to be difficult for a machine to map this if the customer data is not available. The model needs a new shop product inventory count per customer category visit count as training data. But what if the store is just a small local retail shop bootstrapped by a family who doesn't have the customer count, or doesn't have the infrastructure or resources to keep track of the customer categories?

In such cases, you have to resort to models that do not depend on labeled training data, called unsupervised models. The models I have discussed up to now are known as supervised models, as they have proper training data to train your model. And any machine learning model can be divided into one of two types—supervised and unsupervised.

This section shows a popular supervised model and explains how it works.

You need a model that helps you with the following journey, as depicted in Figure 1-18.

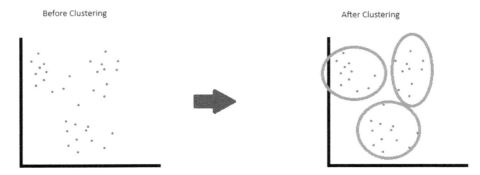

Figure 1-18. *Clustering algorithm*

This algorithm is known as a clustering algorithm; it can separate one cluster from another. Each cluster represents a class category for the dataset.

One of the most popular clustering algorithms used in unsupervised machine learning tasks is the K-Means Clustering algorithm. This chapter explains how this algorithm works intuitively before diving into the Python code.

K-Means Clustering Algorithm

1. Start by initializing centroids randomly. A *centroid* is a data point in a cluster that is equidistant from all the data points in the same cluster. As you have not initialized the clusters yet, you take N data points randomly to be assumed as N cluster centroids (assuming you want the data to be segregated into N clusters).

2. Once you determine the distances of the other data points, you arrange them and assign and divide the data points to clusters according to their distances.

3. Based on the distances, the algorithm assigns new centroids, which have the mean shortest distance with all other data points in its own clusters.

4. The previous steps are iterated until there is no change in centroids. Use the new centroids as a starting point instead of randomly initializing.

Similar to other machine learning algorithms, Scikit-Learn comes to the rescue when you want to implement the algorithm in Python.

```
from sklearn.clussters import KMeans
kmeans = KMeans(n_clusters=k) # k is the number of desired
categories or clusters
y_pred  = kmeans.fit_predict(X) # X is the input dataset
```

This code elegantly shows how simple it is to implement an unsupervised learning algorithm in Python.

It is worth noting that supervised learning algorithms can be measured for their performance using metrics such as accuracy, precision, recall, mean square error, and so on. But all of these metrics require the true labels as well as the predicted ones. Hence, they cannot be used to measure unsupervised algorithms as you don't have true labels in those cases. An alternative way to measure the performance of an unsupervised learning algorithm is using the Silhouette Score.

$$\text{Silhouette Score} = \frac{b-a}{max(b,a)}$$

Where a is the mean distance of centroids with the data points inside the cluster and b is the mean distance of centroids with data points outside the cluster (or in other clusters).

Using the Silhouette Score, you can arrive at an optimal k value. Although you can preset a k value based on your use case, an optimal k value is needed for a perfect model. You can then tune your data to match the optimal k value.

To arrive at an optimal k value, you should use the elbow method, where you can plot the Silhouette Score against k (the number of clusters) and see where the elbow occurs, as shown in Figure 1-19.

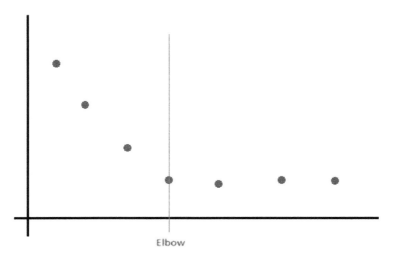

Figure 1-19. *Elbow method*

The elbow shows your optimal k value.

Apart from clustering, unsupervised learning has other applications as well. The following sections discuss some of them very briefly.

Associative Rule Mining

Before the advent of generative AI, building recommendation systems required an excessive use of unsupervised learning. Building recommendation systems was achieved through something known as associative rule mining. Associative rule mining uses large datasets to discern patterns through relationships between the X and Y values without a historical pattern. For example, if you wanted to prepare a recommendation algorithm to map the sales of customers and customer insights, associative rule mining tries to discern a pattern between the relationship between these two parameters—the customer insights (as X) and sales (as Y).

Dimensionality Reduction

Dimensionality reduction is used to model large datasets in terms of a large number of features. When there are a large number of features used to model a certain prediction, it often requires a large amount of memory and processing power. Instead of that, you can compress the feature set. For example, if you have a feature set of N features and you need to prepare a model with limited processing power, you can employ an unsupervised learning technique known as dimensionality reduction, which uses projections of feature sets using eigen vectors and compresses N features to $n<<N$. One such popular dimension reduction technique is Principal Component Analysis (PCA).

Now that you have a fair idea of the various types of machine learning and deep learning algorithms and metrics, you can learn something about their applications, which is covered in the next chapter.

Summary

- Machine learning uses historical data and evidence to discern a pattern using various mathematical models.

- Linear regression is one of the simplest machine learning algorithms and it bases its model on the equation of a line.

- Decision tree is another machine learning model that divides the dataset into features and tries to discern a tree to arrive at the labels. All of these model implementations are available in the Scikit-Learn Python library.

- Ensemble Machine Learning techniques use multiple algorithms on the same subsets of dataset, or the same algorithm on multiple subsets of the dataset and aggregate the results to get a better output.

- Once a machine learning model is selected and trained, evaluation metrics such as accuracy, precision, recall, ROC AUC, and MSE are used to measure the model performance.

- Deep learning tries to imitate the workings of the human brain to create models for AI.

- TensorFlow and Keras libraries are used to implement deep learning models.

- There are also unsupervised models that are used when unlabeled datasets are encountered.

CHAPTER 2

Natural Language Processing Primer

This chapter begins delving into one of the most important applications—natural language processing. Any application of artificial intelligence can be broadly classified into vision and text. Vision applications deal with image and video processing and text applications deal with understanding natural language.

Natural language processing specifically deals with tasks such as the following:

- *Text classification:* Depending on the meaning of the text, a certain decision is automated.

- *Named entity recognition:* Based on the word type (such as country, organization, person, etc.) a certain task is performed.

- *Translation:* Deals with converting languages.

- *Sentiment analysis:* Deals with understanding the tone of a statement (sad, hurtful, happy, etc.) and making some decision based on it.

The list is endless and AI displays new innovations every day.

© Arindam Ganguly 2025
A. Ganguly, *Scaling Enterprise Solutions with Large Language Models*,
https://doi.org/10.1007/979-8-8688-1154-8_2

Steps for an NLP Task

Digital technology understands data in the form of 0s and 1s. These binary digits are interpreted from numbers, and when words are involved, each character has its own numbered code (known as ASCII).

If you require a system that needs to understand words as a whole, the ASCII codes are not very useful, as they represent single letters. For example, the word "FRAUD" would be converted into an array as follows:

[70,82,65,85,68]

This array doesn't make any sense when used with a sentence of several words and a document of multiple sentences. One might argue with a method of aggregating the array of numbers as a representation of a word such as taking the sum of array contents. But that logically doesn't bring meaning to the codes. The reason is that the ASCII characters were not developed keeping in mind the formation of words from letters. Also, it is almost impossible to come up with a system that would assign codes to each letter and number so that they bring meaning to words and in turn bring meaning to a sentence and a document as a whole. Just think about how complex that would be!

In the domain of Artificial Intelligence, we need to come up with a system that can bring meaning to a word or sentence as humans do. Humans do not assign understanding to each single character or letter when they are reading a sentence. They perceive the sentence as a whole, and sometimes a document as a whole. Natural language processing algorithms use systems that do such tasks, similar to how our brains function.

A common natural language processing problem generally boils down to a few steps:

1. Data gathering

2. Cleaning and tokenization

3.   Vectorization and embedding

4.   Model selection, training, and evaluation

You might be familiar with the last two steps, as you have seen them in the previous chapter. The main agenda of the first three steps is to convert the complex textual input into simple machine learning inputs, as seen in the first chapter.

Instead of going down the road where there is a lot of theory without much of an implementation, you'll learn first by implementing. So, open your favorite Python editor and get ready to go through these steps. I recommend using Jupyter Notebooks or Google Colabatory for this chapter.

Data Gathering

As you might know from the previous chapter, data gathering is the first step to any AI problem. It is essential to understand that data gathered must be similar to the data to be encountered in production. If this is not the case, then you must make sure that the training data can be preprocessed to the format of the test data.

A data science team reaches out to the business or domain team to gather data and insights about the training and test data. One of the best and simplest datasets to start the NLP journey is IMDB data. This dataset is easily available in Keras and we take full advantage of this dataset to build your NLP skills. This dataset already has clean data and does not need any preprocessing. So instead we will use the raw IMDB dataset from Stanford University. The link to this dataset is as follows:

```
https://ai.stanford.edu/~amaas/data/sentiment/aclImdb_
v1.tar.gz
```

This dataset is targeted to train a system that can understand a movie review and score the sentiment (the review) as positive or negative.

If you are using Google Colabatory, you can directly download and unzip the contents in the workspace using the following two lines:

```
! wget https://ai.stanford.edu/~amaas/data/sentiment/aclImdb_
v1.tar.gz
! tar -xvzf /content/aclImdb_v1.tar.gz
```

You should be able to see two folders—train and test—consisting of the training and test data, respectively, as well as pos and neg folders inside each of them consisting of positive and negative reviews.

Now it's time to collate the data into a Pandas dataframe. Each of the reviews is in a separate text file. Here's how to read the positive sentiment reviews of the training data:

```
import os

train_pos_reviews_filenames = os.listdir("/content/aclImdb/
train/pos")
train_pos_reviews = []

for filename in train_pos_reviews_filenames:
  with open("/content/aclImdb/train/pos/"+filename) as fd:
    train_pos_reviews.append(fd.readline())
  fd.close()
```

The code is fairly self-explanatory. The list train_pos_reviews holds the reviews from the text files by looping for each of the files in the aclImdb/train/pos folder, which holds all the files storing positive reviews for training.

Similarly prepare the following lists:

train_neg_reviews for negative reviews in the training dataset.

test_pos_reviews for positive reviews in the testing dataset.

`test_neg_reviews` for negative reviews in the testing dataset.

Now you need to create the label data for the datasets. You can use the following code to create a list of labels corresponding to each list (1 is for a positive sentiment and 0 is for negative sentiment).

```
train_pos_reviews_labels = [1]*len(train_pos_reviews)
train_neg_reviews_labels = [0]*len(train_neg_reviews)
test_pos_reviews_labels = [1]*len(test_pos_reviews)
test_neg_reviews_labels = [0]*len(test_neg_reviews)
```

Once this is done, you need to collate these lists into four dataframes— `train_pos_df`, `train_neg_df`, `test_pos_df`, and `test_neg_df` consisting of the positive training dataset, the negative training dataset, the positive test dataset, and the negative test dataset. After that, you need to collate these dataframes into two dataframes—`train_df` and `test_df`—consisting of all the training and the test data, respectively.

Figure 2-1 shows how `train_df` can be created from the training reviews and labels list.

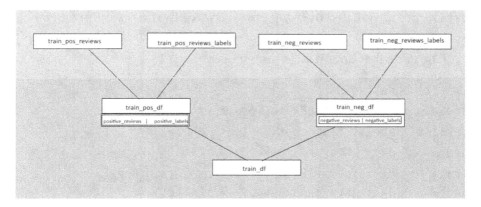

Figure 2-1. *Derive train_df*

Similarly, create the test_df dataframe from the test reviews and labels lists (see Figure 2-2).

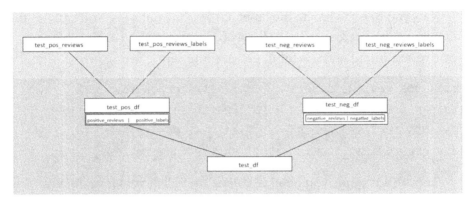

Figure 2-2. *Derive test_df*

These images explain how you should form the final dataframes. The green level infers that the boxes are lists and the blue levels are the dataframes. It is easier to join dataframes than lists, when your final output is supposed to be dataframe.

The train_pos_df, train_neg_df, test_pos_df, and test_neg_df dataframes are created by using the reviews as the first column and labels as the second column, as shown in the image.

The code that does it all is shown here:

```
import pandas as pd
train_pos_df = pd.DataFrame({'reviews':train_pos_
reviews,'labels':train_pos_reviews_labels})
train_pos_df
train_neg_df = pd.DataFrame({'reviews':train_neg_
reviews,'labels':train_neg_reviews_labels})
train_neg_df.head()
test_pos_df = pd.DataFrame({'reviews':test_pos_
reviews,'labels':test_pos_reviews_labels})
```

```
test_pos_df.head()
test_neg_df = pd.DataFrame({'reviews':test_neg_
reviews,'labels':test_neg_reviews_labels})
test_neg_df.head()
train_df = pd.concat([train_pos_df,train_neg_df],ignore_
index=True)
train_df.shape
test_df = pd.concat([test_pos_df,test_neg_df],ignore_
index=True)
test_df.shape
```

Now that you are done with data gathering, the next sections move on to the other steps.

Before proceeding, let's look at the two main libraries used in almost all natural language processing implementations—NLTK and Spacy.

NLTK and Spacy

This section dives into Python. Python has packages and libraries for everything, and two of the most popular Python libraries for natural language processing are NLTK and Spacy.

Install NLTK and Spacy using their websites:

- `https://www.nltk.org/` for NLTK

- `https://spacy.io/` for Spacy

Let's start with the new kid in town—Spacy! Install and import Spacy, then take one review and see how Spacy works.

```
import spacy
review = train_df.loc[50,'reviews']
```

The review consists of the following:

> *Karen goes into a Japanese house as a substitute*
> *nurse to Emma, a strange woman who sleeps at day*
> *and wakes at night. Karen goes upstairs after hearing*
> *noises when she encounters a frightening ghost. She*
> *will learn the house's secrets.

It is very*
> *scary! The scenes are shocking and frightening! The*
> *characters are good. The settings are creepy. I love*
> *the whole plot! The ending was shocking! I paused at*
> *a scene where the little boy meowed so loudly to the*
> *man finding his sister upstairs and I was shocked.*
> *This is the scariest movie I have watched. I did not*
> *see the Japanese version. I recommend this to horror*
> *fans. 10/10 and 5 stars!*

As you can see, there are a lot of sentences in one single review and they consist of HTML tags, exclamation signs, and other nonalphabetical or numeric characters. Hence, getting the tokens out of the reviews by splitting the full text by spaces will not work. A lot of cleaning also needs to be done.

Now, to work with Spacy, you have to import the Spacy model pertinent to the language and type of statements you want to work with. For this example, load the en_core_web_sm model, which is pertinent to the small English model.

```
nlp = spacy.load('en_core_web_sm')
```

Now that the model is loaded, you have to load the text into the Spacy documents. A Spacy document can be considered a single unit of text that you want to work on. You can consider each review as a Spacy document. Spacy understands and analyzes the text in a document and captures insights about the document's contents. Once you have the document loaded, you can also get any insights. These insights consists of tokens, parts of speech of each token, sentences, word shapes, lemmas, and so on. Let's ingest the selected review as a document and print some of the insights.

```
doc = nlp(review)

for token in doc:
  print(token.text, token.pos_, token.tag_, token.shape_,
  token.lemma_)
```

If you run the previous code, the first few lines of the output should be something like this:

```
I PRON PRP X I
can AUX MD xxx can
not PART RB xxx not
say VERB VB xxx say
this DET DT xxxx this
movie NOUN NN xxxx movie
is AUX VBZ xx be
a DET DT x a
disappointment NOUN NN xxxx disappointment
because SCONJ IN xxxx because
I PRON PRP X I
read VERB VBD xxxx read
some DET DT xxxx some
reviews NOUN NNS xxxx review
before ADP IN xxxx before
watching VERB VBG xxxx watch
and CCONJ CC xxx and
it PRON PRP xx it
did AUX VBD xxx do
not PART RB xxx not
do VERB VB xx do
```

```
as ADV RB xx as
well ADV RB xxxx well
as SCONJ IN xx as
I PRON PRP X I
thought VERB VBD xxxx think
it PRON PRP xx it
would AUX MD xxxx would
have VERB VB xxxx have
. PUNCT . . .
```

As you can see, Spacy has extracted the tokens from the document, the part of speech (pos), a code assigned to the part of speech (tag), the word shape (x for small letter, X for capital letter), and the lemma. Note also that Spacy has understood the punctuations over the alphanumeric characters (in the last output). These insights sometimes help in forming feature sets. For example, a model might work better when you include the parts of speech of each token as a feature set along with the tokens. Machine learning models generally work better when you lemmatize the tokens. But the one we use here for leveraging spacy is tokenization.

Let's build a function for tokenization using Spacy.

Now that you have a fair idea of how Spacy works, you can move on to another most widely used natural language processing library, called NLTK.

Installing NLTK is as easy as installing Spacy or any other library for that matter. One thing that NLTK needs to do is download all the pertinent models:

```
! pip install nltk
```

Once NLTK is installed, you can check the various NLP techniques that NLTK helps you provide. But before that I would like to bring to your attention one very important step for any kind of text processing, which is text cleaning. You must have seen that almost all of the reviews have HTML tags, accented characters, and special characters in them. Also, as in real time most of the text inputs will be either OCR text or human written formats, either of which might contain distorted text. There can also be spelling mistakes, grammatical mistakes, and more, which need to be encountered.

Spacy tries to get rid of these discrepancies, but no product is fool-proof until you train it according to your business and requirements or environments. On the other hand, as NLTK does not have an built-in cleansing capability, you need to clean it manually. Next, you'll build some of the functions that help you clean the inputs.

Cleaning Data

Source systems are often not capable of purging junk data, so cleaning that data is an almost mandatory and important preprocessing step. Some of the steps and concepts of text preprocessing are explained in this section.

Removing Accented and Unicode Characters

The Internet is vast and once your NLP system is online you should be wary of all the types of input that can crawl into your system. Although your system should have a validation to accept only text, malicious or unintended text or characters such as control characters can also seep into an input unnoticed, which can break your algorithm. Control characters are nonprintable characters that accompany simple characters with nonalphanumeric keys, such as carriage returns, which is a control character composed of the Ctrl key and R. Control characters are represented in Unicode and they can encode other type of characters that can cause confusion to your system.

Other examples of notorious Unicode characters that are often supported by some programming languages are emojis or special symbols such as ☺ and η, which are composed of nonalphanumeric character keys such as punctuation and character keys. These characters can cause havoc in your system if they are left unaccounted for.

Hence, the first step is to remove any accented and Unicode characters in your text input. This example employs NFKD to normalize any Unicode characters from the unicodedata library:

```
import unicodedata

def remove_splchars(text):
    text = unicodedata.normalize('NFKD',text).
    encode('ascii','ignore').decode('utf-8','ignore')
    return text
```

These accented characters and Unicode data can often disrupt the Python processing, so it is wise to check for such characters and filter them out.

Removing HTML Characters

Now that your text is void of any kind of accented characters, you can start by stripping any HTML characters. To remove HTML tags, you need to use regular expressions, which can remove text with a pattern similar to HTML tags. The following function does this for you.

```
import re
def striphtml(data):
    p = re.compile(r'<.*?>')
    return p.sub('', data)
```

After you run this, you should see the formatted output without the HTML tags.

```
striphtml(review)
'No doubt intended as a totally campy joke, "Full Moon High"
portrays 1950s teenager Tony Walker (Adam Arkin) accompanying
his father (Ed McMahon) on a trip to Romania. Sure enough, Tony
gets bitten, and grows fur and fangs whenever there\'s a full
```

```
moon. A particularly interesting aspect in this
..
and thanked his sons, I wonder whether or not he remembers co-
starring with two of them in this movie (aside from Adam, his
son Anthony also has a small role). Quite funny. Also starring
Elizabeth Hartman.PS: director Larry Cohen is probably best
known for the killer baby flick "It\'s Alive".'
```

It covers removing HTML tags and special characters. Other important cleaning steps, like lowercasing, stemming/lemmatization, and handling contractions, should be mentioned.

You can run these steps together as follows:

```
remove_splchars(striphtml(review))
```

The output should be as follows:

```
'No doubt intended as a totally campy joke, "Full Moon High"
portrays 1950s teenager Tony Walker (Adam Arkin) accompanying
his father (Ed McMahon) on a trip to Romania. Sure enough, Tony
gets bitten, and grows fur and fangs whenever there\'s a full
moon. A particularly interesting aspect in this movie is that
he can\'t age as long as he has the werewolf curse, and that he
...
Also starring Elizabeth Hartman.PS: director Larry Cohen is
probably best known for the killer baby flick "It\'s Alive".'
```

Removing Special Characters

Often your business use case will only deal with textual information, such as a legal contract, and in such cases it will demand the use of only alphanumeric characters. Any other characters should be considered junk. Although some of the special characters should have already been removed from the text when you had filtered accented characters, it never hurts to be extra careful when you want to put something in production. This preprocessing step involves removing these special characters.

This step is not as daunting as the others and a simple regular expression can often do the job, as follows.

```
def remove_special_chars(text):
    pattern = r'[^a-zA-z0-9\s]'
    text = re.sub(pattern, '', text)
    return text
```

This simple function is enough to rid your text of any special characters.

Note that it would be wise to analyze the business use case before proceeding with removing special characters to make sure you really can remove them. For example, systems involving medical or mathematical journals might require these special characters.

Lowercasing

This step is obvious and often is the first one to be included as a preprocessing step. If you let your complete text input be lowercase, it will be easier for the algorithm to handle your input when it is converted into a numeric representation. You will read about vectorization more in the next section.

Python offers an even easier way to implement this step as compared to the previous one.

```
def lowercase(text):
    return text.lower()
```

The lower attribute of a string in Python converts all uppercase characters to lowercase.

Stemming

To understand stemming, you need to know what a morpheme is. A morpheme is the smallest meaningful meaning of a word. For example, the word "unusually" can be divided into "un," "usual," and "ly." Here "usual" is the morpheme that constitutes the word "unusually." Adding prefixes ("un") and suffixes ("ly") to evolve the meaning of the morpheme to something different is known as *inflection*. Stemming is the process of getting morphemes from a word in order to use the morphemes as the unit of input for an NLP sequence.

Stemming is often achieved by running the string through a set of rules that checks for prefixes and suffixes and removes them to get the stem. NLTK provides several stemmers, among which the Porter Stemmer is most frequently used. You can use the Porter Stemmer as follows:

```
def simple_stemmer(text_tokens):
    stemmer = nltk.porter.PorterStemmer()
    text = ' '.join([stemmer.stem(word) for word in text_
    tokens])
    return text
```

In this code snippet, you have to pass the list of words in the function as text_tokens and PorterStemmer from NLTK grabs the stem of the word through the stem() function.

Lemmatization

Lemmatization is similar to stemming, where a word is stripped to get the base form, with a small difference. Stemming is performed through rule engines, where the stemmer only strips the predetermined prefixes and suffixes and presents the output with the form of the word that is left, without any regard to the meaning of the base form outputted by the stemmer. It may so happen that the base form (or the stem) is not a real meaningful word that exists in the English vocabulary. For example, the stem of the word "fancier" is "fanci," which the stemmer will output after passing through the rule to remove "er" from a word form. But "fanci" is not a real meaningful word in the English vocabulary.

Lemmatization is the process of determining a lemma, which is a root word of a word form that also exists in the English vocabulary. Hence, the lemma of "fancier" is "fancy."

Stemming is often used in use cases where the root form of the word does not have to be meaningful, such as with sentiment analysis. Sentiment analysis needs to understand the overall sentiment of a statement without regard to the meaning of each of the base word forms.

On the other hand, lemmatization is necessary for use cases that need to derive the meaning of each word carefully, such as chatbots.

NLTK provides a lexical database known as WordNet, which is a vocabulary that can be used to find lemmas. NLTK also has a lemmatization module that leverages WordNet, known as WordNetLemmatizer. You can use it as follows:

```
from nltk.stem import WordNetLemmatizer
lemmatizer = WordNetLemmatizer()
print(lemmatizer.lemmatize(fancier, 'a'))
```

Here a in the lemmatize() function refers to the part of speech.

Although NLTK has all these processes up its sleeves, Spacy is easier to use when it comes to lemmatization and you can use it similarly to how you used it earlier, as follows.

```
doc = nlp(review)
for token in doc:
  print(token.lemma_)
```

The lemma_ attribute will give you the lemma of the word.

Expand Contractions

An NLP system needs clearly defined words and contractions such as "you're" sometimes confuse the system. It's necessary to expand such contractions to their base words, such as "you" and "are," before processing the rest of the text.

To expand contractions in Python, you can use the `contractions` library, which you can install using `pip` (see `https://pypi.org/project/contractions/`). This library expands a contraction in a sentence into possible words and uses the Word Movers Distance metric to find the best match.

For example, the sentence "They'll get the same prizes due to their similar skills" can be expanded to the following:

> "They will get the same prizes due to their similar skills."

> "They shall get the same prizes due to their similar skills."

> "They are get the same prizes due to their similar skills."

> "They have get the same prizes due to their similar skills."

The Word Mover Distance calculates the distance between these expanded texts. The one with the contracted text and the one closest is chosen as the expanded text. The Word Mover distance calculates the score by using *embeddings*, which you will learn about in upcoming sections.

To use the `contractions` library, start by installing the library using `pip`.

```
pip install contractions
```

Now you can import and use it as follows:

```
import contractions
def expand_con(words):
    expanded_text = []
    for word in words:
        expanded_text.fix(word)
return expanded_text
```

As you can see, here again we are passing the list of words in the function.

Stopword Removal

The last step to consider when cleaning your text is to remove any stopwords. *Stopwords* consist of insignificant words such as "a," "the," and so on. Often it is beneficial to get rid of these stopwords for use cases that need to gather and work on the words that have a weight and significance for analysis.

NLTK makes it very easy to remove stopwords since it contains a predefined list of stopwords that you can use, as follows:

```
stopword_list = nltk.corpus.stopwords.words('english')
```

Then you can use the `stopword_list` to filter out the stopwords when processing.

Tokenization

The problem we are concentrating on is sentiment analysis of reviews and hence the model that we will build will take reviews as the input. Each review can be considered a range of sentences. Hence, the input is a set of sentences.

Almost all of the problems in the real world are similar to this problem, in that they take sentences as inputs. Problems that take documents as inputs can also be broken down into sentences since documents are made up of sentences.

The model should be able to understand these sentences. But sentences cannot be a unit of input. So you have to break down the sentences into words. For example, the sentence "I want to learn machine learning" should be broken down into these tokens:

```
["I","want","to","learn","machine","learning"]
```

These building blocks of inputs (or sentences) are known as *tokens* and the process of breaking down sentences into tokens is known as *tokenization.*

Types of Tokenization

Tokenization does not always mean breaking down a sentence into words. Although the most intuitive idea for a unit of input, as mentioned earlier, is a word, you will often encounter situations where you will need to break down the word units further.

Tokenization ideally can be considered these types:

1. **Word tokenization**

    This is the most intuitive type of tokenization where you have to break down a stream of sentences into words. Word tokenization works well when the language is well defined.

2. **Character tokenization**

   You will at times encounter streams of strings where there is no clear distinctions. In such cases, when you are unable to discern the word boundaries, the best approach is to break down the streams of strings into individual characters. Although it may seem like a naive approach, you can always fall back on this type of tokenization when you are unsure of the structure of the string.

3. **Subword tokenization**

   The previous two types of tokenization represent the best and worst cases, but most of the time you have to deal with systems where you have to break down a word into multiple sections so the model can understand the meaning. Consider the word "radically." The word is a form of the word "radical." In advanced natural language processing systems, after tokenization, each unit is taken through multiple steps so that the system understands the meaning of the word. This is often done through vocabulary. This vocabulary is either prepopulated or sourced from the input; subword tokenization is best in such cases. You will encounter subword tokenization when you learn about advanced NLP models such as BERT.

NLTK also provides a simple way to tokenize text using the default tokenizer. But you have to download the Punkt model of NLTK, which does the tokenization:

```
import nltk

nltk.download('punkt')
```

Now you can use the NLTK tokenizer as follows:

```
tokenizer = nltk.word_tokenize
tokenizer(review)
```

There are other ways to tokenize in NLTK. If you are interested in learning more, check the NLTK library's official website.

Vectorization and Embedding

Even though you have the complete text tokenized into individual units to process, you are still further away from making a digital system understand the tokens or words like humans do. For that, you need to derive numeric features out of these text units. There are various ways to get numeric representations of text inputs, a technique called *vectorization*. Vectorization is a feature engineering technique that converts text inputs into numerical vectors while preserving the meaning of the text. The following sections explain some of the popular vectorization methods used in NLP.

Count Vectorization

This is the simplest vectorization technique. It counts the occurrences of a token in each document (or input row). Scikit-Learn has a wonderful implementation of Count Vectorization.

Start by importing the CountVectorizer class from Scikit-Learn:

```
from sklearn.feature_extraction.text import CountVectorizer
```

Now you can instantiate a count vectorizer as follows:

```
vectorizer = CountVectorizer(encoding='utf-8', decode_
error='ignore', strip_accents='unicode', lowercase=True,
analyzer='word', max_df=1, min_df=1, max_features=None,
vocabulary=None)
```

Here are the parameters passed in to instantiate the vectorizer. Some of these parameters handle some of the text-cleaning methods discussed earlier:

- encoding: Ensures that the encoding to be followed for the input string is in a certain format. By default, the encoding is utf-8.

- decode_error: Lets Scikit-Learn know what to do when it encounters a character that does not follow the encoding. You can use this to ignore harmful characters by passing ignore to this parameter. Other values you can use here are strict and replace. If you set this to strict, Scikit-Learn will raise a UnicodeDecodeError.

- strip_accents: This parameter handles the accented character removal discussed during the text-cleaning methodologies. You can set it to ascii or unicode, depending on your use case. Scikit-Learn uses NFKD for both. You can also use None if you want to ignore the process; this is the default value.

- lowercase: This parameter converts the text to lowercase.

- analyzer: You can pass word, char, or char_wb to this parameter, which uses word-based analysis or character-based analysis. Accordingly, your tokenizer and ngram will work based on characters or words, as explained here:

- tokenizer: You can pass a function as a callback to this parameter, which will use this function to tokenize if you have passed word as the analyzer value. This parameter can only allow tokenization by word.

- ngarm_range: You can pass a tuple in this parameter, which can refer to the range the vectorizer will use while counting. For example, if you have analyzer="word" and ngram_range=(1,1), then CountVectorizer will take one word as a count. On the other hand having ngram_range as (1,2) will let CountVectorizer take both single words (unigram) and two words (bigrams) as one count each. If you used analyzer="character" and the ngram_range set to (1,2), CountVectorizer will take both single character (unigram) and two characters (bigrams) as one count each.

- max_df: This parameter tells CountVectorizer to ignore terms having a document frequency higher than the value mentioned. Here, the value to be mentioned is from 0 to 1.

- min_df: This parameter tells CountVectorizer to ignore terms having a document frequency less than the value mentioned. Here the value to be mentioned is from 0 to 1.

- max_features: The value mentioned here will tell CountVectorizer to ignore terms beyond the term frequency so that it only considers the top max_feature terms. If ignored, the default is None.

- vocabulary: You can pass a mapping (i.e., a dict) with keys as terms and values as indices in a feature matrix to be considered as a vocabulary. The default value is None. If you pass a vocabulary, your CountVectorizer will ignore any out-of-vocabulary words and hence you are safe to let your system only consider the words that are in the vocabulary.

Finally, you can apply the CountVectorizer to your text as follows:

```
X = vectorizer.fit_transform(train_df['reviews'])
print(X.toarray())
```

The output should give you a matrix of word occurrences per document (or row).

```
[[0 0 0 ... 0 0 0]
 [0 0 0 ... 0 0 0]
 [0 0 0 ... 0 0 0]
 ...
 [0 0 0 ... 0 0 0]
 [0 0 0 ... 0 0 0]
 [0 0 0 ... 0 0 0]]
```

To get the shape of the matrix, use this:

```
X.toarray().shape
```

Which should give the following:
(25000, 74849)
You can also get the vocabulary that the CountVectorizer extracted.

```
vectorizer.get_feature_names_out()
```

It's worth noting that we didn't employ tokenization but CountVectorizer did.

Model Selection, Training, and Evaluation

Now that you have a feature matrix ready, you can use a machine learning algorithm on top of it.

If you are working with limited hardware, you can just use 2,000 reviews to see if your POC is working. For that, you need to take a stratified dataset so that you have half negative reviews and half positive reviews. Since you appended positive reviews on top of negative reviews, you need to take the middle part of the dataset. In this case, since the dataset is 25000, the middle is 12500. To take the 2000 stratified data, you can take data points from 12500-1000=11500 to 12500+1000=13500.

```
from sklearn.tree import DecisionTreeClassifier
from sklearn.model_selection import train_test_split
from sklearn.metrics import f1_score

vectorizer = CountVectorizer()
X = vectorizer.fit_transform(train_
df.loc[11500:13500,'reviews'])
y = train_df.loc[11500:13500,'labels']
X_train, X_test, y_train, y_test = train_test_split(X.
toarray(),y,test_size=0.3)
dtree_model = DecisionTreeClassifier()
dtree_model.fit(X_train,y_train)
preds = dtree_model.predict(X_test)
print(f1_score(y_test,preds))
```

This example uses the Decision Tree Classifier and F1 score to see how the model is performing.

Similar to CountVectorizer, another effective text vectorization method is the TF-IDF Vectorizer. TF-IDF stands for Term Frequency-Inverse Document Frequency. Term Frequency is the count of a term (or token) occurring in a document. Inverse Document Frequency is the reciprocal log of the document frequency, which is the number of documents containing a term (token). Scikit-Learn uses the TF-IDF Vectorizer module instead of CountVectorizer for this purpose.

Deep Learning in Natural Language Processing

This section covers deep learning and neural networks from classical machine learning algorithms. A popular class of algorithms for vectorizing text inputs is Word2Vec. It leverages deep learning by dividing the text into sets of neighboring words and the word to be predicted. It uses deep learning to predict a word by leveraging its context words. For example, consider the sentence "I would like to learn AI and ML quickly." The sets of context words are (['I','like'],'would'), (['to','AI'],'learn'), and (['and','quickly'],'ML'). This algorithm is called Continuous Bag of Words (CBOW).

Another algorithm that does something similar is Skipgram. Skipgram attempts to predict context words by leveraging the middle word using deep learning.

Another great NLP library is Gensim, which has numerous functionalities such as vectorization using CBOW or Skipgram.

You can install Gensim using this line:

```
! pip install gensim
```

You have to use the tokenizer to tokenize the text. So, first you need to tokenize it using the following code:

```
tokenized_reviews = []
for i in range(train_df.shape[0]):
    tokenized_reviews.append(tokenizer(train_df.iloc[i,0]))
tokenized_reviews
```

Once the tokenized reviews are in order, you can start using Gensim to vectorize words using the Word2Vec model as follows:

```
from gensim.models import Word2Vec

wv_model = Word2Vec(tokenized_reviews,  window=5, min_count=5,
workers=16, sg=0, negative=5)
```

The following code shows how a single word vector would look.

```
wv_model.wv['Plot']
array([ 0.08990693,  0.25508496,  0.2509542 , -0.05455301,
        0.06975589, -0.51104593, -0.11543421,  1.0389962 ,
       -0.40622306, -1.066329  , -0.28960004, -0.08673833,
       -0.17169608,  0.00749075,  0.28168637,  0.43893206,
        0.4540334 , -0.18602416, -0.1758271 , -0.3663723 ,
       -0.4080482 ,  0.46373916, -0.0285309 , -0.22901495,
       -0.4389961 ,  0.29966518, -0.04618331, -0.47676224,
        0.5549119 , -0.21962325,  0.12367783,  0.1094077 ,
        0.26706585, -0.16847895, -0.4608883 , -0.24890974,
        0.5640716 ,  0.22057909, -0.10006899, -0.39787945,s
        0.16495384, -0.21580067,  0.5167709 ,  0.38862267,
        0.21256255, -0.6272423 , -0.22778796, -0.4818152 ,
        0.5632361 ,  0.07095092, -0.46020564,  0.62135273,
        0.26800495,  0.41899973,  0.5436685 , -0.0673762 ,
       -0.23013812, -0.16339765, -0.33574238,  0.499936  ,
        0.10157613,  0.25957525,  0.7206584 ,  0.20903282,
        0.35593304,  0.47046697, -0.3913343 , -0.22632024,
       -0.85171527, 0.44256178, -0.7991937 , -0.37387526,
       -0.11396343,  0.08097679,  0.03048304, -0.33055916,
       -0.29276899,  0.26041335, -0.00631601,  0.38871458,
        0.30741662,  0.2631277 ,  0.00865427,  0.7148884 ,
        0.5829756 ,  0.16456945,  0.21283737,  0.16670783,
        0.2599439 ,  0.3610271 ,  0.24865824,  0.26855388,
       -0.07378637,  0.11134908,  0.02223351, -0.32067415,
       -0.5192192 ,  0.18481703, -0.23788132,  0.28109246],
      dtype=float32)
```

Let's check the length of such a vector:

```
len(wv_model.wv['Plot'])
```

This outputs 100.

You can also get the vocabulary like this:

```
vocab = wv_model.wv.index_to_key
```

Now you need to use this as embedding for a machine learning input. Considering 25,000 rows, and each row is at least 50 words (which in turn is vectorized into 100 dimension), the train_df vectorized would be 25000*50*100, which is very large. Instead, you can take the mean of all the word embeddings so as to get a dimension of 25,000*100 when all the word embeddings are aggregated. Let's see if we can do the same and form a feature matrix. As before, we take only 3,000 rows of train_df:

```
import numpy as np

X = train_df.loc[11500:13500,'reviews']
y = train_df.loc[11500:13500,'labels']
emb_X = []
for review in X:
    tokenized = tokenizer(review)
    emb = np.zeros(100)
    for token in tokenized:
        if token in vocab:
            emb = emb + wv_model.wv[token]
    emb = emb/(len(tokenized))
    emb_X.append(emb)
```

Let's convert this to a NumPy array for convenience of calculation.

```
emb_X = np.array(emb_X)
```

Now we use a decision tree with this embedding:

```
X_train, X_test, y_train, y_test = train_test_
split(emb_X,y,test_size=0.3)
dtree_model = DecisionTreeClassifier()
dtree_model.fit(X_train,y_train)
preds = dtree_model.predict(X_test)
print(f1_score(y_test,preds))
```

Since we were on the topic of deep learning, let's use this in a neural network. You already prepared the Word2Vec model using Gensim. Since you will be using Keras for deep learning, Keras also has a wonderful API to create embedding layers using the same kind of algorithm that Gensim uses.

Start by installing Keras, initializing the vocabulary as max_token, and calling the embedding dimension embedding_dim.

```
import keras
from keras import layers
import tensorflow.data as tf_data
max_tokens = 40000
embedding_dim = 100
```

Take the same subset of training data as before.

```
X = train_df.loc[11500:13500,'reviews']
y = train_df.loc[11500:13500,'labels']
```

Then use a vectorized layer to split the text into tokens and assign them to number sequences.

```
vectorizer = layers.TextVectorization(max_tokens=max_tokens,
output_sequence_length=embedding_dim)
vectorizer.adapt(X)
```

The output_sequences parameter pads the sequences to a certain length to handle varying length of text sequences. In this case, we fix the length of the sequences to the embedding dimension length.

Now you can use the Keras embedding layer, which will learn the embedding matrix for each input and pass it to the next layers. The advantage of using the text vectorization and embedding layers is that you can embed them in your model and use them as layers in your model.

```
from keras.layers import Embedding

int_sequences_input = keras.Input(shape=(None,), dtype="int32")
embedded_sequences = Embedding(max_tokens, output_
dim=embedding_dim)(int_sequences_input)
x = layers.Dense(128, activation="relu")(embedded_sequences)
x = layers.Dropout(0.5)(x)
preds = layers.Dense(1, activation="sigmoid")(x)
model = keras.Model(int_sequences_input, preds)
```

The model we just built is very simple; it uses the embedding layer to embed the incoming input text and then uses ReLU activation for a network of 128 neurons. Finally, because there are two classes, the model appends another layer of the Softmax activation neurons as output activation functions with just two neurons. The model blueprint is now ready; you can fit it on the subset of the training dataset as you saw for the decision tree classifier.

Leverage train_test_split again to get the middle data points as before:

```
X_train, X_test, y_train, y_test = train_test_split(X,y,test_
size=0.3, stratify=y)
```

Now compile the model by providing the optimizer and evaluation metric.

```
model.compile(
    loss="binary_crossentropy", optimizer="rmsprop",
    metrics=["acc"]
)
```

Finally, use the vectorization layer to vectorize the inputs.

```
model.fit(vectorizer(X_train), y_train, epochs=3)
```

You can check the model performance using the following code:

```
model.evaluate(vectorizer(X_test),y_test)
```

The output shows test loss and test accuracy.

Pretrained Embeddings

The embedding layer learns the embedding for vectorizing the text, which is then passed on to the next layers to learn. But there might be instances where you need to use a pretrained embedding that was previously prepared. For instance, you can try using GLOVE embeddings. GLOVE embeddings are prepared by running an unsupervised algorithm.

To use GLOVE embeddings, you have to download them from the following link and unzip them in your working location:

https://downloads.cs.stanford.edu/nlp/data/glove.6B.zip

The zip that is downloaded consists of a text file that contains key-value pairs in each line separated by spaces. The key is the word and the value is its embedding vector.

While using GLOVE embedding, your system might encounter words that are not in the vocabulary. In such cases, you can either choose to ignore such words or use n-grams to see if they match any of the words in the vocabulary.

A simple way to deal with this is to initialize the embedding matrix as a matrix of zeroes and fill only the words that are found in the GLOVE vocabulary. In that case, the out-of-vocabulary words remain as a vector of zeroes.

Then make a dict, mapping words (strings) to their NumPy vector representation:

```
path_to_glove_file = "glove.6B.100d.txt"

embeddings_index = {}
with open(path_to_glove_file) as f:
    for line in f:
        word, coefs = line.split(maxsplit=1)
        coefs = np.fromstring(coefs, "f", sep=" ")
        embeddings_index[word] = coefs

print("Found %s word vectors." % len(embeddings_index))
```

Finally, prepare a corresponding embedding matrix that you can use in a Keras embedding layer:

```
num_tokens = len(voc) + 2
embedding_dim = 100
hits = 0
misses = 0

embedding_matrix = np.zeros((num_tokens, embedding_dim))
for word, i in word_index.items():
    embedding_vector = embeddings_index.get(word)
```

```
 if embedding_vector is not None:
   # Words not found in embedding index will be all-zeros.
   embedding_matrix[i] = embedding_vector
   hits += 1
   else:
   misses+=1
 print("Converted %d words (%d misses)" % (hits, misses))
```

The last thing you need to do to use a pretrained embedding is use the embedding matrix as weights in the Keras embedding layer. In such cases, you also need to initialize the embedding layer using the embedding matrix that you prepared:

```
from keras.layers import Embedding

embeddings_initializer=keras.initializers.
Constant(embedding_matrix)

embedding_layer = Embedding(
    numtokens,
    embedding_dim,
    weights=[embedding_matrix],
    trainable=False,
)
embedding_layer.build((1,))
embedding_layer.set_weights([embed_mat])
```

I leave the rest as an exercise.

Now that you have a fair idea how a Natural Language Processing problem can be tackled, the next chapter concentrates on the model selection and model building part of NLP.

Summary

- Natural language processing (NLP) deals with processing and understanding textual information in free form.

- The data is gathered from various sources and collated into a single input format and data structure in the data-gathering phase of NLP.

- Once the data is gathered, the text is cleaned to remove unwanted special characters and HTML tags.

- After data cleaning, features are extracted from the text using various methods of vectorization and embedding, such as CountVectorizer, which is the frequency of each term in a document. This method is present in Scikit-Learn.

- You can use Gensim to access advanced deep learning methods of vectorization, such as Continuous Bag of Words (CBOW) and Skipgram.

- You can also learn the embedding by using the Keras embedding layer.

- You can also use pretrained embeddings in deep learning by adding the embedding matrix to the Keras embedding layer.

CHAPTER 3

RNN to Transformer and BERT

At this point, you should have a decent idea how to build artificial algorithms to work like the human brain. In a world waiting to embrace automation to its complete potential, it is necessary to analyze all facets of problem solving to understand how best you can artificially model the various problem-solving approaches.

You have seen how to build neural networks so that they can model the interaction of human brain cells to solve a problem and you have also seen how to model each neuron. But simple artificial neural networks do not excel at modeling sequence problems when the input length is not fixed.

This chapter explains how to attack such problems using state-of-the-art modeling techniques and architectures, such as Recurrent Neural Networks and Transformers.

The chapter starts with RNNs, which give you a unique architecture to model sequences and play a vital role in text sequence modeling. You will then move on to the Transformers architecture and see how it deals with the disadvantages of RNNs. It is the state-of-the-art architecture, even to this day, laying the foundation for architectures such as BERT and Generative AI.

© Arindam Ganguly 2025
A. Ganguly, *Scaling Enterprise Solutions with Large Language Models*,
https://doi.org/10.1007/979-8-8688-1154-8_3

Sequence Modeling

Consider building a model to predict the next word after a sequence of words typed to form a sentence. These systems suggest the next words emails or document editors such as Google Mail and Google Docs. They try to complete your sentence by suggesting the next word. Sometimes they even suggest better words than what you would have written!

Building such a system, even with a large corpus of next word prediction datasets, is daunting, considering the length of input token you would need to set while building your model. You would take a large number and set it as max sentence length, so that whenever an incomplete input sentence arrived, you would fill a set of preceding tokens as blank so they match the maximum sentence length. Another approach is to predict the next word based only on the previous word. But such an approach would fail in accounting for the complete meaning of the sentence.

Consider another task of predicting the next character to autocomplete a word. You cannot consider a fixed length of input and output sequence. The length of words would vary. Another problem is that the successive inputs are no longer independent. For instance, consider suggesting one character at a time while typing the word "Transformer":

> T_
>
> TR_
>
> TRA_
>
> TRAN_
>
> ....
>
> TRANSFORME_

At each step, the character to be predicted depends on the previous set of characters. In such situations, you need to resort to modified versions of artificial neural networks. Recurrent neural networks are the best fit for such situations.

Recurrent Neural Networks

In the previous chapter, you successfully built a model using artificial neural networks to predict the sentiment of movie reviews. There, you used the vocabulary of the corpus to build an embedding matrix. The embedding matrix was trained in every iteration to learn the embeddings of the words (or tokens) in order to make meaningful vectors of the sentences in the reviews. This embedding matrix was then used in the neural network layers downstream to output a sentiment. The problem was pretty straightforward and the embedding matrix was a fixed size since you have already calculated the vocabulary size. Since the inputs are words instead of numbers, there was a need to vectorize the inputs and assign a serial number (or a unique identifier) to each token. The vectorized input was passed to the embedding matrix through the embedding layer to get the embedding vectors and then the neural network layers did the jobs downstream.

An important point to notice is that the input length is almost fixed. You set the maximum token length of an input, i.e. a review. Also, in problems like these, the processing is one-shot, which means you input a sequence of text and you get an output. But in problems such as autocomplete (discussed in the introduction), the processing happens with time. At each timestamp, there is a section of input that requires processing, the output of which may be used in the next timestamp for processing the next section of input. These kind of problems are known as *sequence-learning problems.*

Artificial neural networks can help out in fixed-length or one-shot problems. But when you need recurring processing and variable length inputs, you have to resort to RNNs.

This section explains how recurrent neural networks work. You know that, for a simple neural network, there is an input, a sigmoid neuron (or another dense neuron) layer, and a final output neuron (see Figure 3-1).

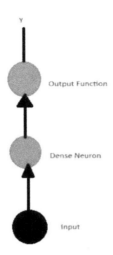

Figure 3-1. *Simple unit of processing*

A careful glance at Figure 3-1 will remind you of the deep learning basics you saw in the previous chapters. If you remember the mathematics, each connection in the figure will have a weight associated with it. Considering an input matrix X, and the final output Y, the dense (or sigmoid) neuron will work as given here:

$$S_i = g(U*X_i)$$

Considering S as the output of the dense neuron, W as the weight matrix associated with the input and g as the dense function (a sigmoid or any other type of function), the output of this state is sent to the output function. This can be a Softmax or linear function based on the problem type (classification or regression, respectively). Considering V as the weight connecting the output of the dense neuron to the output function h, the output should be given by the following equation:

$$Y_i = h(V*S_i)$$

Now, considering a sequence learning problem, the configuration described previously can attend to inputs at each timestamp. Figure 3-2 shows how this configuration can be used with sequence learning problems.

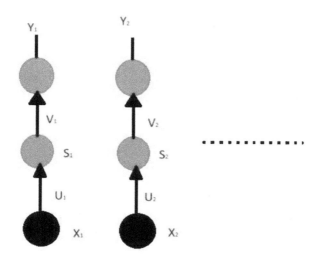

Figure 3-2. *The neural network at each timestamp*

This configuration solves the problem of the variable length input sequence. But the problem with such a configuration is adapting to sequence learning problems such as autocomplete, as mentioned in the introduction. Sequence learning problems need recurrent feedback from the previous states to use them in the next state computations. Recurrent neural networks use the output of the dense state as a parameter while calculating the dense state output of the next state. You also need another weight matrix W at each timestamp to connect the dense state output to the next dense state. Figure 3-3 shows this configuration.

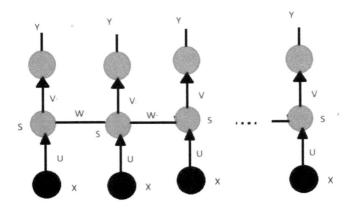

Figure 3-3. *Recurrent neural network*

The only update you need to add to your calculations and dense neuron inputs is the weight matrix W attached to the output of the previous state S. Hence, considering each timestamp from 1,2,3...n as shown in the figure, the dense neuron output computation S_i at timestamp i also needs to consider the weight W and the previous state S_{i-1}, like the following equation:

$$S_i = g(WS_{i-1} + UX_i)$$

The output function calculation remains the same and you get a recurrent neural network capable of sequence learning problems.

Problems with Vanilla RNN

Even though these types of neural networks are some of the best choices for modeling sequence learning problems, there are two problems with these models:

- **Vanishing gradient problem:** There is a complex mathematical analogy behind this problem. But briefly, the problem is due to the fact that each hidden state is dependent not only on its previous hidden state but also on all the states preceding it. Hence, for long sequences, the gradient that flows from the token in the beginning to the end starts fading in the journey. It might so happen that the gradient of the first token almost turns to 0 when the gradient associated with the last token is calculated. This means that the importance of the first token is almost shredded off to zero. This situation is known as the vanishing gradient problem and this leads to losing the information of the tokens, hence losing their knowledge.

- **Exploding gradient problem:** Similar to the vanishing gradient problem, the model might lead to an exploding gradient, where the gradient reaches a huge number, hence crashing the memory.

Exploding gradients can be tackled using a technique called *gradient clipping,* where the gradient is deducted once a certain value is reached. It is intuitive to implement and has been productive in multiple situations. But to address the gradient vanishing problem you have to resort to using LSTMs (Long Short Term Memory Models).

LSTM

As the problem with vanishing gradient is due to the multiple gradients in the flow, if you could only use the gradients that are necessary to carry the information of the input, then you could manage the final gradient from getting unnecessary information that might lead to vanishing gradients of the tokens.

To attain such a configuration, you can introduce three gates:

- **Write gate:** A write gate can filter out the gradients that flow out from one timestamp (or state) to the next. The write gate can be as simple as a gate of real numbers between 0 and 1 of the length equal to that of the incoming gradients that needs to flow to the next state. Each real number represents the importance of carrying the gradient to the next state. This number can also be learned by introducing a weight vector and having an initial value of one for all the gate values.

- **Read gate:** You can use the output of the write gate as an input to the sigmoid (or any other activation function) to get the output of the new state. But before taking this output of the activation function, you can select which of the gradients to pass through according to the new output values. Similar to the write gate, you can introduce another gate to work like a read gate. The configuration is the same as the read gate: you introduce a weight matrix with values between 0 and 1 and initialize the gate with 1s to learn the gate on the go.

- **Forget gate:** The write and read gates take the previous state and manipulates to get a new state after passing it through the gates. After the read gate, you have the new state values. Now you need a gate to combine and filter the previous state and the new state to get the final new state. Although you have selective writes and reads, you can also take the previous state values and let go of some of the values that are not needed (the unnecessary tokens) and concatenate or combine the rest with the new state to get a final new state.

This configuration of RNN is known as LSTM and it is widely used to prevent vanishing gradients.

Figure 3-4 should allay all your doubts about the working of LSTMs.

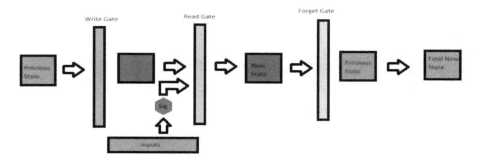

Figure 3-4. *LSTM*

Gated Recurrent Units (GRUs)

It might occur to you that the selective read gate is unnecessary, or the forget gate is unnecessary. GRUs came up with a solution to this confusion. You can use a single gate and combine the outputs of the sigmoid (or activation function) and the previous state values. So instead of using two different weight matrix to learn, you can use a single matrix both as the forget and read gate. This configuration is known as GRU. It's difficult to say which RNN to use—LSTM or GRU. It depends on various factors, such as computation power optimization over faster processing, problem statement, and so on.

The following code shows you how to use these in Python to solve a problem in real life. It uses the problem and dataset from the previous chapter. You will also use the same preprocessing procedures.

```
! wget https://ai.stanford.edu/~amaas/data/sentiment/aclImdb_
v1.tar.gz
! tar -xvzf /content/aclImdb_v1.tar.gz
```

```python
import os
import pandas as pd

train_pos_reviews_filenames = os.listdir("/content/aclImdb/
train/pos")
train_pos_reviews = []

for filename in train_pos_reviews_filenames:
  with open("/content/aclImdb/train/pos/"+filename) as fd:
    train_pos_reviews.append(fd.readline())
  fd.close()

train_neg_reviews_filenames = os.listdir("/content/aclImdb/
train/neg")
train_neg_reviews = []

for filename in train_neg_reviews_filenames:
  with open("/content/aclImdb/train/neg/"+filename) as fd:
    train_neg_reviews.append(fd.readline())
  fd.close()

test_pos_reviews_filenames = os.listdir("/content/aclImdb/
test/pos")
test_pos_reviews = []

for filename in test_pos_reviews_filenames:
  with open("/content/aclImdb/test/pos/"+filename) as fd:
    test_pos_reviews.append(fd.readline())
  fd.close()

test_neg_reviews_filenames = os.listdir("/content/aclImdb/
test/neg")
test_neg_reviews = []
```

```
for filename in test_neg_reviews_filenames:
  with open("/content/aclImdb/test/neg/"+filename) as fd:
    test_neg_reviews.append(fd.readline())
  fd.close()

train_pos_reviews_labels = [1]*len(train_pos_reviews)
train_neg_reviews_labels = [0]*len(train_neg_reviews)
test_pos_reviews_labels = [1]*len(test_pos_reviews)
test_neg_reviews_labels = [0]*len(test_neg_reviews)
train_pos_df = pd.DataFrame({'reviews':train_pos_
reviews,'labels':train_pos_reviews_labels})
train_pos_df
train_neg_df = pd.DataFrame({'reviews':train_neg_
reviews,'labels':train_neg_reviews_labels})
train_neg_df.head()
test_pos_df = pd.DataFrame({'reviews':test_pos_
reviews,'labels':test_pos_reviews_labels})
test_pos_df.head()
test_neg_df = pd.DataFrame({'reviews':test_neg_
reviews,'labels':test_neg_reviews_labels})
test_neg_df.head()
train_df = pd.concat([train_pos_df,train_neg_df],ignore_
index=True)
train_df.shape
test_df = pd.concat([test_pos_df,test_neg_df],ignore_
index=True)
test_df.shape

import keras
from keras import layers
import tensorflow.data as tf_data
max_tokens = 40000
embedding_dim = 100
```

```
X = train_df.loc[11500:13500,'reviews']
y = train_df.loc[11500:13500,'labels']

vectorizer = layers.TextVectorization(max_tokens=max_tokens,
output_sequence_length=embedding_dim)
vectorizer.adapt(X)
```

This code is exactly what you did in the previous chapter. Now you can build your model and use the Keras LSTM layer to use LSTM in the model. You will also use a bidirectional layer so that the LSTM layer performs the RNN from left to right and from right to left. Here's how you can do that:

```
from keras.layers import Embedding

int_sequences_input = keras.Input(shape=(None,), dtype="int32")
embedded_sequences = Embedding(max_tokens, output_
dim=embedding_dim)(int_sequences_input)
# Add 2 bidirectional LSTMs
x = layers.Bidirectional(layers.LSTM(64, return_
sequences=True))(embedded_sequences)
x = layers.Bidirectional(layers.LSTM(64))(x)
x = layers.Dropout(0.5)(x)
preds = layers.Dense(1, activation="sigmoid")(x)
model = keras.Model(int_sequences_input, preds)
```

Now that you have the model ready, you can divide the dataset into training and test sets, compile, fit, and evaluate the model, similar to what you did in the previous chapter.

```
from sklearn.model_selection import train_test_split

X_train, X_test, y_train, y_test = train_test_split(X,y,test_
size=0.3, stratify=y)
```

```
model.compile(
    loss="binary_crossentropy", optimizer="rmsprop",
    metrics=["acc"]
)
model.fit(vectorizer(X_train), y_train, epochs=3)
model.evaluate(vectorizer(X_test),y_test)
```

The output will show test loss and test accuracy. For me, it showed the following output:

```
19/19 [==============================] - 6s 110ms/step - loss:
0.6091 - acc: 0.6689

[0.6091383695602417, 0.6688851714134216]
```

I can say that the test accuracy (0.66 or 66 percent in my case) will definitely be better than what you would have got in the previous chapter.

Attention

RNN and its variants have been extremely popular for solving long-range sequence learning problems without worrying about fixed-length problems. But these models suffer from something known as the long-term dependency problem. The information derived in the beginning is no more relevant when the model reaches the end of the sequence. Although LSTM and GRU manages some of this by introducing gates and filtering out the unnecessary information, they are not enough to capture the importance of tokens.

Another problem with RNNs is that they are relatively slower compared to Artificial Neural Networks, due to temporal processing.

To address these problems, data scientists came up with a wonderful technique known as *attention*. The necessity of attention stems from the fact that temporal processing leads to loss of relevant information.

In simple terms, it becomes too heavy for the last state to capture the information of the entire sequence. Instead of that, a novel solution is to use multiple vectors that represent how each token contributes to the other tokens. This is known as an attention mechanism and the value that represents the contribution is known as the attention score. The following example uses this process to implement an attention mechanism.

Consider each token as a temporal input and each state derived as from each corresponding input. From each of these states, two vector representations (or projections) are derived—key and query (K and Q). Each of these vector representations are learned through weight vectors—one for key and one for query (W_K and W_Q) to be used for all the tokens. Attention scores of a token (or state) are then calculated for each of the other tokens, and they show how the prediction of the token is influenced by the other tokens. To calculate this score, the query vector representation of the token to be predicted is derived, and the key vector of the other tokens are derived. The attention score for each token is calculated by performing the dot product of the query vector with each key vector, combining by scaling, and then normalizing the dot product. This normalization can be done through the Softmax function. Let's look at this calculation in depth:

1. Derive the Key and Query through weight vectors (considering h as state of token):

$$K = W_K * h_t$$
$$Q = W_Q * h_t$$

2. Calculate the dot product as follows:

$$\text{Dot product} = Q * K^T$$

Mathematically, the dot product of two vectors is calculated by the product of one vector and the transpose of another product.

3. You can then scale this by dimension of the key vector (denoted by d_k) as follows:

$$\frac{Q * K^T}{\sqrt{d_k}}$$

4. Finally, you will normalize using Softmax. Why do you even need Softmax? Consider the problem of getting the attention score of a token with respect to the other tokens as a classification problem. In this classification problem, the query vector is the target and the keys are the feature set. The attention score is the maximum probability score derived from the feature vectors. The maximum probability scores are derived using the Softmax function.

   Along with this, another projection of the Key vector (called the Value projection vector or V) is also added as a multiple to add a weight to Softmax. You will realize its significance once you read about self-attention in the next section. Hence, the final attention score is as follows:

$$\text{Attention score} = \text{Softmax}(\frac{Q * K^T}{\sqrt{d_k}})*V$$

Figure 3-5 shows this visually by using the example of a sentence completion problem.

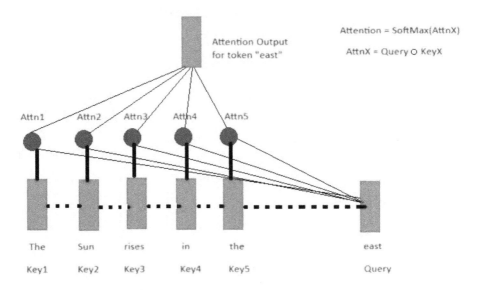

Figure 3-5. *Attention*

As you can see, the attention is calculated in parallel for each token instead of temporal processing. This reduces lag by getting rid of the recurrent connections and computations, which are shown in Figure 3-5 as dotted lines.

If you consider the token predicting the target and the other tokens as a predictor or feature, the attention scores give the feature importance of each of those predictor tokens and hence the Softmax is an obvious choice to gather the final combined attention score. See Figure 3-6.

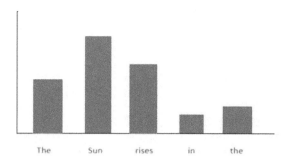

Figure 3-6. *Attention scores of tokens as predictors*

Encoder-Decoder Models

The problems so far have dealt with getting a single output from a range of inputs, for example, predicting the next word of a sentence (similar to autocompletion) and predicting the sentiment in reviews. But in the recent world of AI advancements, these problems are very minimal when compared to advanced AI applications like chatbot. If you think about it for a moment, a chatbot is also a simple AI application where the model is supposed to predict an answer to a query. For a chatbot, the input can be represented in the same way, but the output is a sentence (or a range of tokens) instead of a single token or value. Hence, the problem becomes a multi-output supervised learning problem.

To tackle such a problem, we need to represent and model the output as a sequence of tokens similar to the input. The input model is then considered the encoder model and the output is the decoder model. Since RNN (or its variants such as LSTM and GRU) is the model of choice for sequence learning problems, we can model the encoder as an RNN and the decoder as another RNN. The output of the encoder RNN is taken as the first state of the decoder RNN and the output of the states of the decoder RNN are considered the final output. Figure 3-7 shows how the model is implemented with a simple question answering sample.

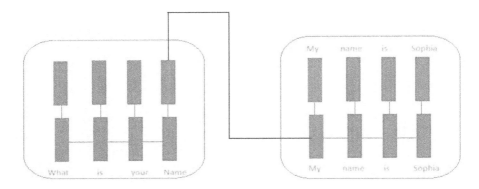

Figure 3-7. *Encoder-decoder models*

Encoder-decoder models use RNNs to train state-of-the-art architectures and are used for advanced AI applications like chatbot.

Self-Attention

Although encoder-decoder models are the foundation for devising modern-day AI applications such as chatbots, simple attention mechanisms cannot be embedded in encoder-decoder models. The reason for this is obvious if you think about it. The output of the decoder is not a single token but a range of tokens as a sentence. So you cannot use a single query vector to map to all the other key vectors of the decoder. Since you have to learn the complete sentence, you have to get query vectors of all tokens, as the desired output will consist of all these tokens. This idea of using query vector representation of all the vectors to get the feature importance of each token with respect to the other is known as a *self-attention mechanism*.

To implement a self-attention mechanism, along with key and query vector representation at each step for each token, you also need a vector representation called the value vector. The *value vector* is used to normalize with Softmax to give a unique value to each of the final attention outputs. The value vector is combined using a dot product and a final neural network layer (a dense layer) is used as the output layer. See Figure 3-8.

$$\text{Attention score} = \text{Softmax}\left(\frac{Q * K^T}{\sqrt{d_k}}\right) * V$$

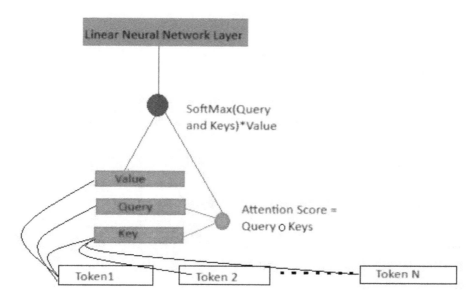

Figure 3-8. *Self-attention*

Why do you need to go to all these lengths when it can be easily accomplished by RNNs? Why do you even need self-attention?

Since all you are doing is creating vector projections using weight matrices, that is, creating simple matrices out of vectors and using these vectors to compute a score and finally a dense and a Softmax layer, you are actually doing everything in one shot. You can create vector projections for all the tokens in one iteration altogether. You can also calculate everything together using matrix multiplication.

Hence you can get rid of the temporal procedures and thus get rid of the recurrent connections because your key vectors take the knowledge of all other successive tokens. See Figure 3-9.

Figure 3-9. *Attention parallel computation*

This mechanism forms the foundation for transformers. Transformers are the basis on which modern AI models such as GPT are built.

Transformers

In 2017, Ashish Vaswani and his colleagues came up with a groundbreaking concept that led to all modern-day architectures. His paper was titled "Attention Is All You Need" and it showed how you can use an encoder-decoder model with self-attention to attain a faster machine translation. You can find the paper at https://arxiv.org/abs/1706.03762.

This chapter has discussed most of the building blocks of this paper in previous sections. This section takes it a few steps further and stitches everything to get the transformer architecture that exists today. See Figure 3-10.

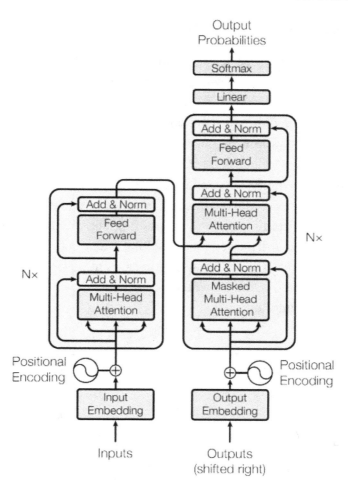

Figure 3-10. *Transformer architecture*

Don't be scared by the complexities of the architecture, as this section dissects all the fine pieces and stitches them together to explain the complete Transformer architecture.

Multi-Head Self-Attention

This chapter has discussed self-attention and how it helps you get rid of the temporal delays by allowing the system to compute attention scores of all the elements in one shot for each training iteration. The Transformer architecture does the same thing, but multiple times in the same step of the iteration. Each time you get an attention score, called the *attention head.*

You create the query, key, and value projection of each token. For ten attention heads, you create ten queries, keys, and value projections and calculate ten attention scores for each training step. All these heads are then concatenated and passed on to the final linear neural network layer.

Figure 3-11 breaks down the attention calculation similar to the procedure discussed in the previous sections and shows how to calculate multi-head self-attention.

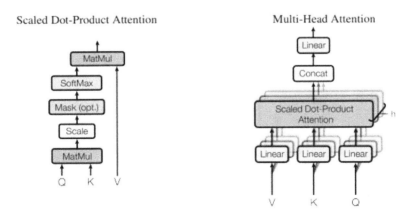

Figure 3-11. *Multi-head self-attention*

In the original Transformer paper, the dimension of the queries, keys, and value vectors was assumed to be 64. Hence the weight matrix for the query, key, and value is used to derive the projections and should be Nx64, where N is the dimension of the token embedding. The number of heads in the original Transformer paper was 8.

The encoder starts with a multi-head attention layer, akin to what was discussed previously. This attention mechanism uses multiple keys, queries, and value projections of the input token embeddings and prepares the attention scores. See Figure 3-12.

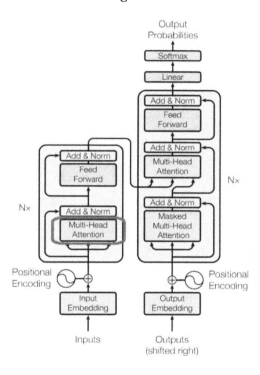

Figure 3-12. *Multi-head attention in encoder*

The next multi-head attention layer is used in the decoder (at the top), which uses cross-attention mechanism. In the cross-attention layer, the multi-head attention uses the output of the encoder and uses these output vector values to create query and key projections for multiple heads. The value is then derived as a projection of the output of the layers preceding this attention layer in the decoder. Figure 3-13 highlights the part where cross-attention is used.

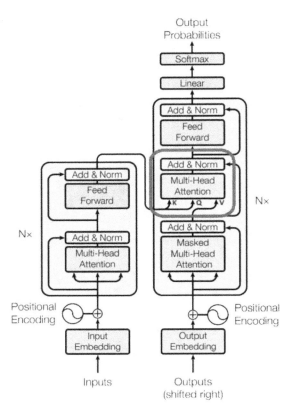

Figure 3-13. *Cross-attention in the decoder*

As you can see from Figure 3-13, the key and query are derived from the encoder outputs and the value vector is derived from the decoder layer outputs. This allows the decoder to acquire and blend the knowledge of the encoder while preparing the final attention scores.

Finally, the masked multi-head attention is used to mask the values of the successive outputs while preparing the attention matrix. Since this is not using temporal processing like RNN and calculating all the attention scores in one go, it is essential to calculate the attention scores for tokens arrived at time t without accounting for the tokens at time t+1. In the attention score matrix, the attention scores for tokens at time t+1 are masked, so the scores don't flow in the next layers.

106

Point-Wise Feed-Forward Networks

You must have noticed that there are feed-forward networks in the Transformer architecture present in the encoder and decoder. These networks are nothing but a combination of three dense layers stacked on top of the other, where a dense layer of ReLU activation function is sandwiched between two linear activation layers.

This section discusses the input and outputs from the feed-forward networks.

Layer Normalization

Normalization is when you need to combine and scale certain elements. Normalization was used when we used Softmax to get the attention scores. There, we used Softmax to essentially combine and get the final probability score out of all the scores. This section looks deeper into what normalization is. You first need to understand what scaling is.

Scaling

Now consider a feature set where the metric is not uniform. A classic example is a feature set that predicts the future price of a stock. This prediction could be based on features such as opening price, closing price, quantity of the stock being traded, and so on. It is worth noting that the quantity of stock traded could be in the range of thousands to millions (for example 120,000), whereas opening and closing price could be just a few hundred at maximum (for example, $125). This means that there is disparity in the metric, which might cause bias toward features having greater values than the others. One way to bring everything into a common range (for example, 0 to 1) is by scaling.

Scaling can be done in two ways:

1. Scaled Value = (value - value_min)/(value_max - value_min)

   Where the range of values in the feature is value_min to value_max.

   This method is known as *min-max scaling* because the range is squeezed between 0 and 1 by scaling the values down within the range. This method is also known as *normalization*.

2. Another method is derived from the statistical calculation of z-score.

$$z = \frac{x - mean}{std}$$

   Where std is the standard deviation of the feature values. This technique assumes that your feature values follow the Gaussian distribution and converts the values to follow the standard normal distribution. Hence, the method is known as *standardization*. A standard normal distribution has a mean of 0 and a standard deviation of 1.

Unlike normalization, standardization does not ensure the scaled values fall in the range of 0 to 1. But standardization is not affected by outliers, which is a possible scenario in case of normalization.

Standardization is sometimes referred to as *z-score normalization*.

It is not untrue to say that almost all machine learning algorithms tend to preprocess the distribution of feature sets to fit the normal curve (or distribution). Hence z-score normalization is an important preprocessing step to perform with a machine learning problem.

Batch Normalization

Consider a neural network layer where the input is a set of N features divided into batches of k. At each layer, batch normalization standardizes the k values corresponding to each feature to a standard normal distribution. Batch normalization is applied as a separate layer; Figure 3-14 illustrates this with an example.

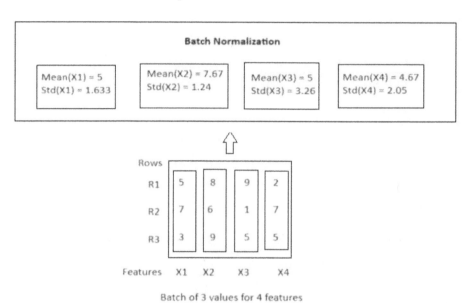

Figure 3-14. *Batch normalization*

Layer Normalization

Although batch normalization attempts to convert each feature at each batch to a standard normal distribution, in sequence learning problems, where the previous inputs carry knowledge about the next inputs, the separation into batches causes this connection of knowledge to break out. Hence, when standardization is done for a batch, the successive inputs in the next batch cannot be accounted for.

Hence, for sequence learning problems, the best approach is to normalize for each row. Figure 3-15 explains this with an example.

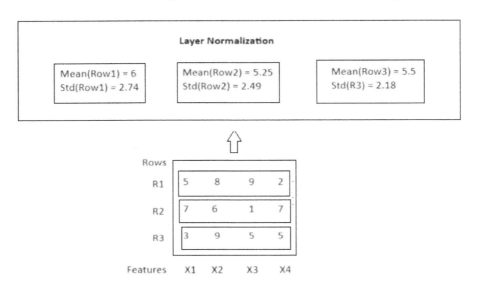

Figure 3-15. *Layer normalization*

After each layer in the transformer architecture, the outputs are passed through the feed-forward layer and a layer normalization. The result of these are concatenated with the original output of the previous layer prior to the feed-forward layer, in order to capture and use the knowledge of the original layer output.

Positional Embedding

As you can see in the Transformer architecture, the inputs and outputs are converted into vector embeddings, called input and output embedding. But there is also a feature added to the embeddings before passing them to the encoder and decoder, which is called *positional embedding*. Positional embedding, as the name suggests, holds the positional information of the tokens. The reason for preserving the position values here is due to the lack of recurrent connections like RNN. Since there are no recurrent connections, there is no way of preserving the order of the inputs. This necessitates the use of positional embedding, which captures the position of the inputs and blends them in the model.

In the original transformer paper, the authors used sinusoidal functions to keep the order of the positions. They simply used two types of positional embedding functions. One for the inputs in even positions, which is passed through the function: $\sin(pos/10000^{2i/d})$, where $2i$ is the position of the input (considering only even positions) and d is the dimensionality of the inputs and output vector. In the original paper d was assumed to be 512.

The other function was for the inputs in odd positions, which is passed through the function: $\cos(pos/10000^{2i/d})$, where $2i+1$ is the position of the input (considering only odd positions).

Leveraging all the previous concepts, the Transformer architecture is implemented with six encoder and six decoder layers in the original paper. During the training, the authors experimented with the ADAM optimizer with $\beta_1 = 0.9$, $\beta_2 = 0.98$ and $\epsilon = 10^{-9}$. Apart from these, the authors experimented with varying parameters—dimension of input and output vector embeddings (d_{model}), dimension of key and value (d_k and d_v respectively), dimension of the sandwiched ReLU layer in a feed-forward layer (d_{ff} which is initially taken as 2048), the number of attention heads (h), a residual dropout with a rate of P_{drop}, and the learning rate. The results are presented in Table 3 in the original transformer paper.

Although the Transformer architecture is a bit convoluted, the inner workings and data flow are very intuitive once you have these concepts in mind. With evolving Python developments, all the models are already implemented by various organizations, including *HuggingFace,* and are open-sourced and available to the general public. If you are still looking to implement the architecture from scratch, TensorFlow has a wonderful tutorial that can walk you through each of the steps while coding along. You can find the tutorial at `https://www.tensorflow.org/text/tutorials/transformer`.

Keep in mind that the transformer was invented to solve a single problem of language translation and the previous link targets solving the same referring to the original paper. But now transformers are used as a foundation for all advanced generative AI models.

The next section discusses how the Transformer architecture began to be used in developing ground-breaking models.

BERT

BERT (Bidirectional Encoder Representations from Transformers) is one of the oldest and best models used, even currently in large enterprise systems. You learned about the inner workings of Transformer architecture and the theories that surround it. This section explains BERT and shows how the Transformer architecture gave birth to numerous models used today.

After all the theories in the previous sections, we finally dive into Python and use these models for practical use cases. But before that, I introduce BERT.

The original paper for BERT introduced by Google can be found here : `https://arxiv.org/abs/1810.04805`

Before BERT, there were attempts to create the perfect model but most of them suffered one problem—they are unidirectional. For models that try to solve problems involving sentence or text inputs, unidirectional models fail to capture the complete meaning of the sentence. But for tasks like sentiment analysis, the complete meaning of the sentence is extracted only when the sentence is processed from both ends.

But previous attempts to process sequences bidirectionally used a naive approach, where the right and left embeddings were concatenated. An example of a model that uses such a technique is ELMO, as shown in Figure 3-16.

Figure 3-16. *Both unidirectional embeddings are concatenated in ELMO*

BERT came up with a novel approach known as Masked Language Modelling to use bidirectional processing in one shot instead of processing them separately and concatenating them. BERT uses two techniques for processing inputs bidirectionally and preserving their knowledge—Masked Language Modeling and Next Sentence Prediction.

Masked Language Modeling

BERT uses masks to hide 15 percent of the tokens at each step of the processing so that there is no need for bidirectional processing. This 15 percent of masking is done in three ways:

- BERT places [MASK] as a special masking token 80 percent of the time

- It replaces masked tokens with a random word from another position 10 percent of the time

- Another 10 percent of the token is kept unchanged

Next Sentence Prediction

During training, BERT is also trained by inputting pairs of sentences from the dataset. It does this by providing two sentences that actually come in order one after the other 50 percent of the time and two random sentences that do not fall in order 50 percent of the time.

With the configurations discussed previously, BERT performs better than almost all other models implemented prior to BERT.

Organizations like HuggingFace have pretrained versions of models like BERT and the pretrained knowledge is used in various industrial use cases where there is no means or infrastructure to train these models from scratch.

HuggingFace Transformers

Let's dive into Python and learn how to use these models in Python.

Similar to all the previous implementation endeavors, you can follow all the steps one by one, starting with data gathering. For data gathering, let me introduce you to Kaggle. Kaggle is a gold mine for data scientists and practitioners. Kaggle lets you avail various datasets, codes, and models over several domains. You will leverage Kaggle to get access to a dataset that predicts whether a news story is fake or not. The application for such a model is endless. Consider building a website that hosts news on a specific domain. Your model can help identify fake news. You can get the dataset from this link:

```
https://www.kaggle.com/datasets/rajatkumar30/fake-news
```

You are welcome to download the dataset and try it on your local system. You can also bring up a notebook from Kaggle itself and write your code to build the model.

But before starting the implementation, I want to introduce you to HuggingFace. It was one of the first organizations to bring a complete library of Transformers for the general public to use. You will use HuggingFace Transformer libraries to build the code.

Since you are aware of the data source, start by checking the dataset through Pandas.

```
data = pd.read_csv('news.csv')
data.head()
```

The output will show you a table with four columns:

Unnamed: 0	title	text		label	
0	8476	You Can Smell Hillary's Fear	Daniel Greenfield, a Shillman Journalism Fello...	FAKE	
1	10294	Watch The Exact Moment Paul Ryan Committed Pol...	Google Pinterest Digg LinkedIn Reddit Stumbleu...	FAKE	
2	3608	Kerry to go to Paris in gesture of sympathy	U.S. Secretary of State John F. Kerry said Mon...	REAL	
3	10142	Bernie supporters on Twitter erupt in anger ag...	— Kaydee King (@KaydeeKing) November 9, 2016 T...	FAKE	
4	875	The Battle of New York: Why This Primary Matters	It's primary day in New York and front-runners...	REAL	

To be on the safe side, you can also load only 500 rows if you are working locally or with limited resources, by adding the parameter nrows=500 in read_csv.

You have to consider the title and text as the input and the label as the target. Specifically, you combine the title and text into a single string and use it as input from a separate column (say desc).

```
data['desc'] = data['title'] + " " + data['text']
```

You might be wondering the reason for choosing a simple text classification problem which can very well be solved by traditional machine learning and NLP toolkits. But let me assure you that Transformers like BERT can give you far better results with minimal preprocessing than with traditional ways of solving the problem.

Now install the Transformer library of HuggingFace.

```
!pip install transformers
```

HuggingFace has a huge repository of advanced and pretrained models and we will use their Transformer library to avail those models. Start by importing the library you will need to use BERT for this classification.

You will use pretrained BERT model available in HuggingFace repository and fine tune it to fit to the dataset to predict the target from the features in the dataset. There are various versions of pretrained models available in HuggingFace. The version of BERT used for this problem is bert-base-uncased. This version is pretrained on Wikipedia, which is a corpus of Wikipedia dumps and Book corpus, which is a corpus of 7,185 unique books. This version of BERT is trained only with English language text and has 11 million parameters.

Import TensorFlow and the Auto class from the HuggingFace Transformers library:

```
from transformers import AutoTokenizer,TFAutoModelForSequenceCl
assification
import tensorflow as tf
```

Auto classes can retrieve the pretrained models from HuggingFace and act as a wrapper to call the HuggingFace model APIs for interacting with the model. Auto classes are available for PyTorch and TensorFlow frameworks, as `AutoModel` and `TFAutoModel`.

Auto classes provide generic wrappers that can be enhanced by adding layers on top of the output of the models for specific purposes like classification, question answering, and so on. HuggingFace also provides specific auto classes for specific purposes, where an extra head is introduced on top of the pretrained model based on a specific purpose, thus preventing you from adding these layers manually. For example:

`TFAutoModelForSequenceClassification` has a classification head on top of the generic Transformer model.

`TFAutoModelForQuestionAnswering` has an additional layer on top of the generic model to support question answering tasks.

`TFAutoModelForTokenClassification` is used for tasks such as Named Entity Recognition.

Since you are dealing with a classification problem from text sequences, you need `TFAutoModelForSequenceClassification`.

Before using the pretrained transformer model for classification, you need to preprocess the text inputs in order to get the tokens properly from each of the sentences. HuggingFace has a wrapper for tokenizers called `AutoTokenizer` that can use subword tokenization algorithms that various Transformer models use. This makes the tokenizer output compatible with the Transformer model that will be used in the next steps. For example,

BERT uses Word-Piece Tokenization, GPT uses Byte Pair Encoding, ALBERT uses unigram, and so on. This example uses AutoTokenizer and leverages bert-base-uncased.

```
tokenizer = AutoTokenizer.from_pretrained("bert-base-uncased")
```

The tokenizer is further wrapped in a function that calls the AutoTokenizer on the concatenated text input. Before using this tokenizer, you need to make the dataset compatible with the HuggingFace model input formats. HuggingFace has a library "datasets" that can ensure that your inputs are in order when you want to input this to the BERT model. Install the datasets library:

```
! pip install datasets
```

You also need to divide the dataset into training and test datasets using train_test_split like you did earlier.

```
from sklearn.model_selection import train_test_split
train_data, test_data = train_test_split(data)
```

Now you can use datasets to let it ingest the training dataset.

```
from datasets import Dataset
train_ds = Dataset.from_pandas(train_data)
```

Now use these tokenizer function to create a preprocess function that can tokenize the combined text using BERT.

```
def preprocess(dataset):
    return tokenizer(dataset["desc"],return_
    tensors="np",padding=True, max_length=512, truncation=True)
```

This code sets a maximum length parameter to 512. If you remember, BERT has been trained in the original paper with dimension of model input set to 512. This is exactly how the versions of BERT models are also trained in HuggingFace. Hence, you need to set the maximum length of the tokens to 512. The `padding` parameter lets the tokenizer pad the sequences having length less than 512 and `truncation` lets the tokenizer remove tokens that exceed the maximum length. Also, note that the example is extracting only the `desc` column while tokenizing and ignoring the other columns.

To tokenize the training dataset, simply call the `preprocess` function on the dataset.

```
tokenized_train_dataset = preprocess(train_ds)
```

For the model to understand the labels, you need to put labels into a NumPy array and convert "FAKE" and "REAL" to 1 and 0.

```
train_labels = np.array(train_ds["label"])
train_labels_modified = []
for tl in train_labels:
    if tl=='FAKE':
        train_labels_modified.append(1)
    else:
        train_labels_modified.append(0)
```

You also need the text dataset to be converted to `dict`.

```
tokenized_train_dataset = dict(tokenized_train_dataset)
```

Do all of this to your test dataset as well.

```
test_ds = Dataset.from_pandas(test_data)
tokenized_test_dataset = preprocess(test_ds)
test_labels = np.array(test_ds["label"])
tokenized_test_dataset = dict(tokenized_test_dataset)
```

```
test_labels_modified = []
for tl in test_labels:
    if tl=='FAKE':
        test_labels_modified.append(1)
    else:
        test_labels_modified.append(0)
```

Now you are ready to bring the model to the ground and fine-tune the model with the dataset.

As discussed, this example uses TFAutoModelForSequenceClassification.

```
from transformers import TFAutoModelForSequenceClassification

model = TFAutoModelForSequenceClassification.from_
pretrained("bert-base-uncased")

model.compile(optimizer="adam")

model.fit(tokenized_train_dataset,np.array(train_labels_
modified))
```

It took me around five hours to train on CPU. I suggest you change your environment to GPU and try the same.

Once it's done, you can also evaluate your model with your test dataset.

```
test_loss = model.evaluate(test_tf_dataset,np.array(test_
labels_modified),verbose=2)
print('\nTest Loss:', test_loss)
```

You can assume that it's fairly easy to fine-tune any transformer model with your dataset of choice using HuggingFace libraries. But you were lucky enough to match the business requirement exactly with one of the model wrappers provided by HuggingFace and hence you were directly able to use TFAutoModelForSequenceClassification.

But what if you need something other than plain classification, or question answering, or anything that can fit with the specific model wrappers? In that case, you have to take the model without any specific head and add a few layers to top of it to match the business use case. In such a case, you need to use the TFAutoModel wrapper of HuggingFace, which gives you the model outputs. You can add the custom layers on top of it to fit your needs.

TFAutoModel

Let's see how to do that. This example uses the same problem you just read about for sequence classification of fake news detection, but it uses TFAutoModel instead of TFAutoModelForSequenceClassification.

To begin, you read and preprocess the data using the HuggingFace datasets library exactly like you did in the previous section.

```
import pandas as pd
```

```
data = pd.read_csv("news.csv", nrows=500)
data['desc'] = data['title'] + " " + data['text']
```

This time I suggest that you download and install only a specific version of HuggingFace Transformers.

```
!pip install transformers==4.37.2
```

Next, you'll import AutoTokenizer and prepare the tokenizer.

DistilBERT

This time you'll use another Transformer model devised by data scientists to overcome one of the major disadvantages of BERT, namely the resource utilization. BERT was definitely ground-breaking in terms of performance and accuracy but it was really a struggle for small enterprises and development teams to use the model with limited resources and infrastructures. Hence, DistilBERT was introduced in the paper "DistilBERT, A Distilled Version of BERT: Smaller, Faster, Cheaper and Lighter," by victor, lysandre, julien and thomas from HuggingFace. You can read the DistilBERT paper at `https://arxiv.org/pdf/1910.01108.pdf`.

With model training and maintaining becoming more and more expensive with BERT, data scientists came up with a novel approach to bring forward a smaller, faster, cheaper, and lighter transformer trained by distilling BERT. The approach is known as *knowledge distillation* and it is defined as a compression technique in which a compact model—the student—is trained to reproduce the behavior of a larger model—the teacher—or an ensemble of models.

The two main parts of the knowledge distillation architecture used by DistilBERT are as follows:

- **Teacher model**: The large and expensive model trained on a huge corpus.

- **Student model**: A relatively smaller model that uses a different type of training called "distillation" to transfer knowledge from the teacher model to the student model.

The distillation is done after training the teacher model with the complete large corpus, by taking another set of training data smaller than the full corpus and using this data to train both the teacher and student models, by leveraging a combined loss function.

Now that you have a very basic idea of what DistilBERT does, and continuing with the coding, you can use DistilBERT in the tokenizer.

```
from transformers import AutoTokenizer
import tensorflow as tf
tokenizer = AutoTokenizer.from_pretrained("distilbert/
distilbert-base-uncased")
```

You can also split the data into training and test datasets, install the HuggingFace datasets library, and ingest the data after tokenization as you did earlier.

```
! pip install datasets
from sklearn.model_selection import train_test_split

train_data, test_data = train_test_split(data)

from datasets import Dataset

train_ds = Dataset.from_pandas(train_data)

def preprocess(dataset):
    return tokenizer(dataset["desc"],return_
    tensors="np",padding=True, max_length=512,truncation=True)

tokenized_train_dataset = preprocess(train_ds)

import numpy as np

train_labels = np.array(train_ds["label"])
tokenized_train_dataset = dict(tokenized_train_dataset)

import numpy as np

train_labels = np.array(train_ds["label"])
tokenized_train_dataset = dict(tokenized_train_dataset)

train_labels_modified = []
for tl in train_labels:
    if tl=='FAKE':
        train_labels_modified.append(1)
    else:
        train_labels_modified.append(0)

test_labels_modified = []
for tl in test_labels:
```

```
if tl=='FAKE':
    test_labels_modified.append(1)
else:
    test_labels_modified.append(0)
```

These preprocessing steps should seem familiar to you, as you are doing the preprocessing steps you did in the previous section.

Next, download the DistilBERT model and wrap it with TFAutoModel.

```
from transformers import TFAutoModel

auto_model = TFAutoModel.from_pretrained("distilbert/
distilbert-base-uncased",output_attentions=True,output_hidden_
states=True)
```

Notice that two new parameters have been added—output_attentions and output_hidden_states—which allow AutoModel to return the attention scores as a separate vector and return the last hidden states respectively.

You can check the attention scores and the hidden states using this code snippet:

```
hidden_states = auto_model_output.hidden_states
attentions = auto_model_output.attentions
```

You have to build your model by leveraging the AutoModel class and other Keras layers.

```
import keras
from keras import layers

max_length=512

auto_model.trainable = False
```

```
input_ids = keras.Input(shape=(None,), dtype="int32",
name="input_ids")
attention_masks = keras.Input(shape=(None,), dtype="int32",
name="attention_mask")
auto_model_output = auto_model(input_ids, attention_
mask=attention_masks)
sequence_output = auto_model_output.last_hidden_state

dropout = tf.keras.layers.Dropout(0.3)(sequence_output)
preds = layers.Dense(1, activation="sigmoid")(dropout)
model = keras.Model(inputs=[input_ids, attention_masks],
outputs=preds)

model.compile(loss="binary_crossentropy",optimizer="adam")
```

Let's analyze this code snippet carefully.

In the beginning, you set the `AutoModel` to nontrainable since you do not want to mess with the weights and biases of the pretrained DistilBERT.

After that, you prepared two input layers to accept the input IDs and attention masks from the Transformer tokenizer. This is also one of the reasons for using AutoTokenizer, as it can return the tokenized dataset in the format that the HuggingFace Transformer models expect as inputs. Almost all of the Transformer models expect the following input formats:

- **Input IDs:** These are the tokenized and vectorized sequences derived from text.

- **Attention Masks:** These are the masks that a transformer model needs for multi-head masked attention.

- **Token Type IDs:** These are used by Transformers when the input is a collection of sequences and the model needs to differentiate tokens of one sequence from the other.

125

Since you are building a model leveraging a pretrained Transformer model, you need to pass these input formats separately. Also, since your final model input is only a single sequence, you can leave the Token Type IDs.

Once you have placed the Transformer model using the `AutoModel` wrapper instance, you need to get the last hidden state to pass it on to the next layers. These layers will determine the output of your final model based on business requirements.

Since you are referring to the same problem and same dataset, you can use a simple dropout and a sigmoid output layer for binary classification. Hence, you finally add a dropout and a dense layer and compile the final model with binary cross entropy loss and ADAM as the optimizer.

You can now go ahead and fit your model to your dataset and you are good to go.

```
model.fit([tokenized_train_dataset['input_ids'],tokenized_
train_dataset['attention_mask']],np.array(train_labels_
modified).astype("float16").reshape((-1,1)))
```

Notice that since you have explicitly added input layers to capture the input IDs and attention masks, you need to pass the input IDs and attention masks separately from the dataset dictionary.

Because of this, you need to reshape and pass the labels, because you do not have HuggingFace dataset as inputs to do these adjustments.

I prepared and ran the code in Google Colab and used TPU as a runtime instead of CPU, which took 624 seconds to run.

```
12/12 [==============================] - 624s 50s/step -
loss: 0.7244
```

You can also leverage a `Trainer` class provided by HuggingFace to train an LLM using this code snippet:

```
from transformers import Trainer, TrainingArguments

training_args = TrainingArguments(
output_dir='./results',
num_train_epochs=3,
per_device_train_batch_size=16,
per_device_eval_batch_size=64,
weight_decay=0.01,
logging_dir='./logs',
logging_steps=10,
)

trainer = Trainer(
model=model,
args=training_args,
train_dataset=train_dataset,
eval_dataset=eval_dataset
)

trainer.train()
```

You should now have a good idea how to use HuggingFace Transformers to level up your NLP applications. The next chapter covers Large Language Models.

Summary

- Recurrent Neural Networks (RNNs) are the ideal neural network models to work on sequence inputs. Vanishing gradient is one of the common problems in RNN. LSTM and GRU are the two variants of RNNs that can help minimize vanishing gradient issues.

- RNNs are good for sequence-to-label problems, but when it comes to sequence-to-sequence problems, the encoder-decoder architecture shines as an obvious solution.

- For long-range sequence problems, it is very difficult to manage the context, as the knowledge at the beginning of the sequence starts to fade when the temporal processing reaches the end. An attention mechanism helps in mitigating the problem by figuring out attention scores of one token to the other.

- Attention can be used in sequence-to-sequence problems by using the self-attention mechanism. In the self-attention mechanism, all the tokens are scored with respect to all the others.

- Leveraging the encoder-decoder architecture and a self-attention mechanism, models can completely get rid of temporal processing by leveraging the Transformer architecture.

- While the Transformer was already popular, BERT was introduced by Google and it raised the bar by coming up with state-of-the-art performance.

- HuggingFace has a huge repository of pretrained Transformer-based models and wrappers for developers to leverage the power of models like BERT and DistilBERT.

CHAPTER 4

Large Language Models

Artificial intelligence has come a long way from predicting simple weather temperatures using meteorological factors to generating poems and songs from a single line of text. Natural Language Processing as a domain of AI started by predicting sentiment analysis from statements. Such problems dealt with text inputs as complete sentences and a number as an output, which determined the positive or negative tone of the sentences, that is, a simple classification problem. Once we could determine or categorize text based on some classes, we could apply the same technique to other problems, such as statement comparisons that determine whether two statements are similar or different. There again, the input is a combination of text (two sentences) and the output is a number determining the class. Taking this a step further, a similar technique can be applied to extract intent and entities from text. Intent and entities are basic building blocks of chatbots and you will see them in detail in a later chapter.

Now that you know how to derive a complex system out of AI models, you should be confident enough to tackle any system that your business might need.

Assume that you are working as a data scientist and building AI models day in and out. Suddenly your supervisor comes up with a problem to create an automation system to generate marketing content for your

© Arindam Ganguly 2025
A. Ganguly, *Scaling Enterprise Solutions with Large Language Models*,
https://doi.org/10.1007/979-8-8688-1154-8_4

client's products. Now you are dumbfounded! Your confidence is down to zero as none of your experience or expertise seems to apply. What do you do now?

Your answer now resides elsewhere. Welcome to the world of Generative AI and Large Language Models!

Language Models (LLMs)

Necessity is the mother of invention and Transformers were invented as a solution to efficiently and accurately translate text from one language to another. As data scientists and industry professionals tried the architecture and its variations on other problems, they realized that simple variations and improvement techniques could easily break the previous benchmarks. These improvements mainly depend on your goals, business requirements, or constraints. Large Language Models (LLMs) revolutionized natural language processing, enabling tasks like text generation, translation, and question-answering with remarkable accuracy and fluency. For example, in the past DistilBERT was a successor to the vanilla BERT architecture, where the idea was to optimize on the infrastructure while achieving a similar performance. Most of these language models follow a technique known as Masked Language Modelling as opposed to traditional string sequence predictive analysis. The next section explains how.

Masked Language Modeling

Chapter 2 discussed how string sequences are processed for predictive analytics. For example, autofill works by predicting the next word while typing a sentence in real time. LLMs, on the other hand, adopted a technique known as Masked Language Modeling, where instead of predicting the next upcoming word at the end of the sentence, it tries to predict a random word somewhere in between the sentence in question.

For example, consider a dataset containing numerous sentences to train a model for autofill. If you focus on a single sentence such as, "Learning Generative AI is more fun than necessary," your traditional modeling should have the following X (independent variable) and Y (dependent variable):

> X = "Learning Generative AI is more fun than __",
> Y="necessary"

A Masked Language Modeling technique, on the other hand, will try to predict each of the words as follows:

> X = "__ Generative AI is more fun than necessary",
> Y="Learning"

> X = "Learning __ AI is more fun than necessary",
> Y="Generative"

> X = "Learning Generative __ is more fun than necessary", Y="AI"

> X = "Learning Generative AI __more fun than necessary", Y="is"

> X = "Learning Generative AI is __ fun than necessary", Y="more"

> X = "Learning Generative AI is more __ than necessary", Y="fun"

> X = "Learning Generative AI is more fun __ necessary ", Y="than"

> X = "Learning Generative AI is more fun than __",
> Y="necessary"

Other variations in MLM can sample 80 percent of the words in random as Y and keeping the rest intact as X.

Based on such ideas and generalizing on a broader level, language models are classified into sequence models and autoregressive models.

Sequence-to-Sequence Models

Sequence models can be either autoencoding models or sequence-to-sequence models. Autoencoding models borrow the encoder part of the Transformer architecture and are pretrained on various tasks. These tasks can vary based on constraints and requirements. For example, BERT uses Next Sentence Prediction, but DistilBERT uses Sentence Ordering and this helps optimize the infrastructure. But at the heart of the pretraining process, these models play with the input tokens (such as masking) and/or sentences (bidirectional read/write) to understand the text.

Sequence-to-sequence models are best for tasks that expect a text sequence as output from an input sequence of text, such as translation, question answering, and so on. These models leverage both the encoder and decoder parts of the Transformer architecture and are pretrained with input and output text sequences.

Autoregressive Models

Autoregressive models, on the other hand, use only the decoder part of the Transformer architecture; they use the idea of predicting the next element based on the previous set of elements in a sequence (hence the name autoregressive). They use masks to hide the next elements when using the previous elements to determine the current element. These models are now the foundation of Generative AI and are best suited for generative tasks. The following sections discuss how they led to the foundation of the generative AI models that we see today.

GPT

GPT (Generative Pretraining) doesn't sound like anything that we might have thought of after the rise of ChatGPT. This chapter explains how advanced models like ChatGPT came into existence and the concepts that helped form the gears that drive LLMs today.

The first version of GPT was a simple autoregressive model, which was pretrained on the Books Corpus, which consisted of text from more than 7,000 unique books. The pretraining strategy was divided into three steps:

1. Language Modeling

   Language modeling leveraged text prediction using log probability. The model used at this step was the decoder part of the transformer and predicted the next word from a long sequence of preceding text regarded as context.

2. Supervised Learning Task

   Here again the decoder was used as a classifier to be applied to the following tasks:

   - Sentence similarity

   - Entailment detection (Sentence A implies Sentence B or not)

   - Multiple choice question answering

3. Combine the previous tasks and use weighted evaluations to get the final model.

This example uses GPT with HuggingFace and the Transformer library. It will again use one of the auto classes, specifically `AutoClassForCasualLM`, which is appropriate for handling autoregressive models. Since you have already seen how the auto classes can be used for classification and fine tuning, you will see how to use GPT for text generation, which autoregressive models excel at.

Let's start by importing the auto class and use GPT2 for this now.

```
from transformers import AutoModelForCausalLM

gpt2 = AutoModelForCausalLM.from_pretrained("gpt2")
```

To use the LLM, you need to use input IDs for this similar to the one you did in the previous chapter.

```
input_ids = tokenizer("It was stormy", return_tensors="pt").
input_ids
```

You can now use the input IDs to generate the rest of the sentence.

```
output_ids = gpt2.generate(input_ids, max_new_tokens=20)
decoded_text = tokenizer.decode(output_ids[0])

print(decoded_text)
```

The decoded text should be something starting with the phrase, "It was a stormy."

Although this seems impressive, you will not get the kind of generations that you get when using ChatGPT. For readers who have not encountered or used ChatGPT, let me take you through ChatGPT and how to use them.

Open AI introduced ChatGPT around 2024 and it changed the paradigm of AI completely. Open AI is now known by almost everyone due to the incredible accomplishments that ChatGPT can achieve. But before ChatGPT, OpenAI had always been working on a special field of machine learning known as *reinforcement learning*. It was reinforcement learning that sparked the idea of how Chatbots can converse and learn like human beings.

Reinforcement Learning

Have you seen computers playing video games? If you feel this is a bit far-fetched, I urge you to search for the advancements that industries like NVIDIA and DeepMind are cooking up. In 2003, researchers from DeepMind devised a model that learned to play Atari. In 2016 and 2017 their system was able to defeat the world champions at a game of Go. This took the world by storm.

Until the 1900s, data scientists could devise a system, namely neural networks, that could mimic the workings of a human brain based on how biological neurons work.

Babies learn to walk by taking a first step, falling, and standing up. Through various rewards and failures, a person learns their way through life.

Data scientists took this idea into consideration and came up with reinforcement learning. The model doesn't learn from traditional labeled data in one go. Instead, a software agent takes an action to move from its current state to the desired state in a predefined environment. The reward received by the agent decides whether it has succeeded or not.

We can have a predefined set of actions that the agent can take at any point in time; we call that set an action space. The action space can be discrete or continuous. If a system is attempting to play a game of Chess, the action space is definitely discrete, as it can traverse right, left, up, or down by a certain number of steps and pattern. But if you consider a system generating sample text, the action space is continuous, based on probability distributions of tokens and vector embeddings that you saw in the previous chapters.

This behavior of the agent to take certain steps and discard others can be accumulated in a policy. A *policy* determines the strategy that maps states to actions. Relating to the same examples discussed previously, the policy can be deterministic or stochastic. A stochastic policy will give a probability distribution for all possible actions and a deterministic policy will show the definite action to be taken at a certain state.

Reinforcement learning is a paradigm where an agent learns to take actions in an environment to maximize a cumulative reward. In reinforcement learning, the model learns by trial and error. Each trial can be considered as an episode and each episode contains a trajectory, which is a set of actions, states, and rewards. To evaluate a policy, you have to use a Value function $V^\pi(s)$. The Value function estimates the expected cumulative reward R from a given state for a certain policy π. This can be expressed mathematically as follows:

$$V^\pi(s) = E[R(\pi,s)]$$

where $V^\pi(s)$ is the Value function for policy π for a given state s and $R(\pi,s)$ is the Reward achieved by the policy at state s.

To get the optimal policy, you use the policy with the maximum value.

A similar evaluation parameter is the Q function. It estimates the expected cumulative reward from a given state-action pair. It records the value of a certain policy π from a specific state to another, but also for a certain action. This also can be mathematically expressed as follows:

$$Q^\pi(s,a) = E[R(\pi,s,a)]$$

where $Q^\pi(s,a)$ is the Q Function of a policy π for a state s performing an action a and $R(\pi,s,a)$ is the Reward achieved by the policy at state s performing an Action a in order to transition to another state.

If you consider the set of all the possible policies as a policy space, then the Q value allows you to pick the best policy by taking into account not only the complete trajectory, but also the states it is visiting and the action it's taking for each state traversal.

The Q function to evaluate the maximal Q value is also known as the Q* function.

$$Q^*(s,a) = maxQ^\pi(s,a)$$

Your objective is always to get the optimal policy. Consider the Q function parameterized by a weight matrix so that it can learn to pick the Q* value based on the probability distribution of state-action pairs for a continuous action space. But how do you fit in a network for the weight matrix?

You need a supervised learning algorithm for learning the weight matrix through an artificial neural network. For this, the dataset will be a buffer consisting of source state, destination state, action, and reward. You also need a loss function that uses Q* values. The algorithm uses a weight parameter to calculate Q* as follows:

$$Loss(max(Q^*(a,s), Q^*(a,s))$$

The first Q* contains the true values and the second one contains the predicted values. They both use the weight matrix as a parameter to calculate Q* values.

To help the model balance the evaluation of loss, the weight matrix should differ for both the Q* values and hence there has to be another neural network for the target (or true) value. This algorithm is known as *Deep Q Network* (DQN).

If you have a stochastic policy, you can allow weight matrices as parameters to the stochastic policy space. An algorithm that learns the policy by using the gradient of weight matrix for policy is known as a *policy gradient method.* There are numerous other reinforcement learning algorithms, including Actor-Critic, Advantage Actor Critic, and TRPO. Discussing all the algorithms and their implementations would require a separate book and is out of scope. But the next section does discuss one algorithm called Proximal Policy Optimization (PPO) when we dig deep into ChatGPT. Before discussing PPO, you need to understand Reinforcement Learning through Human Feedback (RLHF).

OpenAI Gym

Before OpenAI came up with their disruptive idea to incorporate reinforcement learning into chatbots for AGI, they released a framework to implement reinforcement learning models, known as OpenAI Gym.

Just like Scikit-Learn has some datasets (such as iris, boston housing, etc.) for you to work your initial modelling journey, OpenAI Gym also has a wide range of preconfigured environments for your initial reinforcement learning journey.

This section illustrates a simple reinforcement learning algorithm in Python using OpenAI Gym. This is a relatively small exercise and I recommend you use the Google Colab, as OpenAI Gym is preinstalled in Google Colab.

Start by importing Gym as follows:

```
import gym
```

You need an environment to simulate your reinforcement learning algorithm. This exercise uses the Cart-Pole environment, which simulates the cart pole game, where one needs to balance a pole on a moving cart.

```
env = gym.make("CartPole-v1")
```

The next step is to reset the environment so that every time you run this code, it starts from the beginning.

```
observation = env.reset()
```

The system needs to take a random action from the action space. You will keep this running in a loop 100 times, as shown here.

```
for _ in range(100):
  env.render() # Render the environment (optional)
  action = env.action_space.sample() # Sample a random action
  observation, reward, done, info = env.step(action)
  # Take action
  print(observation, reward, done, info)
```

Now let the system take a random action from the action space. You will keep this running in a loop also for 100 times, as shown here.

You should see the observation as a tuple containing four values representing a state in the form of cartesian coordinates and the reward as a value.

Finally, make sure you close the environment to prevent any hanging resources.

```
env.close()
```

This is a very simple demonstration of OpenAI Gym and a simple reinforcement algorithm. I urge you to explore OpenAI Gym if you want to get your hands dirty on game automation or robotic automation technology such as self-driving cars.

Reinforcement Learning Through Human Feedback

You now know that reinforcement learning is based on how humans learn using trial, error, and experience. Human knowledge, however, is also guided by other humans. Our parents taught us basic virtues and helped us make good decisions. Our teachers guided us in understanding the correct meaning of materials in books.

Reinforcement Learning through Human Feedback (RLHF) borrows the idea that there needs to be manual feedback to improve the learning and training processes. Human feedback can be provided in various forms, including demonstrations, reward shaping, critiques, and preference rankings. One of these techniques widely used in Generative AI is preference ranking, where a human in the middle checks the output of the generated text and ranks them based on requirements, such as accuracy. This feedback is then taken into the system to update the reward and target network (in the case of DQN) and the training continues until convergence.

Reinforcement learning was mastered by data scientists at OpenAI. Now you are ready to understand how ChatGPT works. ChatGPT is an interface that lets you chat with a bot akin to a human. The model under the hood is Instruct GPT. The next section explains how Instruct GPT works.

Instruct GPT

ChatGPT was an application born out of an RLHF model known as Instruct GPT. Instruct GPT uses GPT3 for training. GPT3 had certain shortcomings such as misalignment of context, which means it could not follow the instructions provided in the inputs. Instruct GPT used RLHF to allow models to abide by the instructions and be precise and concise in their responses (see Figure 4-1). Instruct GPT was pretrained using the following steps:

1. **Supervised Pretraining**

   A set of instructions are considered the input dataset and a human is introduced in this step to prepare the response of the instructions. This dataset of instructions and their response is then trained using supervised pretraining. The model used here is GPT3.

2. **Reward Model Training**

   In the second step, a dataset of instructions or prompts and the generated responses are accumulated. Multiple responses are generated as variations and a human is introduced to label and rank these responses from best to worst. Once the ranked results are tallied, the reward model is trained with the ranked dataset.

3. **Policy Optimization**

In the final step, a prompt is sampled from the
dataset and a policy from a policy space is chosen
to generate the response. A reward model is used
to assign a reward for this generation. This reward
is leveraged to optimize the policy using Proximal
Policy Optimization (PPO).

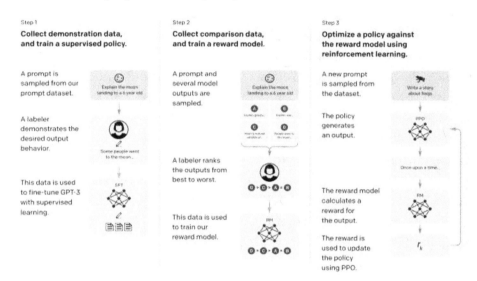

Figure 4-1. *Instruct GPT (Source: `https://arxiv.org/pdf/2203.02155`)*

PPO uses the trust region method to check whether the new policy
is within the trust region. A loss function, specifically KL Divergence, is
used to evaluate the differences with the old (or previous) policy. Trust
region is a predefined threshold that is used to check how much a value
of a function can diverge. PPO checks whether the gradient of a policy
defies the trust region. This policy is then considered optimal and is used
further in trajectory selection. In the case of ChatGPT, this trajectory is the
response to the instructions or prompts in the final step of Instruct GPT.

Now that you know how ChatGPT works internally, gear up to see how you can use ChatGPT.

OpenAI

OpenAI started a new paradigm of technical development through LLMs by using prompt engineering. Instead of learning through the theory of prompt engineering, you'll now get your hands dirty and learn by doing.

When OpenAI introduced LLMs through ChatGPT, they opened ChatGPT to the public through OpenAI Playground. Getting access to OpenAI Playground is easy. You have to create an account and register at `https://platform.openai.com/`. OpenAI Playground is an interactive interface for users to test and play around with OpenAI models.

Once you register, you should get a $5 credit under the Free Trial usage. I recommend that you add more credits to move on to the paid account, so that you don't have any constraints in experimenting with LLMs. You can do that from the Billing section.

Once you have your account set up, you can go to OpenAI Playground using this link: `https://platform.openai.com/playground`.

OpenAI Playground is shown in Figure 4-2.

Figure 4-2. *OpenAI Playground*

As you can see, OpenAI lets you test models for Chat, build assistants, and run completions (which are considered legacy now). This chapter uses Chat to test the models. There is a drop-down to select the model you want to test. OpenAI hosts the top-performing models and these models are deployed in their servers for general use.

You might be wondering why we don't use our knowledge of model building to rent our own servers and build our own models. As easy as it might sound, they are often not economically feasible since training such large models with such a huge number of parameters would require a fortune in hardware. Apart from the economic constraints, industries often detest reinventing the wheel and let firms such as OpenAI worry about hosting and maintaining the models. Driving the applicability of the models often requires more hustle than training and hosting these models. Apart from some basic security concerns, which I discuss later, you can use your skills to fine-tune and apply these models to achieve wonders!

On the right tab in Figure 4-2, you should see some parameters. These parameters are going to be one of the crucial factors that tunes the model to fit your purpose.

Finally, you should see two text areas in the middle—one for System Instruction (or prompting) and the other for User Message. The user message is the user input you want to test with your selected model and its configuration. The system instruction is known as prompting. Let's discuss prompting in detail.

Prompting

A *prompt* is a specially crafted instruction given to an LLM, which decides how to use the user input to get the desired output. Prompt engineering is a discipline of designing a prompt and has been one of the foremost demanding skills in the world of LLMs since Generative AI came to existence. There has been lots of research in the field of prompt engineering, leveraging LLMs that are tuned to perform interesting tasks just by manipulating the prompts. You learn about some of them in the next chapter.

To understand prompt engineering, you need to understand notable concepts:

1. **Few shot prompting**: Just like with supervised learning, LLMs work best when you provide them with some examples to show what it should do with the inputs. Although the concept might sound similar to supervised learning, keep in mind that these models are pretrained with lots of data. You are only providing it some instructions to nudge the model to fit your purpose. Hence your examples cannot be as large as the training data, but must fit the input length of the model. Each model has a specific maximum input length that must be respected to not cause errors and your prompt along with inputs that should fit in that range.

A simple example of few shot prompting follows. Say you are an IT assistant and your task is to extract the employee number, location, and issue occurring from the call transcript. You can use the following examples as your reference.

Example 1:
Transcript: "Hey this is 1745 from the Delaware office. I have been facing some issues with my monitor. It shows some green lines in the middle."
Extracts:
Employee Number: 1745
Location: Delaware
Issue: Issue with monitor. It shows some green lines in the middle.

Example 2:
Transcript: "Hi, I'm not sure why my laptop is not booting up. Can you please check it? I'm in Dallas and my ID is 5122."
Extracts:
Employee Number: 5122
Location: Dallas
Issue: Issue with monitor. Laptop is not booting up.

The examples are your few shots (two shots to be specific) and the instruction is the prompt instruction.

You can enter this few shot prompt in the system instruction text area in OpenAI Playground and test a model.

2. **Zero shot prompting**: In this case, you provide instructions but do not provide any examples. The model uses its pretrained knowledge to perform actions mentioned in the instructions.

Other than prompting, your model also needs to tune a few parameters pertinent to tune the model to the needs. Let's now discuss a few parameters that you can see in the right tab of OpenAI Playground.

Temperature

This is a crucial parameter that's tuned based on your use case. Temperature determines the amount of creative freedom that should be given to the model while generating the output. A lower temperature (under the range of 0 to 0.9) restricts randomness of the output and is generally used for use cases that require factual and traceable outputs. Some examples of such use cases are entity extractions and data analysis. Medium temperature values are generally used for chatbot-like use cases where you require factual answers but in a conversational way. Temperatures above 1 are used for creative use cases, such as poetry generation, song composition, marketing slogan generation, and so on.

You can tune the temperature parameter in the previous example of few shot in OpenAI Playground and see the differences.

Top P

Top P is used instead of temperature to determine the randomness of the generation in a quantitative way. Top P mainly allows the generation to generate tokens having cumulative probability greater than P. This seems a bit intricate and mathematically heavy, but the idea is almost same.

Frequency Penalty and Presence Penalty

Frequency penalty restricts the model to generate the same words or phrases multiple times or too frequently. It acts on the output as a whole as a flat reduction on the frequency of the tokens and phrases.

Presence penalty allows the model to generate varied forms of words, hence increasing the creativity.

Stop Sequences

Since the models are trained for output generation, they might choose to generate unwanted sections of text. Sometimes you might see your model appending the question along with the answer. In such cases, when you see a part of text being generated often, you can use some part of the starting text as a stop sequence so that your models stop generating whenever it encounters that particular text sequence.

Maximum Tokens

You can restrict your model to generate up to a certain number of tokens. Although, generally you might not restrict your model in generating text, you have to keep in mind that all your model executions incur cost. The cost is based on the number of tokens and adjusting your token count is crucial in developing your application for obvious budgetary concerns.

Assuming that you will work with other LLM providers such as Anthropic, Mistral, WatsonX, and so on, the parameters are almost the same. For example, IBM WatsonX has something known as Prompt Lab, where you can test your prompts with their parameters. If your firm has an IBM WatsonX subscription, you can create a project. While creating an asset, choose Chat and Build Prompts with Foundation Models (see Figure 4-3). Foundation models is another phrase often used to describe LLMs.

Figure 4-3. *IBM WatsonX Prompt Lab selector*

Once you select this, you should be able to access Prompt Lab, which is similar to OpenAI Playground, as shown in Figure 4-4.

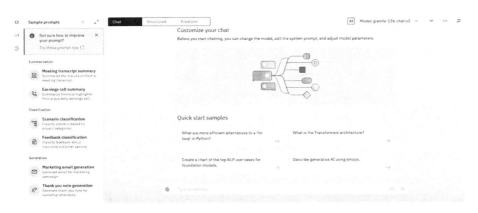

Figure 4-4. *The IBM WatsonX Prompt Lab*

Similar to OpenAI Playground, you will see three ways to experiment with your prompt—Chat, Structured, and Freeform. You should use the structured form to make your experience similar to OpenAI Playground. You will also see a drop-down with the model names to change your models and the button at the top-right allows you to access and tune the model parameters. See Figure 4-5.

Figure 4-5. *WatsonX Prompt Lab, Structured pane*

As you might have guessed, Repetition Penalty corresponds to frequency penalty for OpenAI models and Decoding allows you to tune the temperature categorically. Sampling corresponds to higher temperature values and Greedy corresponds to higher temperature values. Stop Sequence and Min and Max Tokens are the same as those in OpenAI Playground.

If you are in the Structured pane, as shown in Figure 4-5, you will also be able to see the parts where you can provide the prompt instruction (Instruction). The examples should be separated as inputs and outputs and your user inputs go in the Input Text pane at the bottom. Once you click Generate, you will be able to see the output in the Output pane at the bottom.

My intention of showing you the WatsonX playground is to emphasize that no matter which LLM provider or hypervisor you choose, your models will adhere to the input and parameter formats.

OpenAI API

Now that you have a place to experiment and choose the correct LLMs and parameters, this section shows you how to use them in enterprise applications.

All the LLM providers allow you to use their hosted LLMs through API endpoints. These APIs allow you to pass the prompt instructions, few shots (if needed), and the tuning parameters. In the next section of this chapter, you will attempt to develop and build an application using these APIs. But before that, you see how these APIs look and how to use them.

To start with experimenting with LLM APIs, you need two things:

- An API key from an OpenAI account.

- A tool such as Postman to test the API responses.

To begin, you need to get an API key from an OpenAI account.

Create Your API Key

1. Go to `https://platform.openai.com` and log in to your OpenAI account.

2. Go to your profile at the top right.

3. In your profile page, click Create New Secret Key.

4. Give your key a descriptive name (e.g., `IT Assistant Project`).

5. Copy the key immediately and store it securely—you won't be able to see it again.

To start experimenting with OpenAI APIs, you need Postman. Postman is a widely used API testing tool and many developers use it when building web applications. The next section explains how to set up Postman.

Setting Up Postman

Postman is a widely used tool for testing HTTP requests. It provides a user-friendly interface to enable developers to send HTTP requests and analyze the responses.

To set up Postman, navigate to `www.postman.com` and download the setup file to install Postman on your computer.

Alternatively, you can create an account in `www.postman.com` and you should be able to access the Postman application through your browser in your Postman account.

Follow these steps to start using Postman:

1. Open Postman (either through your browser or from the application installed on your computer).

2. Select Workspaces from the top and click Create Workspace.

3. Select Blank Workspace and then click Next.

4. Give the workspace a name, select Personal, and then select Create.

Open Postman to start testing your few shots example through the API endpoint. The API endpoint you are going to use is the chat completion API and you can use this API endpoint most of the time while calling your model inferences. The chat completion API can be invoked through the endpoint `https://api.openai.com/v1/chat/completions` as a POST method. You need to pass your API key as a bearer token and you can pass the parameters (model identifier, temperature, stop sequence, etc.) as JSON objects in the body. The prompt instruction, few shots, and user inputs all need to be passed inside an array named messages. Each object in messages can be of several object types. Your prompt instruction should be as system message (object) type; your examples should have an input as user message type; and your output should reside as assistant message type. Your final user input will also be passed as user message type. Each of these types can be discerned by assigning the role field as "assistant" or "user" for each object. The request for the few shot example should therefore look like this:

```
{
    "model": "gpt-3.5-turbo",
    "messages": [

      {
        "role": "system",
        "content": "You are an IT assistant and your task is
        to extract the employee number, location and issue
        occurring from the call transcript. You can use the
        below examples as your reference."
      },
      {
        "role": "user",
        "content": " Hey this is 1745 from the Delaware office.
        I have been facing some issues with my monitor. It
        shows some green lines in the middle."
      },
      {
        "role": "assistant",
        "content": "Extracts: Employee Number : 1745, Location:
        Delaware, Issue: Issue with monitor. It shows some
        green lines in the middle."
      },
```

```
  {
    "role": "user",
    "content": "Hi I'm not sure why my laptop is not
    booting up. Can you please check. I'm at Dallas and my
    ID is 5122."
  },
  {
    "role": "assistant",
    "content": "Extracts: Employee Number : 5122, Location:
    Dallas, Issue: Issue with monitor. Laptop is not
    booting up."
  },
  {
    "role": "user",
    "content": "Hi my ID is 4412 and I'm not able to
    connect to the internet hence I had to call you
    directly. Please check, It's urgent. Oh I'm in the
    New York office now."
  }
],
"temperature":0
}
```

Let's break down the key components of the API request:

- model: Specifies which model to use (e.g., gpt-3.5-turbo)

- messages: An array of message objects, each with a role and content

- temperature: Controls randomness (0 for deterministic, 1 for more random)

Additional parameters you can use include:

- `max_tokens`: Limits the length of the generated response

- `stop`: Specifies sequences where the API should stop generating further tokens

- `presence_penalty` and `frequency_penalty`: Adjust the model's focus on new or repeated information

Experiment with these parameters to fine-tune the model's responses for your specific use case.

Remember to set the authorization as bearer token and add your API key as a token.

As you can see, I used GPT3.5 Turbo and the temperature is set as 0 since you want factual extractions from the transcript. Note that all the examples are passed as user and assistant messages with inputs (the transcripts) as user message and the expected extractions as assistant message. The final user input is then passed as a user message.

The list of model IDs can be found at `https://platform.openai.com/docs/models`.

You can also access the API documentation at `https://platform.openai.com/docs/api-reference/chat`. You might find some additional parameters useful.

The results should look something similar to this response:

```
{
    "id": "chaxxxxxxxxxxxxxxx8fznO3sZnOP61EMGR1SK",
    "object": "chat.completion",
    "created": 1718807108,
    "model": "gpt-3.5-turbo-0125",
    "choices": [
        {
            "index": 0,
```

```
        "message": {
            "role": "assistant",
            "content": "Extracts: Employee Number : 4412,
            Location: New York, Issue: Unable to connect to
            the internet."
        },
        "logprobs": null,
        "finish_reason": "stop"
    }
],
"usage": {
    "prompt_tokens": 220,
    "completion_tokens": 24,
    "total_tokens": 244
},
"system_fingerprint": null
}
```

You can see there are some obvious output parameters sent by OpenAI, including prompt_tokens, completion_tokens, finish_reason, and so on. Your desired output will reside in the message field. If there is any discrepancies due to token length or plan limitation, you should be able to judge that from the finish_reason value.

Handling Rate Limits

When using the OpenAI API in production, you need to be aware of rate limits. OpenAI imposes limits on requests per minute and tokens per minute, which vary based on your account type and the model used. To handle rate limits:

- Implement exponential backoff for retries

- Use a queue system for high-volume applications

- Monitor your usage and adjust your application's behavior accordingly

Keep in mind the following best practices while building your application.

LLM API Best Practices

Best practices for efficient API usage include:

- Batching requests when possible

- Caching responses for identical or similar queries

- Using the smallest model that meets your needs

- Optimizing your prompts to reduce token usage

By following these practices, you can manage costs and ensure smooth operation of your application.

When working with the OpenAI API, you may encounter various errors. The next section looks at some of the common issues.

Common Issues

Common issues include:

- **Authentication errors:** Check your API key and ensure that it's correctly set

- **Rate limit errors:** Implement backoff and retry logic

- **Context length errors:** Reduce your input or use a model with a larger context window

- **Content policy violations:** Review and adjust your prompts

To debug API requests:

- Use logging to capture full request and response details

- Implement verbose error handling to provide meaningful error messages

- Use tools like Postman to test API calls independently of your application

Remember to sanitize any logged data to avoid exposing sensitive information.

Although this is pretty easy to use, you need to build applications in code and not in Postman, so you need an SDK for the APIs. Since this example has been using Python all along (and OpenAI has a wonderful Python SDK), you are going to use the OpenAI Python SDK. You will build the application using this SDK and see how you can get the most out of OpenAI LLMs to build a production-grade business enterprise application.

The IT Assistant

The example in this chapter pertains to a necessary business requirement relevant in almost all industries today. IT is an indispensable part of any firm in today's world and keeping the IT infrastructure in order is necessary for all firms. This section expands on this example to make it relevant to the real world.

You will add all the necessary gears to make the system production ready. This section explains the brief architecture of the application you are going to build. I assume you are mostly aware of all the elements needed in a basic web application because introducing all of them is out of scope of this book.

You are going to create a system that can refer to a set of knowledgebase documents, such as system manuals, and talk to users to solve their problems. A few years back, this would not have been possible and you would have needed a human in the loop to find the relevant document and reply to the user's queries. With the emergence of LLMs, it is now possible to pass on the relevant document and the LLM can answer queries referring to the text from the document.

To get the relevant document, you are going to refer to a database. This database keeps track of all the system manuals in the firm. It consists of all the details of the knowledgebase (i.e., the documents/system manuals) and you will allow users to choose the document from the set of documents they want their assistant to refer to when answering their queries.

Since the target of this book is to show how Generative AIs can fit in large enterprises, you need this system to be production ready and easily pluggable. A brief architecture of the system is shown in Figure 4-6.

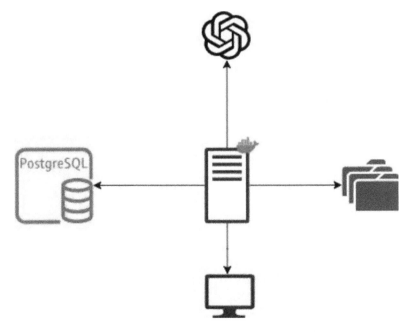

Figure 4-6. *Simple IT assistant architecture*

Let's start building this application step by step.

The demo limits the application to three device manuals so that it can solve any problem occurring in any of those devices. It uses WikiHow `www.wikihow.com/Main-Page` to prepare the manuals.

Go to each of the following links and save these pages in the form of PDF.

- `www.wikihow.com/Fix-a-Keyboard`

- `www.wikihow.tech/Solve-Common-Printer-Problems`

- `www.wikihow.com/Repair-LCD-Monitors`

In case you are wondering, you can open the links in the browser and simply try to print them (by pressing Ctrl+P). Instead of printing, you can ask to save them as PDFs. As you can figure from the links, these are the knowledgebase documents that the system would use to answer the user queries and try to solve their problems.

Save the first link as `keyboard.pdf`, the second one as `printer.pdf`, and the third one as `monitor.pdf`.

Once you have the documents ready, create a workspace and a folder inside the workspace called `docs`. Copy these documents into that folder.

Preparing the Database

Now that you have the knowledgebase ready, you can prepare a database that will consist of the details of the documents and the devices they refer to. You might have figured out that the first link refers to fixing a broken keyboard, the second link is to fix a printer, and the third link is for repairing a LCD monitor. Hence, in the database, you will tag them to the specific devices in the form of a table that should look like this:

```
doc_id |   doc_name   |     doc_url        |  topic
--------+--------------+--------------------+----------
1       | keyboard.pdf | docs/keyboard.pdf  | keyboard
2       | monitor.pdf  | docs/monitor.pdf   | monitor
3       | printer.pdf  | docs/printer.pdf   | printer
(3 rows)
```

The table has a document ID, the name of the document or the file name, the URL or path to access, and the topic, which is the device it attempts to refer to. You will use the last two columns in this application.

You can use any database, but the codebase I prepared uses Postgres. If you are new to Postgres and want to set it up in your environment and learn, I suggest you refer to this link:

https://www.w3schools.com/postgresql/postgresql_install.php

It doesn't matter where you have set up your Postgres instance (local or otherwise)—you will be able to access it through the credentials of the database, namely database user ID, password, database name, the host URL, and the port. Generally, all databases even have a command-line interface. To create the table, open your Database shell and use the following query:

```
create table tst_index_tab (doc_id varchar, doc_name varchar,
doc_url varchar, topic varchar);
```

You can check your table using the following:

```
Select * from tst_index_tab;
```

You will be able to see a blank table if the table was created.

```
 doc_id | doc_name | doc_url | topic
--------+----------+---------+-------
(0 rows)
```

Now you can fill up the table with data using SQL `insert` statements shown here:

```
insert into tst_index_tab values ('1','keyboard.pdf',
'docs/keyboard.pdf','keyboard');

insert into tst_index_tab values ('2','monitor.pdf',
'docs/monitor.pdf','monitor');

insert into tst_index_tab values ('3','printer.pdf',
'docs/printer.pdf','printer');
```

Preparing the Backend and Orchestration Layer

Now that your database and knowledgebase are ready, you need to prepare the backend or orchestration layer with microservices. Let's start by preparing the functions to retrieve data from the database when required. The database connection needs to know the database credentials, but exposing database credentials is a potential risk if you consider your system running in production. Security is obviously a concern.

There are two ways to prevent credentials and secrets from being leaked. You can either create an environment variable or an environment file. Creating an environment variable requires administrator system access. You can instead create an environment file and hide it from your codebase repository or your source code management (SCM). In this project, you are going to use git as the SCM, so you need a `gitignore` file containing your environment file path. The steps are as follows:

1. Create a file named `.env`, which will contain the application secrets in a key value pair as follows:

    ```
    DB_USER=<Your Database User Name>
    DB_PASSWORD=<Database Password>
    DB_NAME=<Database Name>
    ```

```
DB_HOST=<Database URL>
DB_PORT=<Database port>
OpenAI_API=<The OpenAI API Key we created in the
previous section>
```

2. Create a file named .gitignore, which will contain just one line:

    ```
    .env
    ```

This will ensure that your credentials are safe, even if you push your codebase to an external repository such as GitHub.

Creating a Python File

In this section, you create the Python file containing the database functions. You cannot use Jupyter Notebook or any other similar experimentation environment, as you are building a complete application to run in production.

The first task is to include the libraries you are going to use. This example uses psycopg2 to connect to the Postgres database from Python. You also need the dotenv package to access the environment file through the load_dotenv function.

One last thing I recommend using is a logger to keep a track of your system errors while the application is running. This example uses the logging package, which is included with the basic Python installation.

Start by installing the packages you will need. You need to install the following packages using pip on your command line:

```
pip install Flask
pip install openai
pip install PyPDF2
```

Open your code editor and create a file named db_functions.py. Then follow these steps:

1. import your packages

   ```
   import psycopg2
   import os
   import sys
   from dotenv import load_dotenv
   import logging
   ```

   You have read about all these packages already except for os and sys, which are needed to support the load_dotenv function to access the environment files.

2. Now configure logging using the following code. The comments should make the code self-explanatory.

   ```
   # Create and configure logger
   logging.basicConfig(filename="assistant.log",
                       format='%(asctime)s %(message)s',
                       filemode='w')

   # Creating an object
   logger = logging.getLogger()

   # Setting the threshold of logger to DEBUG
   logger.setLevel(logging.DEBUG)
   ```

   The logger configuration in the first line allows your logs to be saved in a file named assistant.log in the format <time> <output log>.

An example of the contents of the log is as follows:

```
2024-06-21 10:01:46,350 load_ssl_context verify=True
cert=None trust_env=True http2=False
```

3. Now load the env file using the load_dotenv function:

```
load_dotenv()
```

4. As your environment file is now loaded, you can assign the environment file secrets in global variables as follows:

```
# Now get all the database Configs from .env file
host = os.getenv("DB_HOST")
port = os.getenv("DB_PORT")
user_name = os.getenv("DB_USER")
pass_word = os.getenv("DB_PASSWORD")
db_name = os.getenv("DB_NAME")
```

5. Now you'll create a function to connect to the database. This function will be used to create a database connection in your Python program and send that connection for use. You will use the global variables created from the environment file values to create a connection using the psycopg2.connect function. A cursor will also be created with the connection, which is a tracker or identifier to access each row returned by the SQL queries.

```
# Function to generate a DB connection
def get_connection():
```

```
con = psycopg2.connect(database=db_name,
user=user_name,password=pass_word,
host=host,port=port)
cursor = con.cursor()
return (con,cursor)
```

6. The final function in this file is the get_topic_
   details function, which will take the topic as a
   parameter, use the get_connection function to get
   a connection and a SQL query to get the row values
   corresponding to a topic. The topic is selected from
   the frontend by the user.

```
# Now get all the topics and their document
details (id, name and URL/path)
def get_topic_details(topic_id):
    try:
        con,cursor = get_connection()
        cursor.execute(f"SELECT doc_id,
        doc_name, doc_url FROM tst_index_tab
        where topic='{topic_id}'")
        row = cursor.fetchall()
        con.close()
    except Exception as e:
        logger.error("get_topic_details()|"
        +repr(e))
        con.close()
        return False
    return row
```

As you can see, the code uses exception handling to log errors using the `logger`. `repr(e)` ensures that you get the details of the exception (or error occurred) in the string. Note also how the query string is formatted. The code uses f-string instead of string concatenation and placeholders for variables as { }.

Creating Microservices

Now that `db_functions.py` is ready, you can create the microservices that will drive the web app. You need to establish methods that can initiate a server, listen for HTTP requests, and send a response. Using bare HTTP methods in Python can be a bit of a hassle, so you are going to use Flask in this case, which has simple methods that do all of the hard work for you. Start by preparing the backend code:

1. Create the `index.py` file in your workspace:

    ```
    import all the libraries as follows.
    from flask import Flask, request, render_
    template, session
    import psycopg2
    from db_functions import get_topic_details
    import os
    import sys
    from dotenv import load_dotenv
    from openai import OpenAI
    from PyPDF2 import PdfReader
    import io
    ```

The first `import` line imports the desired functions from Flask. The `request` module is used to access the HTTP request and its parameters and `session` is used to hold the web session as long as the application is running. It will help you persist certain values, such as the topic (or device) selected to use the proper knowledge document. Finally, the `render_template` is used to render a template, which is the frontend web page to be displayed to the user. Flask uses Jinja2 templates to pass the Python variables and perform manipulations on DOM elements based on the variable values. This makes the web page dynamic. You can read more about Flask and Jinja2 templates at `https://flask.palletsprojects.com/en/3.0.x/tutorial/`.

The second `import` is `psycopg2`, which we already discussed.

The third `import` lets you use the function you created in the `db_functions.py` file.

The fourth, fifth, and sixth `imports` are similar to the ones you saw in the previous section.

Since you need to use OpenAI, you need a Python package for OpenAI, which is imported in the seventh line.

The final package that's imported is PyPDF2, which is a Python package that can extract text from a PDF. Since PDFs are unstructured documents, you need a Optical Character Recognizer (OCR) to extract text from PDFs. OCRs use machine learning algorithms to decipher the image content and extract the characters in that unstructured document. You can read more about PyPDF2 at `https://pypdf2.readthedocs.io/en/3.x/`.

2. Since you need the API key stored as a secret in the .env file, you need to load the environment variables and store the API key in a variable.

```
# Load .env file
load_dotenv()

# Now get the OpenAI API from .env file
apikey = os.getenv("OpenAI_API")
```

3. Now you need to initialize the web application in Flask.

```
app = Flask(__name__)
```

4. You also need to set an app secret key to use the web session in Flask.

```
app.secret_key = "index"
```

It's actually better to use a random string as a secret key. For demo purposes only, I use a simple string.

5. Now you need to create some utility functions. The first utility function you need to create will use PyPDF2's OCR to extract text from a PDF.

```
def get_text(pdf_url):
    reader = PdfReader(pdf_url)

    context = ""
    #For each page get the text and add it to context
    for page in reader.pages:
```

```
    context = context + page.extract_text()
return context
```

The parameter you need to pass to this function is the PDF URL, which as you might have already guessed, you will get from the database, given the topic leveraging the function from the previous file.

6. Now you use the OpenAI model to generate query results. Up to now, you have used HTTP requests and Postman to call OpenAI APIs, but now you will use Python to do this, by utilizing the Python library called openai, which provides Python functions to seamlessly invoke OpenAI models, just like we did using Postman. This makes your life easier by abstracting the intricacies needed to invoke OpenAI using HTTP requests and will allow you to use OpenAI models in different applications.

```
def get_openAI_completion(context, query,
chatlog=""):
    client = OpenAI(api_key=apikey)
    if chatlog=="": # For first time
        prompt_instruction = "You are an IT
        Assistant and you are provided a
        knowledge text and a user query. Your
        task is to use the knowledge text to
        answer the user query."
        user_content = "Knowledge Text:\n"
        +context+"\n\nUser Query:"+query
    else:
```

```
            prompt_instruction = "You are an IT
            Assistant in conversation with a user.
            You are provided a knowledge text, the
            previous chat conversation and user query.
            Your task is to use the knowledge text to
            answer the user query as a continuation
            to the previous chat conversation."

            user_content = "Knowledge Text:\n"+context+"\n\
            nChat Conversation:\n"+chatlog+"\n\nUser
            Query:"+query

    # Call OpenAI model below:
    response = client.chat.completions.create(
        model="gpt-3.5-turbo",
        messages = [
            {
                "role":"system",
                "content": prompt_instruction
            },
            {
                "role":"user",
                "content": user_content
            }
        ],
        temperature=0.6,
        top_p=1
    )
    return response.choices[0].message.content
```

There are a couple of things to understand about
this function. It will be used whenever a query
is sent to the assistant. Since you are building a
conversational assistant, to attain the conversation

flow, the assistant needs to keep in mind the previous dialogues that have been exchanged. This conversation context is provided in the chatlog variable, which persists the log of any conversations. But when the conversation starts, the chatlog variable should be empty and at that time no conversation context needs to be passed to the LLM. The prompts are designed conditionally, keeping in mind this criteria. The context should also include the document text that the assistant should refer to, as discussed previously. This document knowledge is passed in the context variable. Finally, the chat completion URL is invoked with the chat.completion.create() functions and the parameters passed are similar to the ones discussed in the previous section.

7. Now that the utility functions are ready, you need to create the HTTP routes for the Python server in the same file. To create a route in Flask, you need a @app.route decorator. The route along with the HTTP method is passed and the respective HTML template should be rendered along with the variables to be passed. The first route is the entry point /index.

```
@app.route("/index",methods=['GET'])
def index():
    return render_template("index.html")
```

8. The index template should have a drop-down to
    allow the users to select the appropriate device.
    Create a folder called templates and place a
    file called index.html into it with the following
    contents:

```html
<html>
    <head>
        <title>Topic</title>
    </head>
    <body>
        <h3>Select Topic</h3>
        <form action="get_doc_detail" method="POST">
            <select id="topic" name="topic">
                z<option value="keyboard">KEYBOARD
                </option>
                <option value="monitor">MONITOR
                </option>
                <option value="printer">PRINTER
                </option>
            </select>
            <input type="submit" value="submit"/>
        </form>
    </body>
</html>
```

As you might have guessed, the starting template or
frontend allows the user to select between keyboard,
monitor, and printer. It passes the selected value to a
HTTP route /get_doc_detail.

9. To create the /get_doc_detail route, go back to the
   index.py Python file and add this code:

```
@app.route("/get_doc_detail",methods=['POST'])
def get_doc_detail():
    topic = request.form['topic']
    row = get_topic_details(topic)
    if not row:
        return render_template("index.html")
    doc_obj = {"doc_id":row[0][0],"doc_name":row
    [0][1],"doc_url":row[0][2]}
    session['doc_url'] = doc_obj['doc_url']
    session['chat_history'] = [{"user":"",
    "assistant":""}]
    return render_template("chat_template.
    html",chat_history=[])
```

As you can see, this is a POST method and hence
the data (the topic value received from the index.
html template) is sent here, which is set in a topic
variable. The function then utilizes the get_topic_
detail() function from the db_functions.py file to
get the document details and saves it in a variable
named row. Just to keep error handling in place,
the row variable is checked and the URL is saved or
persisted in the Flask session in order to persist it in
the full lifecycle of the web application. An empty
session with empty dialogs is also set in session as
an initial chat log. The chat template is rendered in
chat_template.html.

10. Now you'll create the chat_template.html Jinja
    template. Create the chat_template.html file in the
    templates folder and add this code:

```html
<html>
    <head>
        <title>Chat</title>
    </head>
    <body>
        {% if chat_history!=[] %}
            {% for c in chat_history %}
            <p>
                {% if c['user']!="" %}
                <b>User: </b>{{ c['user'] }}
                {% endif %}
            </p>
            <p>
                {% if c['assistant']!="" %}
                <b>Assistant: </b>{{ c
                ['assistant'] }}
                {% endif %}
            </p>
            <hr/>
            {% endfor %}
        {% endif %}
        <p>
            <form method="POST" action=
            "/message">
                <b>Enter Your Message</b>
                <input type="text" name="user_
                message" id="user_message" />
```

```
            <input type="submit" value=
            "submit">
        </form>
      </p>
    </body>
</html>
```

The code is almost self-explanatory. The chat history is shown as a combination of user and assistant dialogs in a loop and the form in the end allows the user to send the query. This form leverages another route, called /message, to send the query to the system.

11. Finally, go back to the index.py Python file and add this code to create the /message route:

```
@app.route("/message",methods=['POST'])
def assistant():
    doc_url = session['doc_url']
    chat_history = session['chat_history']
    user_message = request.form['user_message']
    knowledge = get_text(doc_url)
    chatlog = "user: " + chat_history[-1]
    ["user"] +"\nassistant: " + chat_history[-1]
    ["user"]
    result  = get_openAI_completion(knowledge,
    user_message,chatlog)
    chat_history.append({"user":user_message,
    "assistant":result})
    session['chat_history'] = chat_history
    return render_template("chat_template.html",
    chat_history=chat_history)
```

This function uses the last chat conversation as the conversation context derived from the chat_history session and the document URL from the session is leveraged to point to the document that the assistant should refer to while answering the queries. This document URL is then sent to the get_text utility function to get the text of the PDF. All of these are sent to the get_openAI_completion utility function to get the response.

12. The last step is to allow the server to listen to a certain port. In Flask, you need to add a main function with this code:

```
if __name__ == '__main__':
    app.run(host="0.0.0.0",port="3000")
```

You are now ready with your application; your working directory should look like Figure 4-7.

Figure 4-7. *The workspace*

You can run the Python file index.py in the console and open your browser to point to 127.0.0.1:3000/index. You should see something like Figure 4-8.

Figure 4-8. *The index page*

You can select a topic from the three and the web application will redirect you to /get_doc_detail, where you can start chatting with your assistant. You should see your conversation being answered, based on the corresponding document you selected. See Figure 4-9.

Figure 4-9. *The Chat page*

Mission Accomplished

Congratulations! You have successfully built an IT assistant and eradicated your Level1 Support team!

The application you created uses a document to retrieve relevant text and augment it with context to get the desired response. This technique is known as *retrieval augmented generation* and this is the topic of discussion in the next chapter, which introduces modern toolkits to improve on this system you built.

But before that, as promised, you need to containerize your system so that it's compact, replicable, and has cross-platform consistency. A container is the best way to achieve such advantages and Docker is one of the best tools to do this.

It is best to assume that you are familiar with Docker and Kubernetes. If you aren't, I strongly recommend you picking up some resources on Docker and Kubernetes and building your skills for deployment. Covering Docker and Kubernetes is out of the scope of the book and a complete subject altogether.

Here is the Dockerfile you need for this application:

```
FROM python:latest
WORKDIR /app
COPY requirements.txt /app/
RUN pip install -r requirements.txt
COPY . /app
CMD ["python", "index.py"]
```

The Dockerfile is simple and it requires that you create a requirements.txt file to let Docker install all the required Python libraries. Add the following contents to your requirements.txt file:

```
requests
Flask==2.0.2
Jinja2==3.0.2
psycopg2==2.9.9
python-dotenv==1.0.1
MarkupSafe==2.0.1
Werkzeug==2.0.2
openai
PyPDF2
```

Most of the libraries are discussed except a few—MarkupSafe, Werkzeug, and Jinja2—and they assist Flask in performing their jobs smoothly. If you are getting errors when running the application locally, it is quite possible that you are missing one of these Python libraries.

Although Kubernetes is a default choice for container orchestration, docker-compose is a simpler choice. If you are ready to use docker-compose, use the following docker-compose.yml file:

```
version: "3.3"
services:
  application:
    build:
      context: .
      dockerfile: ./Dockerfile
    ports:
      - '3000:3000'
    image: it_assistant_application
    container_name: it_assistant_application
    extra_hosts:
      - "host.docker.internal:host-gateway"
    networks:
      - net

networks:
  net:
    external: true
```

Note the line in the docker-compose.yml file that says

```
  extra_hosts:
      - "host.docker.internal:host-gateway"
```

If you have your Postgres deployed in the localhost, you need Docker to reach out to your host system's localhost; this line will enable that process. Along with this, you should also edit your environment file for DB_HOST as follows:

```
DB_HOST=host.docker.internal
```

This will allow your Python code to access your localhost from the Docker container.

To run `docker-compose`, you can simply run this line:

```
docker-compose up - -build
```

Open your browser to `127.0.0.0:3000/index`.

You will find this code using the GitHub link at `https://github.com/gangulyarin/IT_Assistant_Simple`.

With this, let's move on to Retrieval Augmented Generation (RAG) in the next chapter.

Summary

- Language models are either sequence-to-sequence models like Transformers or they use only the decoder part of the Transformer architecture. These are called autoregressive models and they specialize in text generation such as GPT.

- Reinforcement learning is a discipline of machine learning that uses trial and error to understand patterns, similar to how humans learn from experience.

- Reinforcement Learning through Human Feedback (RLHF) introduces a human in the loop to criticize the model performance and allows the model to correct itself.

- Instruct GPT uses RLHF to allow models to converse, similar to humans, which gave rise to ChatGPT and other LLMs.

- OpenAI hosts LLMs and exposes APIs to use them. It allows APIs to configure the LLM through parameters like temperature, top p, presence penalty and frequency penalty, stop sequences, and maximum tokens.

- OpenAI APIs can be accessed through HTTP requests as well as from the Python package called `openai`.

- You can leverage `openai` for LLMs, PyPDF2 to extract text from PDFs, and Flask for Python HTTP request and response handlers to create a RAG application.

CHAPTER 5

Retrieval Augmented Generation

The previous chapters provided a foundation of intelligent applications and thus far a machine learning hobbyist should be able to confer their understanding with you. But the agenda of this book is to look beyond machine learning model building. We have only scratched the surface and the next chapters take you into the trench.

In the previous chapter, you built a chatbot that not only responds to casual conversations but can also refer to a knowledge source and retrieve the exact excerpts that might assist the LLM in generating answers. Prompt engineering plays a big role here. Your prompt should instruct your LLM to use the excerpts from the knowledge sources to answer the customer queries.

Prompt engineering has itself emerged as a new domain in the seemingly ever-growing field of artificial intelligence. This chapter attempts to give you an idea of what prompt engineering is and how various prompting techniques can tune an LLM to render good results.

I introduced and talked about prompts in the previous chapter, but I will reiterate them once more and expand on a few more techniques for prompt engineering.

© Arindam Ganguly 2025
A. Ganguly, *Scaling Enterprise Solutions with Large Language Models*,
https://doi.org/10.1007/979-8-8688-1154-8_5

Prompt Engineering

There are several movies and books about how machines will surpass human intelligence and trick us into causing a doomsday. With generative AI growing at a faster pace than ever in the history of human civilization, computer scientists and philosophers have been discussing how machines are continuing to take over tasks that were previously thought of as impossible for them.

Previously, during the age of traditional machine learning, many industries rejected models due to the high cost of maintainability and lack of skilled computer scientists who could understand the intricacies of the models. Then came deep learning, where models started getting more complex, and it was almost impossible to track and trace back to the output they had produced. The models were then accepted as black boxes, with certain hyperparameters to be tuned to reach the desired outcome. But this didn't stop mathematicians from coming up with new sets of modifications to certain parts of the models such as a modified activation function, a new optimizer function, or a new neural network architecture altogether.

There is a new discipline called *Explainable AI* (often abbreviated XAI), which tries to explain how the model came up with the output that it did. These techniques are never fool-proof and are still an active area of research. With generative AI and LLMs, computer scientists can see that models are almost completely behaving like humans.

You can think of the LLM as your assistant and your prompt as a carefully crafted instruction to get your models to behave the way you want. A prompt is the input given to an LLM; it consists of an instruction and some examples. These examples are technically called *shots* and you can have zero (only the instruction is provided) to one, to few shots (more than one). These examples are your LLM's way of understanding how you want your inputs and outputs.

These are some of the concepts you have already seen and even used in the previous chapter. The next section discusses some of the popular prompt engineering techniques and you can then try them in OpenAI Playground.

Chain of Thought Prompting

Although it's impossible to trace back and understand how your LLM came up with its outputs, you can ask the LLM to give you its reasoning in a manner you seem fit. To do so, you have to give the LLM a way to present the pattern. Consider this example:

```
Instruction:
You are given a math problem. Your task is to solve them by
showing the step by step thought process.
```

```
Example 1
Question
A rabbit has 13 carrots and he wants to share them amongst his
family - his mom and dad. He wants to share all of them and eat
the ones that are left after distributing them equally. Can the
rabbit keep a carrot for himself.
```

```
Answer
13 carrots can be divided into two members as 13/2 which is
6 and 1 is the remainder. Hence after sharing them equally
amongst his mom and dad he has 1 left with himself.
Yes, he can have 1 carrot for himself.
```

```
Question
A kingfisher has captured 4 fishes and wants to distribute them
with his wife. How many can each of them eat?
```

With this, your LLM should respond with the answer along with the reasoning. I encourage you to try this in OpenAI Playground. When I did so, I got the following result:

```
Answer
Since there are 4 fishes and 2 to be distributed among 2
members, we divide 4 by 2 which equals 2.
Each of them can eat 2 fishes.
```

You can refer to the original paper published by Wei et al. (2022) at `https://arxiv.org/abs/2201.11903`.

The author of that paper provides a wonderful example, as shown in Figure 5-1.

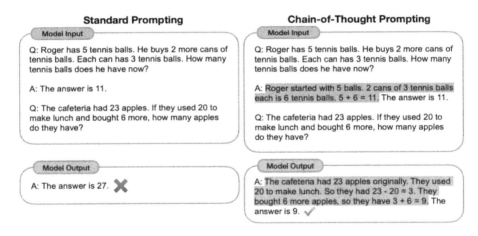

Figure 5-1. *Chain of thought prompting*

Tree of Thoughts Prompting

Prompt engineers and computer scientists have come up with different variations of Chain of Thoughts to fit the purpose of some more complicated prompt engineering techniques. One such modification is the Tree of Thoughts. There are often problems that require the system to devise a tree of decisions to be made to arrive at an appropriate response.

Tree of Thoughts allows the LLM to reach the proper response by creating intermediate decision trees of thoughts and then combining them with search algorithms (e.g., breadth-first search and depth-first search) to enable systematic exploration of decision points.

Yao et al. (2023) came up with Tree of Thoughts (ToT) in the paper titled "Tree of Thoughts: Deliberate Problem Solving with Large Language Models," which you can access at https://arxiv.org/abs/2305.10601. The ToT framework from the same paper is illustrated in Figure 5-2.

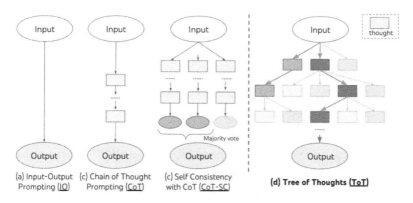

Figure 5-2. *Tree of Thoughts prompting*

There are a plethora of prompt engineering techniques that you can explore and are popularly published. You can come up with novel ideas to arrive at unique prompt engineering techniques that best fit for your system.

If you can recollect from the previous chapter, you used a database to store the mapping of the knowledge source to the topic that the user was referring to. Although the prompt could direct the LLM to gather proper resources to answer the user queries, the document needed to be selected manually by the user to map the topic. Now, this is fine until you have finitely distinguishable topics. But when you are building systems for a large industry, your knowledgebase should be finitely uncountable.

The reason for this is your system must have a provision to add documents and other formats of knowledgebases such as Excel, docs, pictures, transcripts, and so on, on the fly.

For example, say your manager asked you to design a chatbot that listens to customer care call transcripts and assists data analysts to gather certain insights from them. The data analysts are placed to gather insights about the performance of the products. One of their queries is, "How many times have the customers expressed their discomfort while using the Product A in the past two weeks?" As you might have guessed, your system is continuously transcribing customer care calls and storing the information in the knowledgebase. You need to design a system to extract the topics out of each call transcript. Even if you think of achieving this by using a machine learning model, maintaining the model is another headache and a burden for the team.

To address such issues, you need something to store the knowledgebases, index them for faster retrieval, and do a semantic search instead of topic mapping. These tasks can be easily achieved by using something known as *vector databases.*

Vector Databases

You have likely worked with relational or nonrelational databases. However, even if you haven't, it is impossible to ignore the fact that any application needs a place to store data. Data is conventionally stored in databases, which allow easy retrieval and storage of data, as opposed to storage mediums such as raw or formatted files stored in the hard disk.

Disadvantages of Traditional Databases in Intelligent Applications

Storage of data in databases is managed by various complex data structures. Such data structures ensure that the storage is optimal in terms of space and efficiency when it comes to retrieval.

Even though these data structures are well researched to optimize retrieval, sometimes it falls on the user to ensure the retrieval is efficient, by adding indexes. Indexes can be assigned to a single or composite set of columns so that the database can prepare a dictionary of index columns and the corresponding record for easy retrieval. For example, in a search application, the database designer inquiries about the columns that are used to filter the records. The database designer then assigns indexes to these database columns so that the database engine internally arranges the records according to the index column. See Figure 5-3.

Database Indexes

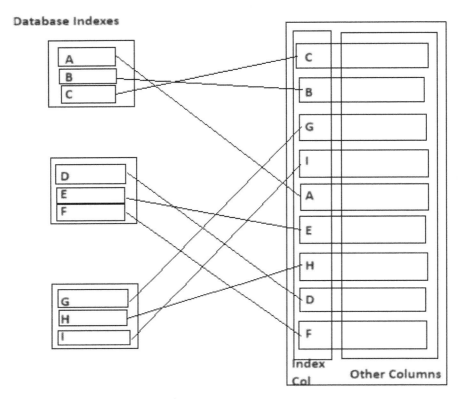

Figure 5-3. *Traditional database indexing*

With the indexing in place, the database can easily retrieve a record, by just looking at the indexes instead of looking at all of the records.

Although the concept of indexing in traditional databases can ensure performant retrieval, retrieval demands of a structured language such as SQL are more complicated. You usually query a row where the search values match in the database.

Even though databases are almost inescapable when building any kind of application, retrieval procedures in intelligent systems need more than rule-based matching techniques. Of course, you need to retrieve the data you are storing (or there is no point in storing data). But the in-memory storage and retrieval needs to be shifted to something intelligent for the kind of applications you are targeting.

Imagine a system that can do semantic searches from a database of paragraphs. Can you think of some of the ways you could use traditional databases to perform this task?

Well, one way is to allow the users to manually select the set of documents and then let the LLMs take the whole set of text from the selected documents as context and answer the user search queries accordingly. But, as discussed, this is infeasible for large enterprises that have terabytes of documents. The LLMs will not be able to fit the data in context. This approach is just not practical.

Semantic search systems need to understand the text from the documents. For a machine learning model to understand the text, it needs to be preprocessed and vectorized using embeddings. Once the text is vectorized, the embedding space can be searched by a similarity algorithm.

In a very crude way, you can use an embedding algorithm to convert all the text into vector embeddings and store them in your database after somehow partitioning them. You can partition them based on documents, that is, each row in the database will consist of three columns—document IDs, vector embeddings of the complete document text, and the text. If the documents are huge, you can partition each document further into paragraphs. In that case, you would add a column called paragraph ID.

In either of these two cases, you need your system to follow these steps:

1. Take your documents and prepare vector embeddings from them.

2. Ingest these document embeddings into the database.

3. Your search input needs to use this embedding algorithm to convert the search query into vector embedding using the same embedding algorithm.

4. Finally, you use a similarity score and a threshold to output your result. See Figure 5-4.

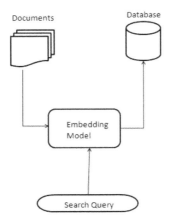

Figure 5-4. *Semantic search using a traditional database*

Although this algorithm seems straightforward and simple, there are a lot of intricacies that you will encounter once you start implementing it. You can try to start implementing this and I will not discourage you. But I will not resist from revealing the warning signals beforehand.

You need to have a middle layer that does the embedding, which is not an easy task. Your middle layer needs to sit actively intercepting all the text coming in from any new documents, every time a new query is made by the user in the system. This poses a great deal of concern in terms of performance, scalability, and maintainability. Your system needs to perform the algorithm dynamically on the fly for every request and, on top of that, you have to manually add the similarity algorithm and metric to get your desired result. All the individual components need to work in sync. Maintaining these gears can be really stressful. Finally, if your system has incoming documents from a lot of lines of businesses, maintaining them will be almost impossible.

Vector databases provide an easy way out, as explained next.

How Vector Databases Work

Vector databases use a pipeline of preprocessing, ingestion, indexing, and retrieval.

You will need to decide how you want your documents to be partitioned and chunked initially while you enter the pipeline to ingest your set of documents. For example, you can partition on paragraphs from your combined set of text, just like in the database scenario.

Vector databases then can use vectorization algorithms to embed text using any of the embedding models. You can include metadata to supplement your search capability while ingesting your documents. Each chunk being ingested is similar to the columns we talked about while building the traditional database, apart from the fact that they are ingested as JSON instead of columnar values. Hence, your metadata includes the document ID, paragraph ID, and the text itself. The real search utilizes your text embeddings. But then why do you even need them if you get the same result using a traditional database?

The answer is simple. You get the complete package under one roof. Vector database can preprocess, vectorize, embed, and ingest altogether.

The real juice comes with what happens next.

Once the documents are chunked and ingested into a vector database, the vector database uses machine learning and clustering algorithms to form index clusters. There are multiple algorithms that different vector databases use. I cover one of them that some popular vector databases such as ChromaDB or Pinecone use—HNSW.

Hierarchical Navigable Small Worlds (HNSW)

The Hierarchical Navigable Small Worlds (HNSW) algorithm is one of the best performant algorithms for ingestion and similarity search and the one that most popular vector databases use. In this algorithm, the text embedding space is divided into clusters as nodes. These nodes are placed in a graph-like structure with edges connected between nodes having high similarity scores. Once a query enters a system, the query embedding searches for the most similar node through graph traversal algorithms such as BFS (Breadth First Search) to get the best result. See Figure 5-5.

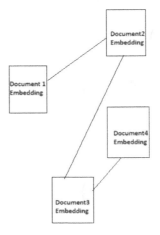

Figure 5-5. *HNSW graph like embedding space*

Internally, the graph is created through multiple layers of linked lists. The top layer connects the start node to the last, the next layer has more nodes in between the start and end, and so on. The hyperparameter here is the number of layers, which needs to balance traversal cost with overlapping nodes. Once a node (or a new text embedding) enters the system, the algorithm must decide the levels it needs to reside in based on this tradeoff. See Figure 5-6.

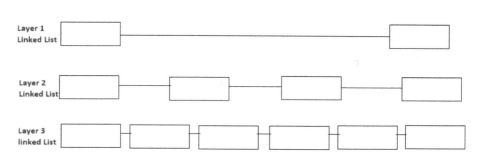

Figure 5-6. *HNSW internal linked list structure*

Similarity Measures

Finally, this section covers two of the famous similarity measures that some of the vector databases use:

- **Cosine similarity**: Considering each embedding as an N-Dimensional vector, cosine similarity measures the cosine of the angle between the embedding vectors to arrive at a score.

- **Euclidean distance**: It computes the straight-line distance between the embedding vectors.

Vector databases attempt to preserve all of the features boasted by traditional databases, such as atomic transaction, scalability, fault tolerance, and so on. Some vector databases, like Pinecone, use a middle caching layer called a freshness layer that caches an incoming text vector until it can properly decide to cluster and place it appropriately within its existing embedding vector space.

Vector databases come in serverless and on-premise flavors. Serverless vector databases also ensure data replication, data security, compliance, and protection. Offline vector databases leave it up to you to manage.

Now that all the concepts are more or less clear, you can get your hands dirty and build a production-based application. In the previous chapter, you attempted devising a small application but it is far from being production grade. You used a traditional database to store the data and had to make do with selecting the topics manually from a small set of documents. Now you'll use a vector database instead of the production database and see if it makes a difference.

The current technical landscape looked something like Figure 4-6 from the previous chapter. As you are attempting to build a production-grade application, you need to make some changes to the current application.

This book assumes you are well aware of all the components required for a bare minimum production application, such as a CI/CD pipeline like Jenkins and Kubernetes or Docker Compose and Docker for containerization. A Docker compose file can be converted into a Kubernetes file with ease if your preference is Kubernetes (as production applications reside well in Kubernetes as opposed to Docker Compose). Your CI/CD pipeline also needs a source-code management tool such as Git or Bitbucket to store and track your source code changes.

OpenShift has emerged as an advanced platform for deploying containerized applications. You get all the features of Kubernetes without the code-level intricacies that you need to manage in a Kubernetes Cluster.

Containerization is advocated and used in most production grade applications now. Even if you have a cloud environment such as AWS set up, you should go for EKS clusters to support containerization.

You also need to make sure that some of the configurations are set in advance, which I mentioned at the end of the previous chapter—the Dockerfile, the docker compose file (with the external hosts configuration set), and the `requirements.txt` file for the Python packages. These are some of the minor details you have to keep in mind to keep your container in check.

Returning to the application, you will now try to get rid of the manual topic selection that you had to use in the last chapter. I guide you now to include a vector database instead of a traditional one. You will start out with a Jupyter Notebook instead of a full-blown production application. This is the experimentation phase of the development lifecycle. You can try your code in Jupyter Notebooks before actually building Python files to stick it to your production pipeline. Some cloud environments even allow Jupyter Notebooks to be used as a part of the production pipeline instead of insisting on using Python files. Although I still advocate using Python files for cleaner and structured source-code management.

LangChain

Before starting, there is one last thing you need to know about—LangChain.

In recent times, with generative AI models being the forerunner of almost all the industries, there has been an increasing emergence of popular frameworks that allow you to encapsulate everything under one roof. One such popular framework is LangChain. It allows you to think of your generative AI application pipeline as a chain. They have now also come with their own expression language to make development easier. It's called the LangChain Expression Language (LCEL). LangChain also has other supplementing frameworks, such as LangGraph, LangSmith, and so on, and you'll explore some of them in the upcoming chapters.

In the previous chapter, you saw how to use OpenAI and its API to use LLMs and build an intelligent application. The APIs exposed by OpenAI are often sufficient and very extensive. But with the growing demand and exposure to generative AI, every organization wants to embed LLMs in their applications and enterprise applications are complex enough to use plain OpenAI APIs.

Similar to how JavaScript developers came up with frameworks such as Angular JS, React JS, Vue JS, and so on, to cope with the ever-increasing complexity of frontend applications, machine learning engineers came up with LangChain to cope with the increasing complexity needed to integrate LLMs into complex applications.

It might sound a bit paradoxical when you think of the main idea of introducing LLMs into a large enterprise application is to get rid of the complexities and let the LLMs handle the tough job, but you need to handshake all the complex wheels with your LLM while attaching your LLM, which ultimately attends to the complexities.

The following section explains some basic features that LangChain provides out-of-the-box so that you can get comfortable using LangChain instead of OpenAI APIs.

LLM Development Lifecycle

You use Jupyter Notebook in this chapter for all applications since you have not yet learned about some of the MLOps concepts (covered in the next chapter).

If you think about it, you can use Jupyter Notebook to build the application (at least the backend part) from the end of the previous chapter. Once you have the backend of the previous application at hand, you can take it into a Python file and add a frontend to make your application whole. Similarly, whatever you build in this chapter in a Jupyter Notebook can be brought into a Python file and combined with a frontend to have a complete application. This is exactly how an AI application development lifecycle works. You have an experimentation environment, which is actually your Jupyter Notebook, where you can work on building your skeleton and see how each part works in isolation. Once you are ready, you can move your code to a final Python file and start your integration for the complete application. Of course, you can have some of the parts in both your environments in common, such as the database. Your database will reside in a database server from the beginning. Your client may have an existing database which you will need to connect to. Both your experimentation and production environment will connect to this database server. Similarly, you may have an input and output system that you need to connect to, which is supposed to be common for both. You may have a streaming service and hence you will need a message queue service that will be common input for both. A vague representation of such a setup is mapped in Figure 5-7.

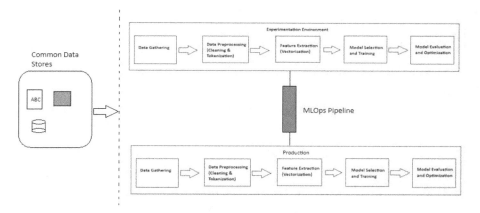

***Figure 5-7.** Intelligent application development lifecycle setup*

We discuss this in detail in the next chapters. Open your Jupyter Notebook and get ready to build a bare minimum featured generative AI application. This will help you get familiar with LangChain.

A Bare Minimum Chatbot Using LangChain

Since this is a demo application to get you accustomed to the basic features of LangChain, you can use Jupyter Notebook, as previously discussed.

Start by installing the LangChain Python SDK, which has integration with OpenAI. LangChain has Python libraries, which can also work with other LLM providers, including Anthropic, Cohere, and so on. Since you have been using OpenAI in this book, go ahead with that.

```
! pip install langchain-openai
```

You now need to set the OpenAI API key to the environment as a variable.

```
import os
from dotenv import load_dotenv

os.environ["OPENAI_API_KEY"] = '<Your API Key>'
load_dotenv()
api_key = os.getenv("OPENAI_API_KEY")
if not api_key:
        raise ValueError("OpenAI API Key not found")
```

You can now initialize the LLM.

```
from langchain_openai import ChatOpenAI

model = ChatOpenAI(model="gpt-3.5-turbo")
```

GPT3.5 Turbo is one of the models of the GPT family early release. You can use any other model, such as GPT4 or so on.

The ChatOpenAI class ensures integration and usability of the LLM in the format of a chat application. In most cases, you will be using ChatOpenAI unless you have a very specific requirement from any of the other interfaces. You can think of the ChatOpenAI interface as the programmatic version of the OpenAI platform. You need to add Assistant and User sections as inputs and your LLM will respond similar to how it does in OpenAI.

If you want to test your model, you can use the interface as follows.

```
model.invoke("Tell me about langchain.")
```

You should get a response in this format:

```
AIMessage(content='Langchain is a decentralized language
learning platform that utilizes blockchain technology to
connect language learners with native speakers around the
world. Users can take lessons,
....
Langchain aims to make language learning more accessible,
affordable, and engaging for people of all ages and
backgrounds.', additional_kwargs={'refusal': None}, response_
metadata={'token_usage': {'completion_tokens': 81, 'prompt_
tokens': 13, 'total_tokens': 94}, 'model_name': 'gpt-3.5-
turbo-0125', 'system_fingerprint': None, 'finish_reason':
'stop', 'logprobs': None}, id='run-410ef98d-e553-4a7d-
ae20-3640fd189542-0', usage_metadata={'input_tokens': 13,
'output_tokens': 81, 'total_tokens': 94})
```

As you can see, your response arrives wrapped in an AIMessage interface, which you can think of as the output from the OpenAI platform. You should see lots of metadata along with your text content response such as total_tokens, model_names, and so on.

You know what prompts are and how prompt engineering can bring out the best. You can use the ChatPromptTemplate interface of LangChain, which will allow you to build a prompt template wherein you can insert your queries and other data points to adjust to your dynamic query requirements.

```
from langchain_core.prompts import ChatPromptTemplate
prompt = ChatPromptTemplate.from_messages([
```

```
    ("system", "You are a computer science trainer. You will
    be asked to provide some technical documentation and your
    task is to explain those technical concepts in layman's
    terms."),
    ("user", "{input}")
])
```

As the prompt template is ready, you can use chains to create a pipeline using LCEL (LangChain Expression Language). The paradigm of programming using LangChain is by using these pipelines, called *chains* (and hence the name LangChain), which are the way to prepare your orchestrations in LangChain. In this book, I use pipeline and chains interchangeably when I am talking about LangChain.

```
chain = prompt | model
```

This chain will create a pipeline to take the input, fit it into the prompt template you created in place of the input placeholder, and pass it to the LLM through the ChatOpenAI interface class.

Finally, you can use the pipeline using the invoke function as follows:

```
chain.invoke({"input": "What is deep learning?"})
```

This should respond to your input query as you have instructed in the prompt (in layman's terms, in this case). Your response format should be similar to the one you received by invoking the model directly using the ChatOpenAI interface.

```
AIMessage(content='Deep learning is a subfield of machine
learning that involves training artificial neural networks to
learn and make decisions in a way that mimics how the human
brain works. These neural networks are composed of layers of
interconnected nodes that process data and extract features
to make predictions or decisions. By using deep learning
```

techniques, computers can be trained to recognize patterns and make decisions without being explicitly programmed to do so. This allows them to perform tasks such as image recognition, speech recognition, and natural language processing with a high level of accuracy.', additional_ kwargs={'refusal': None}, response_metadata={'token_usage': {'completion_tokens': 103, 'prompt_tokens': 47, 'total_ tokens': 150}, 'model_name': 'gpt-3.5-turbo-0125', 'system_ fingerprint': None, 'finish_reason': 'stop', 'logprobs': None}, id='run-de6a30b1-1228-4f3f-9328-a821a08376cb-0', usage_ metadata={'input_tokens': 47, 'output_tokens': 103, 'total_ tokens': 150})

LangChain also allows you to format your responses using output parsers. You can transform the output generated by the LLMs into a predefined format of your own using output parsers.

Now you'll see how to use an output parser, which takes the response from the LLM and gives you only the string content.

```
from langchain_core.output_parsers import StrOutputParser

output_parser = StrOutputParser()
```

StrOutputParser takes the response from the LLM and gives you only the string contents of AIMessage.

You have to build another chain (or pipeline) to output the LLM response through the output parser.

```
chain_1 = prompt | llm | output_parser
```

If you invoke your chain with some input, you should only see the string message without the other metadata.

```
chain_1.invoke({"input": "What is deep learning?"})
```

You should see something just like this:

```
Deep learning is a type of artificial intelligence (AI) that
is inspired by the way the human brain works. It uses neural
networks, which are algorithms that mimic the structure and
function of the human brain, to learn from large amounts of
data and make decisions or predictions without being explicitly
programmed to do so.

In simpler terms, deep learning is a technology that allows
computers to learn and make decisions on their own by analyzing
vast amounts of information, similar to how our brains process
and learn from the world around us.
```

Building Your First RAG Application

Instead of understanding how each of the parts of LangChain work individually, this section takes you through the code directly and builds a RAG application. RAG applications leverage the power of vector databases to ingest and retrieve documents through popular embedding models and prompt engineering. They use the retrieved document excerpt as context for the final LLM in order to answer the user's queries.

The complete application process is visually imagined in Figure 5-8. You can refer to this figure anytime while developing your application.

Open your Jupyter Notebook and let's start by installing the required Python libraries. I introduce some libraries that you didn't use in the previous application of this chapter when you started with LangChain.

```
! pip install langchain langchain-community chromadb pypdf
```

Consider the libraries you installed in this line. LangChain has a Python SDK called langchain, which has the core features of LangChain but some of the helper functions are found in another library, called `langchain-community`. The vector database you will use is ChromaDB. ChromaDB is an open-source vector database and has a Python SDK called `chromadb`. You will also need an OCR that can extract text from PDFs. You will use PyPDF for this, which also has a Python SDK called `pypdf`.

Now install the library you used previously:

```
! pip install langchain-openai
```

Since you are building a RAG application, you need some data sources. Allow me to digress for a moment and talk about the data source I planned to use (unless you have some other document at hand to try this out on).

Since I was a kid, I have always been interested in mathematics. I was not a very bright student and my report cards will support my case. But I was keen on learning various avenues that mathematics can lead to. Although I was always quick on my feet when it came to programming, and I had always secured the top spot when it came to computer science, I always had this deep in my heart that programming is just a tool to use math in the real world.

Now that I am a professional data scientist and a technical specialist, I keep myself updated on the advances of mathematics, particularly something that involves the best of both worlds—mathematics and data science.

A topic that had interested me for quite a bit is algebraic topology (groups, rings, etc.) even though my friends used to consider this field of mathematics not as worthy as statistics or combinatorics. And I admit that you won't find any layman talk about this subject even though they may know about the other subjects of mathematics.

Now, coming back to the application, the data source I used is a wonderfully written paper titled "Algebraic Topology for Data Scientists," by Michael S. Postol. The link to the paper is here: `https://arxiv.org/abs/2308.10825`.

Although this is a single paper, it contains almost all the topics of algebraic topology that a data scientist may find useful, similar to a complete book.

But this is just my personal preference. You are welcome to use any PDF from your library and query your system accordingly.

You might be wondering why this example uses a single document instead of multiple ones like in the previous chapter. You are welcome to use multiple documents or a single one. You just need to ingest in a loop and add it to your document store. Don't worry, I will point out where you need to do this!

Let's start by ingesting the document:

```
from langchain_community.document_loaders import PyPDFLoader

try:
    loader = PyPDFLoader("mypdfpaper.pdf")
    pages = loader.load_and_split()
except Exception as e:
    logging.error(f"Failed to load PDF: {str(e)}")
```

PYPDFLoader is a helper function in the langchain-community library and it uses PyPDF library internally. You might not see importing PyPDF library explicitly even though you have installed it separately. But this helper function leverages the installed library internally and extracts the text from the PDF document.

The loader uses the load_and_split() method to split the documents into chunks and return an array of chunks (or pages), which you store in the pages variable.

Here, you can load any PDF document of your liking. If you want to load multiple documents, you can have a master array (or list) of pages that you can keep extending after every loader loads and splits a document at each iteration.

```
master_pages.extend(pages)
```

Now you need to set the OpenAI API key in an environment variable and use `ChatOpenAI` again, as you did in the previous application, to choose an OpenAI model.

```
import os

os.environ["OPENAI_API_KEY"] = '<Your API Key>'

from langchain_openai import ChatOpenAI

model = ChatOpenAI(model="gpt-3.5-turbo")
```

These two sections of code should look familiar. I don't have anything new to explain here.

Now you'll use a vector database called ChromaDB, as discussed previously, to store the document chunks and create a clustered embedding space. Don't not get worked up on choosing and defining a complex embedding model; just use the OpenAI embedding models in this case.

OpenAI has three embedding models specially curated to vectorize text into embeddings and use them for semantic retrieval using similarity metrics:

- `text-embedding-3-small`
- `text-embedding-3-large`
- `text-embedding-ada-002`

They differ mainly on performance and cost and you can get details about them from this OpenAI link: `https://platform.openai.com/docs/guides/embeddings/embedding-models`.

You will use the `OpenAIEmbeddings` interface of `langchain-openai` to add the OpenAI embeddings to this application. The default model that the interface functions fall back to if no embedding model is chosen is `text-embedding-3-large`.

```
from langchain_openai import OpenAIEmbeddings
from langchain_community.vectorstores import Chroma
```

```
vectore_store = Chroma.from_documents(documents=pages,embedding
=OpenAIEmbeddings())
```

The Chroma interface from `langchain_community.vectorstores` allows LangChain to leverage the `chromadb` library. It is installed to prepare and ingest the chunks into ChromaDB as collections. This LangChain interface does all the heavy lifting, from preparing the chunks into a format fit for `chromadb` to preparing and/or ingesting into the appropriate ChromaDB collection.

Alternatively, if you have a list of text, you can have more control over how you want your text source to be ingested and chunked through `RecursiveCharacterTextSplitter`.

To begin with using `RecursiveCharacterTextSplitter`, start by installing the library.

```
pip install -qU langchain-text-splitters
```

You can start adding the configuration parameters to control your text chunking next:

```
# Add configurable parameters
CHUNK_SIZE = 1000
CHUNK_OVERLAP = 200
```

The `CHUNK_SIZE` variable determines the number of characters each chunk should have and the `CHUNK_OVERLAP` determines the maximum number of characters that two consecutive chunks can intersect or overlap.

You can add them to `RecursiveCharacterTextSplitter` as follows:

```
text_splitter = RecursiveCharacterTextSplitter(
chunk_size=CHUNK_SIZE,
chunk_overlap=CHUNK_OVERLAP
)
```

Finally, you can use them to create chunked ingested documents as follows:

```
text_splitter.create_documents([text_list])
```

Now that your vector database is ready and the documents have been ingested, you need to have a LangChain retriever to query and retrieve document chunks from the vector store. LangChain uses a special kind of interface known as a LangChain retriever to do this. Retrievers connect with vector databases and allow a chain to return document chunks based on a prompt or a query from the vector database. They then pass it on to the next feed in the pipeline (the chain).

It sounds complex—connect to the vector database, get the query, and pass it to the vector database, and use the similarity score to get the best answer. However, retriever can be set up using the following line of code, which you need to add to your application:

```
retriever = vectore_store.as_retriever()
```

Your retriever is ready!

It is worth mentioning that the code shown here doesn't persist the vector store and hence you have to parse and ingest the PDF documents or text sources every time you want to run your application. Hence you should also be aware of the way to persist your vector store once you have created it. You can do that using the persist_directory parameter when you are creating your vector store, as follows:

```
# Add persistence and optimization
vectorstore = Chroma.from_documents(
documents=pages,
embedding=OpenAIEmbeddings(),
persist_directory="./chroma_db",
collection_metadata={"hnsw:space": "cosine", "hnsw:m": 16}
)
vectorstore.persist()
```

Now you'll set up the prompt template using the same old ChatPromptTemplate and the same output parser (the StrOutputParser).

Start by defining the prompt.

```
template = """Answer the question based only on the following
context:
{context}

Question: {question}
"""
```

As you can see, the prompt not only needs the query but also a reference or context to answer the query. In this case, this context is gathered from the vector database. Hence, your prompt needs to add two things—a question from the user and the context from the vector database.

```
from langchain_core.output_parsers import StrOutputParser
from langchain_core.prompts import ChatPromptTemplate

prompt = ChatPromptTemplate.from_template(template)
output_parser = StrOutputParser()
```

The final LangChain concept to understand are the runnables. Runnables are a kind of protocol that LangChain devised for using and building custom chains. It must have occurred to you that while you are building chains using LCEL, there are several input and output formats that the parts of the chains can understand and interact between. Runnables allow you to add custom components and build custom chains if needed.

Figure 5-8 shows a diagrammatic view of the runnables.

In this case, you have to feed the prompt part of the chain two things—the context from the vector database and the query from the user. The context needs to be placed from the retriever that you set up. You can pass these prompt inputs into a runnable interface known as RunnableParallel, which ensures proper formatting of the inputs and returns a dictionary representation of these prompt inputs. The user query that is to be passed to the prompt needs to be gathered from the user input (a variable). The RunnablePassthrough interface allows you to insert a variable value unchanged and use it in a runnable interface (RunnableParallel in this case).

```
from langchain_core.runnables import RunnableParallel,
RunnablePassthrough
```

```
sr = RunnableParallel({"context":retriever, "question":Runnable
Passthrough()})
```

Finally, you have to build the chain and invoke it as you did previously.

```
chain = sr | prompt | model | output_parser
```

```
chain.invoke("What is a group?")
```

Congratulations! You have a fully functional RAG application. See Figure 5-8.

You don't need a database anymore for storing document topics like you did in the previous chapter.

I leave it to you as an exercise to add the frontend and prepare the backend from the Notebook you created.

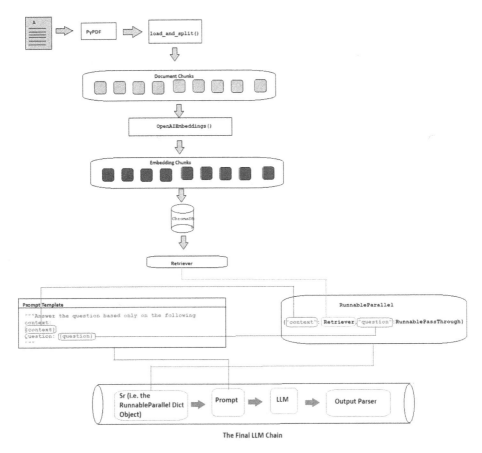

Figure 5-8. *The RAG application workflow*

Isn't it easier to understand a complex application when you can map the workflow in your mind? What if I tell you that LangChain developed a graph-like framework where you can build your application as if it were a workflow of graphs? This framework is known as LangGraph and you will see how to use it to build LLM evaluations in the next chapter.

Summary

- Prompts are an essential part of a generative AI application that helps to fit an LLM to a specific purpose. Prompt engineering is the discipline where data scientists devise various prompting techniques to best fit a business or technical requirement for an LLM to work.

- There are various prompting techniques, such as Chain of Thought and Tree of Thought prompting. They instruct the LLM to lay out the reasoning that led the LLM to the response.

- Although traditional databases are best fit for storing and retrieving data, they fail miserably when it comes to semantic searches from a specific set of documents. Semantic search can be best achieved when a document is divided into chunks and vectorized into embedding so that they can reside in an embedding space based on semantic similarities. Vector databases allows you to do this using several algorithms, including Hierarchical Navigable Small Worlds (HNSW). They use several similarity measures such as Euclidean distance and cosine similarity.

- When you have a vector database and an LLM, you can build an application that refers to the document stores to answer queries. These applications are known as Retrieval Augmented Generation (RAG) applications.

- LangChain is a popular framework often preferred over RAG and other Generative AI applications due to its immense capability for abstracting complex functionalities.

CHAPTER 6

LLM Evaluation and Optimization

This chapter focuses on getting the maximum efficiency from Generative AI with minimal resource consumption. Achieving maximum efficiency involves getting the best results out of the LLM. Hence, this chapter starts by explaining the need to evaluate an LLM. It also discusses *hallucinations*, which are made-up results that are not factual.

You learn a new framework from LangChain, called LangGraph and how it can be used to evaluate an LLM using a technique known as LLM as a judge. LLM as a judge can in turn be achieved for a RAG application by a technique known as Corrective RAG.

The chapter also discusses benchmarking LLMs as a standard way to evaluate their performance. This is often necessary when you are using a new LLM from scratch.

The chapter then introduces MLFlow, which is one of the go-to tools for MLOps to track your model and workflow. You will start by using MLFlow with earlier machine learning algorithms and optimize them using hyperparameter tuning. Then you will learn how to use MLFlow in a complete end-to-end intelligent enterprise application. After that, you will use MLFlow for Generative AI to optimize and track the RAG application.

© Arindam Ganguly 2025
A. Ganguly, *Scaling Enterprise Solutions with Large Language Models*,
https://doi.org/10.1007/979-8-8688-1154-8_6

Additional features, such as load balancing and caching, can optimize your application resource usage and they are best done in another platform, called Portkey.

Finally, you will learn how to deploy your model locally to optimize it on the LLM provider charges.

The Need for LLM Evaluation

Generative AI and LLMs are the youngest descendants in the field of AI. The term artificial intelligence was coined in 1956 by John McCarthy. Hence, you can imagine how old traditional AI is. In 2017, Vaswani et al. introduced the Transformers architecture, which can be considered the epitome of Generative AI. OpenAI bundled all the state-of-the-art machine learning architectures such as Transformers with reinforcement learning into Instruct GPT and ChatGPT toward the end of 2022. At the time of writing this book, Generative AI is just three years old but AI itself is 68 years old.

Thus, Generative AI and LLM developers are still exploring the various parts of application development. When OpenAI almost broke the Internet with ChatGPT, scientists and philosophers around the world started to discover various drawbacks with LLMs. Some of the philosophical debates sprung up about machines taking over the manual job and hence the world. But developers and practitioners were more concerned with generative issues such as hallucination, which was one of the most concerning drawbacks with LLMs. In fact, it is still worrying large industries and preventing them from adapting such intelligence in their ecosystem. This chapter discusses hallucinations and other such issues and prevention mechanisms. Hallucinations were accompanied by qualitative drawbacks in responses such as toxicity and profanity.

Practitioners who were happy letting LLMs do the heavy lifting without a whiff of concern were considering alternative routes. Data scientists started thinking about evaluation strategies, some of which are covered in this chapter.

LangGraph

Before diving into the actual evaluation, you need to be familiar with LangGraph. LangGraph is a library built to support LangChain, which can support multiple agents' stateful workflows for LLM applications. You can think of LangGraph as the tool that can create workflows to drive your LLM applications. This workflow can persist states and use multiple agents. Agents are a new concept in LangChain where you can create various tools.

You can consider tools as one action that you have programmed your LLM to work on. Agents allow your LLM to decide which tool to invoke, as opposed to chains, where your tool chain is hardcoded. You can read more about LangChain agents at `https://python.langchain.com/v0.1/docs/modules/agents/`.

Although this chapter does not use agents to keep things simple, you can set up your functionalities as tools and hence as agents.

This section explores LangGraph and shows you how you can leverage LangGraph to perform LLM evaluations. The concept used here is Corrective RAG.

Recall that Retrieval Augmented Generation (RAG) uses vector stores to chunk and store embeddings of documents or other data sources. RAG works in the following two phases. In the first phase, the query is passed to the vector store and it retrieves document chunks based on the embedding space. In the second phase, the LLM takes over the document chunks and generates chunks to produce a conversational summary. See Figure 6-1.

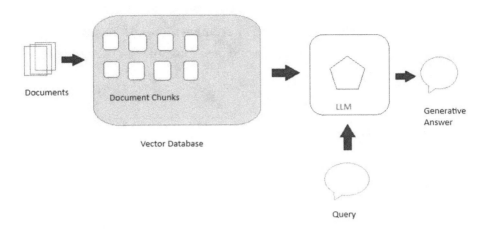

Figure 6-1. *Retrieval Augmented Generation (RAG)*

RAG suffers from a long-term issue, known as hallucinations, covered in this next section.

Hallucinations

When an LLM generates a response, the LLM can introduce information it thinks is relevant, but is actually not factual. For example, if you have a document covering various mathematical topics and you ask something specifically that might require inference and reasoning, there are two issues that can come along with it for the two steps of RAG. First, the similarity algorithm might retrieve chunks of text that's closer in the embedding space due to some of the words that relate to the query better than other chunks that actually do contain something more relevant but don't contain the key terms. Second, the LLM can generate a response from this even though it is not factually relevant and correct.

Consider a document that explains traditional machine learning techniques and models such as linear regression, SVM, random forests, and so and which is fed into the RAG system. Also consider that the document doesn't contain the chronology of the inventions of the models and why SVM was invented. It only discusses the functional methodology and formula that work underneath.

The user asks, "Is linear regression inspired from SVM?". The vector store retrieves the two document chunks that discuss SVM and linear regression. It is quite possible that the LLM might wrongfully infer that linear regression was inspired from SVM due to the notion that SVM tackles nonlinear boundaries and linear regression could be the successor to the SVM, which started tackling the linear boundary problems quicker.

Had the document contained the idea of how machine learning came into being and how SVMs were considered, the RAG could infer correctly. But due to the missing knowledge, LLM cannot infer correctly and might make up an inference on its own, even though there is nothing mentioned in the document about it.

This phenomena is known as hallucinations, where a RAG system makes up information on its own.

LLM as a Judge

Traditional AI evaluation techniques have been around for quite some time and there are quantitative measures that determine how your model performs. Some of these techniques were discussed in previous chapters, including precision, recall, F1 score, and so on. These metrics tackle issues such as false positives, which are also quantitative in nature.

But when it comes to Generative AI, there isn't one quantitative metric that can measure its efficiency. Precision, recall, F1 score, and other traditional AI metrics need a mathematical formulation on the quantity of elements produced and how they differ from the ground truth quantitatively. With Generative AI, you can't gather a ground truth since the answer is generated from the documents and a predefined response can't be considered the ground truth since it would not match the generated answer word for word.

Hence, it makes more sense to somehow measure the RAG performance qualitatively. At the time of writing this book, there is no such mathematical breakthrough that can quantitatively measure the quality of the answer.

One way to address this conundrum is to have another LLM (or even the same model that is performing the LLM) review the response it generated. You can think of it in this way—suppose that you are a teacher. You ask your student to write an answer to a question by referring to the book. Once it's done, you give the answer and the response to another student (maybe in the same class) to verify the other student's response.

It might be quite possible that the other student (and hence the LLM) is also wrong. But let's settle for at least one round of a second opinion.

This procedure is exactly how LLM as a judge works. You employ an LLM to perform RAG and other LLMs to check on qualitative feedback such as hallucination, relevance, and so on. It is all a matter of how you engineer your prompts at different stages. Corrective RAG is an improvement on top of conventional RAG that can use LLM as a judge to refine RAG responses.

Corrective RAG

As mentioned in the previous section, Corrective RAG or C-RAG uses the LLM as a judge strategy to refine RAG responses. This technique can be used to evaluate LLM applications. You will use LangGraph to see how to implement this.

The workflow that you need to build using C-RAG can use the following steps to ensure refined LLM responses:

1. The query is routed to the system, which is taken over by the vector store.

2. The vector store returns the document chunks fetched by the LLM and the LLM responds with a conversational summary referring to the document chunks as context.

3. Another LLM (or maybe the same one) fetches the response and tries to determine how much the LLM is hallucinating.

4. If the LLM is hallucinating, the LLM tries to regenerate the answer.

5. If the LLM is not hallucinating, the LLM tries to determine whether it is on point and resolves the user's query.

6. If the answer does not resolve the user's query, the system (an LLM) tries to regenerate the query so that the vector store can retrieve more relevant chunks.

This process can be explained in the form of a graph, as shown in Figure 6-2.

```
A[Start] --> B(Retrieve);
B --> C(Generate);
C -->| "not supported" | C
C -->| "not useful" | D(Transform Query);
C -->| "useful" | E(End);
D --> B;
```

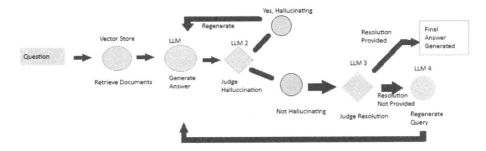

Figure 6-2. *Corrective RAG*

It's time to get dirty with a Jupyter Notebook. Start by installing the appropriate libraries.

```
! pip install -U langchain_community langchain-openai
langchainhub chromadb langchain langgraph pypdf
```

Most of these libraries should be familiar to you:

- `langchain_community`
- `langchian-openai`
- `chromadb`
- `langchain`
- `pypdf`

The ones that need introduction are these:

- `langchainhub`: LangChain Hub is a crowdsourced collection of prompts, agents, and other elements often used for preparing recipes including LangChain.

- `langgraph`: The official library to install the LangGraph Python SDK.

Now you can set the OpenAI API key.

```
import os

os.environ["OPENAI_API_KEY"] = '<Your API Key Here>'
```

I referenced a wonderful paper on the survey of various activation functions used in neural networks. (You can get it at https://arxiv.org/abs/2109.14545.) You can also use your own source documents.

This example uses PyPDF to extract the text from the PDF:

```
from langchain_community.document_loaders import PyPDFLoader

loader = PyPDFLoader("Activation_Functions.pdf")
pages = loader.load_and_split()
```

Now set up the LLM from OpenAI:

```
from langchain_openai import ChatOpenAI

model = ChatOpenAI(model="gpt-3.5-turbo")
```

You also need to set up the vector store and initialize the LangChain retriever:

```
from langchain_openai import OpenAIEmbeddings
from langchain_community.vectorstores import Chroma

vectore_store = Chroma.from_documents(documents=pages,embedding
=OpenAIEmbeddings())
retriever = vectore_store.as_retriever()
```

Finally, you need to prepare the chain (the LangChain pipeline) exactly like you did in the previous chapter. I try to keep it simple this time.

```
from langchain_core.output_parsers import StrOutputParser
from langchain_core.runnables import RunnableParallel,
RunnablePassthrough
```

```
generate_template = """Answer the question based only on the
following context:
{context}

Question: {question}
"""

generation_prompt = ChatPromptTemplate.from_template(generate_
template)
output_parser = StrOutputParser()

generation_chain =  generation_prompt | model | output_parser
```

The previous lines of code should be very familiar to you, as all you have done is set up a simple RAG pipeline. Next, you add the RAG improvements.

Before getting to that, let me share a technique that's useful for many applications that require LLM responses to perform middle layer calculations. LLMs respond in a string format; if you are looking to use the response to get a specific value for some kind of calculation, you have to parse it from the response. LangChain can help you with this by allowing your LLMs to render structured responses. The trick is to prepare a JSON schema (or a Python class) and pass it to the ChatOpenAI interface method with_structured_output().

You will leverage Pydantic library, which allows to prepare a model for a schema to be used in Python. You can think of it as a converter from a JSON schema to a Python class. A Pydantic model is a class simply derived (inherited) from pydantic.BaseModel and it has fields (defined by the Field interface of the Pydantic library) for class attributes. You can read more about Pydantic at https://docs.pydantic.dev/latest/.

```
from langchain_core.pydantic_v1 import BaseModel, Field
```

```
class GradeHallucinations(BaseModel):
  binary_score:str = Field(description="Answer is grounded in
  the facts, 'yes' or 'no'")
```

As you might have already inferred from the description of the class (or schema suggests), this model stores "yes" or "no" based on whether the response is factual or not, that is, whether the LLM is hallucinating or not.

Now you'll use this schema and set up a LangChain pipeline to grade hallucinations from an LLM response.

```
llm_grader = model.with_structured_output(GradeHallucinations)
```

```
system = """You are a grader assessing whether an LLM
generation is grounded in / supported by a set of retrieved
facts. \n
    Give a binary score 'yes' or 'no'. 'Yes' means that the
    answer is grounded in / supported by the set of facts."""
```

```
hall_prompt = ChatPromptTemplate.from_messages([
    ("system",system),
    ("human","Set of facts: \n\n {documents} \n\n LLM
    generation: {generation}")
])
```

```
hallucination_grader = hall_prompt|llm_grader
```

Similarly, prepare a chain to determine whether an LLM response resolves the user's query:

```
class GradeAnswers(BaseModel):
  binary_score:str = Field(description="Answer addresses the
  question, 'yes' or 'no'")
```

```
llm_grader_ans = model.with_structured_output(GradeAnswers)
```

```
system = """You are a grader assessing whether an answer
addresses / resolves a question \n
     Give a binary score 'yes' or 'no'. Yes' means that the
     answer resolves the question."""

answer_prompt = ChatPromptTemplate.from_messages([
    ("system",system),
    ("human", "User question: \n\n {question} \n\n LLM
    generation: {generation}")
])

answer_grader = answer_promptIllm_grader_ans
```

Finally, prepare a prompt and a chain to rewrite the user query.

```
rewrite_template = """You a question re-writer that converts an
input question to a better version that is optimized \n
     for vectorstore retrieval. Look at the input and try to
     reason about the underlying semantic intent / meaning."""

rewrite_prompt = ChatPromptTemplate.from_template(rewrite_
template)
output_parser_rewrite = StrOutputParser()

sr = RunnableParallel({"question":RunnablePassthrough()})

rewrite_chain = sr I rewrite_prompt I model I output_
parser_rewrite
```

Now you'll concentrate on preparing the workflow and graph using LangGraph.

The first step is to prepare a state. You can think of it as a session store that stores the attributes that need to be accessed by all the nodes of the graph or all the tasks in the workflow.

```python
from typing import List

from typing_extensions import TypedDict
from langchain.schema import Document

class GraphState(TypedDict):

    question: str
    generation: str
    documents: List[Document]
```

This state is similar to a dictionary that flows throughout the edges of the graph and is accessible to all the nodes that the graph refers to. When you set up the functionalities for each of the graph nodes, your state will be used to access the query, generated response, or the retrieved document at every point of the graph.

For example, say you have to create a function that can access the user query from the state and use the LangChain retriever that you created earlier to extract relevant document chunks from the vector database.

```python
def retrieve(state):
    question = state["question"]
    documents = retriever.invoke(question)
    return {"documents":documents,"question":question}
```

You also need to prepare a document aggregator that can join all the source documents returned by the vector database. You'll now prepare a utility function for that.

```python
def format_docs(docs):
    return "\n\n".join(doc.page_content for doc in docs)
```

You now have to create all the other functions that use the LangChain chains (or pipelines) that you created earlier.

Create the following function to leverage the generation_chain to generate answers from the retrieved document chunks and the user query, which you can access from the state.

```
def generate(state):
  question = state["question"]
  documents = state["documents"]

  generation = generation_chain.invoke({"context":format_docs(d
  ocuments),"question":question})
  return {"documents": documents, "question": question,
  "generation": generation}
```

Now create the following function, which will rewrite the query using rewrite_chain.

```
def transform_query(state):
  question = state["question"]
  documents = state["documents"]
  better_question = rewrite_chain.invoke({"question":question})
  return {"documents": documents, "question": better_question}
```

Finally, create a function that can decide and act upon the correction in the C-RAG approach. As discussed, you need the system to check for hallucinations in the LLM response. It will either rewrite the query or regenerate the answer. This function handles the machineries behind it.

```
def grade_generation_v_documents_and_question(state):
    question = state["question"]
    documents = state["documents"]
    generation = state["generation"]

    hg = hallucination_grader.invoke({"documents":documents,
    "generation":generation})
    if hg.binary_score=="yes":
```

```
    ag = answer_grader.invoke({"question":question,
    "generation":generation})
    if ag.binary_score=="yes":
      return "useful"
    else:
      return "not useful"
  else:
    return "not supported"
```

If you carefully look at the if-ladder, you should be able to relate it to the C-RAG workflow.

It's time to create the graph exactly according to the C-RAG figure. The grade_generation_v_documents_and_questions function does most of the heavy lifting. Hence, you can assign this function as a conditional edge in the graph and the rest of the functions as nodes of the graph.

To start, you need to import certain elements from the langgraph. graph library:

```
from langgraph.graph import END, StateGraph, START
```

Here, END and START are string constants that act as virtual start and end nodes. StateGraph is used to initialize the graph, which you need to do to start your graph development, as shown here:

```
workflow = StateGraph(GraphState)
```

Now, as discussed in the previous section, you have to create the nodes by assigning the functions that you created (except the one that needs to be added as a conditional edge) to each of the nodes so that they can be invoked by the node when the workflow encounters them.

```
workflow.add_node("retrieve",retrieve)
workflow.add_node("generate",generate)
workflow.add_node("transform_query",transform_query)
```

Now let's concentrate on developing the edges.

The first edge should connect the START node to the retriever.

```
workflow.add_edge(START,"retrieve")
```

Now that the document chunks are retrieved, the workflow should generate the LLM response using the generate function and node.

```
workflow.add_edge("retrieve","generate")
```

You can add your conditional edge by leveraging the grade_generation_v_documents_and_question function:

```
workflow.add_conditional_edges("generate",grade_generation_
v_documents_and_question,
                              {
                                      "not supported":"generate",
                                      "not useful":
                                      "transform_query",
                                      "useful":END
                              })
```

As you can see, if the answer really turns out to be useful even after all the checks, you can definitely ask the workflow to stop, and hence call the END node at the "useful" check.

Finally, you can compile your workflow:

```
app = workflow.compile()
```

Now you can test your workflow by sending a user query. It would be best if you could add some logging (print statements) for each function to see how your workflow flows.

```
inputs = {"question": "What is Activation Function?"}
for output in app.stream(inputs):
  print(output)
```

The `app.stream` function will show all the logs (if you have set any) and the final output.

For each node, you should see what the function associated with that node returns.

Using LangGraph is a crude way of evaluating LLMs, where you create workflows and design them according to your needs. This way of evaluating intelligent systems has its own advantages and disadvantages. You can definitely design your workflow in your own way and add a few diversions along the way to suit your needs. This might be suitable for a developer and a unit tester. But when it comes to valuing and verifying from the business perspective, this might lead to some unending adjustments when the business requirement keeps changing and your evaluation strategies are tightly coupled with your workflow. If you can separate the evaluation part and the rest of the system workflow, you can handle adjustments at any point in time as easily as any other task.

Benchmarking

LLM evaluation is an active area of research and one way of separating the evaluation part with the model development is using benchmarks. Various benchmarks have already been agreed upon for several early ML models. For example, MNIST was considered one of the benchmarks that used to decide how your AI model performed. Data scientists used to test their models using popular datasets such as MNIST and calculating precision, recall, F1-Score, and AUC to benchmark their models. They had been used for a long time and various papers and journals validated published models using these datasets and the metrics.

With the growing branches of machine learning, AI started taking over (rather solving) previously untackled problems, such as question answering and summarization, and it became difficult to benchmark models based on generic metrics and simple datasets.

Popular datasets such as SQuAD (Stanford Question Answering Dataset) started to serve as benchmarks to validate the worthiness of a model.

Some popular benchmarks were derived from calculating scores using new metrics, including BLEU (Bilingual Evaluation Understudy) for machine translation and ROUGE (Recall Oriented Understudy for Gisting Evaluation) for summarization. Data scientists used to calculate the scores and benchmark the efficiency of a model specifically designed for a particular task based on the score. These metrics made more sense than simple precision and recalls as they couldn't target specific domains and tasks.

There are numerous such evaluation metrics and explaining each of them is out of the scope of this book, but I urge you to search for their papers and try to understand at least a few of them.

After the advent of the Transformers architecture, models started targeting specific tasks and metrics such as ROUGE and BLEU became the norm for evaluating AI models. Various tools sprung up to ease the pain of evaluation; machine learning development became more fluent and systematic.

Machine learning ops emerged as a new discipline, with new challenges to embed CI/CD into intelligent systems that include model building and development. Productionizing these models required extra precaution and MLOps started gaining attention. MLOps tools came out with features to solve these intricacies and they included evaluation metrics to make everything streamlined.

The next section covers one such MLOps tool.

MLFlow

MLFlow is an open-source, all-inclusive tool that streamlines your machine learning development pipeline. MLFlow can track and manage your machine learning development lifecycle and can ensure that each phase is traceable and reproducible. You will embed MLFlow in your development from now on in this book and use its myriad range of evaluation strategies to perfect your model iteratively if needed.

You can check out the MLFlow documentation at `https://mlflow.org/docs/latest/index.html`.

MLFlow starts by tracking the model building right from the beginning and it can help evaluate your models and save them in their own managed repositories. You can perform versioning of your models and monitor how they are doing. MLFlow supports traditional as well as Generative AI pipelines.

MLFlow for Scikit-Learn Models

Without further ado, let me show you how you can use such a powerful tool. You will learn how MLFlow can take care of your machine learning development pipeline if you are planning a Scikit-Learn traditional AI model, a TensorFlow deep learning model, or an LLM.

You have to use Python files instead of Jupyter Notebooks when you start building your MLFlow components. MLFlow, which comes after the experimentation and model building phase, mainly deals with tracking the runtime model performance and usability. Hence, once you are done with your experimentation and model selection, you will embed model tracking in your final application as a complete project.

But just like with any other data science project, you'll start your experimentation and model building and selection phase.

Pull up your Jupyter Notebook; you'll start by exploring how a simple Scikit-Learn model can use MLFlow to track its development lifecycle. You created and reviewed various Scikit-Learn models in the first chapter. For the purposes of demonstration, you'll use the iris dataset and a random forest classifier in this chapter.

Setting Up Data-Gathering Modules

You'll make a small modification where you will modularize the code:

```
from sklearn.datasets import load_iris

def get_data():
  iris = load_iris()
  return iris.data, iris.target

X,y = get_data()

print(len(X))
print(len(y))
```

This should output:

```
150
150
```

The data gathering is now separated into a function. The code is pretty straightforward. You can also place it in a separate file and use it as a package or library.

Next, you learn about hyperparameter tuning and then you will initialize the model.

Hyperparameter Tuning

Let's first identify the difference between a model parameter and a hyperparameter.

You must have heard of various LLM announcements stating that a model contains a certain number of parameters. At the time of writing this book, these parameters have reached billions. For example, the Llama model from Meta has upped their game by incrementing the number of parameters and as of now, Meta has announced Llama 3.1 with three versions—8 billion, 70 billion, and 405 billion. When you use these models, you often ID these models using these parameter versions such as `meta-llama/Meta-Llama-3-8B`, which refers to the 8 billion parameter version of Llama 3 from the `meta-llama` library.

Recall that a deep learning model relies on the number of weights and biases that are learned during the training phase. These weights and biases are initialized randomly and the gradient method allows the model to learn the appropriate values of these weights and biases to model the training data as accurately as possible with each iteration or epoch. The weights and biases learned during training are model parameters. Sometimes you can include other parameters that accompany the weights and biases to learn their values as well, such as the read/write gates in an RNN.

On the other hand, other parameters, such as the number of neurons, the optimizer, number of epochs, the number of layers, and so on, in the same ANN need to be decided from the beginning. Similarly, if you consider a simple model such as a SVM, the C parameter decides how soft or hard your decision boundary is. You fix the value of this parameter from the start according to your needs or business requirements and the rest of the parameters are learned. These parameters are known as *hyperparameters* and they are determined from the beginning of the training phase and don't change.

What if you could experiment with the hyperparameters as well and let the system determine which is the best configuration for a certain use case?

One way to do this that you possibly have already imagined is using an array of hyperparameters and manually looping over all their configurations for a particular model.

Scikit-Learn enables you to tune the hyperparameters in the same way automatically as well, by allowing the model to be trained with several configurations of hyperparameters. It shows the evaluating metrics by using a method known as a grid search. You need to tell the hyperparameter configuration and the estimator you are using to train. Your estimator can be a model instance or a pipeline (it may consist of preprocessors and model instances).

Grid Search can be done in Scikit-Learn using the GridSearchCV class. Now you'll see how to use GridSearchCV for the iris classification. You'll try a random forest classifier with several configurations of hyperparameters.

To begin, you need to instantiate the random forest classifier model:

```
from sklearn.ensemble import RandomForestClassifier

rfc = RandomForestClassifier()
```

Now, like any responsible data scientist, you have to split your dataset into a training and test set.

```
from sklearn.model_selection import train_test_split

X_train, X_test, y_train, y_test = train_test_split(X,y)
```

You now have to decide on the hyperparameters to try for the random forest models. Some of the popular hyperparameters that you can meddle with are n_estimators (signifies the number of trees), max_features (specifies the maximum number of features it can assume to take from the dataset), and max_depth (tells the model the maximize size to allow the trees to grow).

Start by preparing the configuration for these hyperparameters:

```
param_rfc = {
    'n_estimators': [10,20,30,40],
    'max_features': ['sqrt','log2'],
    'max_depth': [3,6,9,12,15]
}
```

As you can see, each hyperparameter is assigned to a key value pair in the configuration, with the key being the name of the parameter and the value being the array of values of the hyperparameter.

For example, this example sets the n_estimators to 10, 20, 30, and 40, so max features should be considered square roots of the total number of columns (or features) in the dataset and a logarithm of the total number of features, and max_depth can be between 3, 6, 9, 12, and 15. GridSearchCV will try all permutations of all the hyperparameters and find the best model.

To accomplish this, you need to initialize your GridSearchCV with the model and hyperparameter configuration.

```
from sklearn.model_selection import GridSearchCV

gs = GridSearchCV(rfc,param_rfc,scoring='accuracy',cv=5,
n_jobs=-1)
```

The first line of code is definitely the one you need to import GridSearchCV with. The second line of code ensures that you can use grid search. The first two parameters are well understood—the model (estimator) and the parameter configuration dictionary. You need to provide a metric for GridSearchCV to pick the best hyperparameter configuration, which you have done using the scoring parameter. GridSearchCV uses cross-validation, which is one way of trying the permutations of all the parameters. During cross-validation, grid search uses holdout data to check how the model configuration performs by leveraging the scoring method. This holdout data is set aside from the training data and used as a small test set every time GridSearchCV trains the model with a particular hyperparameter configuration. Finally, n_jobs tells GridSearchCV to use a certain number of parallel jobs while it's training the model. -1 signals GridSearchCV to use as much as it can.

Now you have to fit your dataset to gs:

```
gs_fit = gs.fit(X_train,y_train)
```

This will start the grid search process with the model and the hyperparameter configuration provided.

Now that the grid search is done, let's see how it has performed. GridSearchCV has a myriad of several metrics to check the performance and evaluation of hyperparameter values for the estimator.

> `gs_fit.best_estimator_` tells you the best model configuration it has picked based on the metric (scoring parameter value of `GridSearchCV`).
>
> `gs_fit.best_params_` gives you the hyperparameters that gave the best result on the holdout data that `GridSearchCV` used during cross-validation.
>
> `gs_fit.best_score_` shows you the score (accuracy in this case) of the best model configuration.

You can try to see the score (accuracy) your test data gives by using your own test dataset that you kept aside in the beginning, by using the following line of code.

```
gs_fit.score(X_test,y_test)
```

You can also leverage the `predict` and `predict_proba` functions to get the prediction on your test set.

```
gs_fit.predict(X_test)
```

Figure 6-3 runs the same lines of code described earlier.

```
[11] gs_fit.best_estimator_
```

```
          •                    RandomForestClassifier
     RandomForestClassifier(max_depth=3, max_features='log2', n_estimators=10)
```

```
[12] gs_fit.best_params_
```

```
     {'max_depth': 3, 'max_features': 'log2', 'n_estimators': 10}
```

```
[13] gs_fit.best_score_
```

```
     0.9727272727272727
```

```
[14] gs_fit.score(X_test,y_test)
```

```
     0.9736842105263158
```

```
     gs_fit.predict(X_test)
```

```
     array([0, 1, 0, 1, 1, 2, 0, 1, 1, 1, 1, 1, 2, 1, 2, 2, 2, 0, 2, 1, 1, 0,
            1, 1, 1, 0, 2, 0, 2, 1, 2, 2, 1, 0, 1, 0, 1, 2])
```

Figure 6-3. *Grid search evaluation*

The Complete Intelligent Application with MLFlow Tracker

Now that you have the model ready and with hyperparameter tuned, you'll put all these components into a Python project.

Pull up your favorite Python IDE and get ready to write the same lines of code that you wrote earlier.

Just to give a sense of how a complete intelligent application is structured in a production environment, I urge you to divide your modules into separate files in the following manner.

Start by preparing data_gathering.py, which can reside in your project workspace. This file ensures data gathering. In a practical scenario, this file might contain modules to connect to a database or another external data source/sources. This file will also have the required mechanisms to get the data from those sources and outsource them from the entry function of this file. This file might have various table joins, big data manipulations, or message queues to gather streaming data.

This case is much simpler, as you are getting the data directly from the Scikit-Learn library.

Here are the contents of `data_gathering.py` that pertain to this project.

`data_gathering.py`

```
from sklearn.datasets import load_iris

def get_data():
  iris = load_iris()
  return iris.data, iris.target
```

As a next step, create a separate file for the data preparation stage. This file might contain steps to mingle with the data to format the dataset into a suitable structure. In case of unstructured data such as PDFs, images, and so on, this file will take the of activities such as OCR (Optical Character Recognition), convert pixel data into dataframes in the case of images, extract important features from the datasets, and so on. This Python file sets the stage for the models to access the training and testing data directly. Hence, it also contains the train and test split and stratification methods.

Again, since this case is simpler than what you might encounter later, you already have the data in the required format, courtesy of Scikit-Learn, and you only have to perform the train and test splits.

`data_prepartion.py`

```
from sklearn.model_selection import train_test_split

def prepare_data(X,y):
    X_train, X_test, y_train, y_test = train_test_split(X,y)
    return X_train, X_test, y_train, y_test
```

Now you move on to the exciting part of this project, where you will need to train the model. You have already selected and experimented with this model and have decided on the process for training (including the hyperparameter tuning), so you will simply use the code written earlier during the experimentation phases pertaining to model training and tuning in `train.py`. Along with this, you also include the model tracking steps. You can separate the model training and tracking in separate Python files, but this example keeps things simple for now and keeps them together.

train.py

In this section, you create a file called `train.py` and add all the imports. The imports will contain the libraries you used in the experimentation phase, as well the data gathering and data preparation files, since you need to access and prepare the data for training.

Add the Scikit-Learn modules as you did earlier:

```
from sklearn.ensemble import RandomForestClassifier
from sklearn.tree import DecisionTreeClassifier
from sklearn.model_selection import GridSearchCV
import datetime
```

In Python, once you have a file with the required functions in place, you can use them in another file by treating them as any other libraries. Include the data gathering and data preparation functions from data_gathering.py and data_prepration.py:

```
from data_gathering import get_data
from data_preparation import prepare_data
```

Finally, include MLFlow library that you have been waiting eagerly for.

```
import mlflow
```

After all these imports, you need to start your model selection. You have already experimented with random forest classifier. But just to make things a little more interesting, you'll also add a decision tree classifier, assuming that you have also tried the decision tree classifier in the experimentation phase.

241

Add the following lines of code, which will instantiate the model classes from Scikit-Learn:

```
rfc = RandomForestClassifier()
dt = DecisionTreeClassifier()
```

Now you'll prepare the parameter configurations for the decision tree classifier and random forest classifier. The parameters from the random forest classifier have already been explored in the experimentation phase. The parameters for the decision tree classifier are similar to the random forest classifier, apart from the n_estimators parameter.

As you already know, the n_estimators parameter defines the number of trees to be used in a random forest classifier. As the decision tree classifier deals with a single tree, n_estimators makes no sense here. Instead, you'll use a parameter called criterion, which defines the criteria that the tree uses to split, namely entropy or gini impurity.

You can add the following code to add the model configurations:

```
param_rfc = {
    'n_estimators': [10,20,30,40],
    'max_features': ['sqrt','log2'],
    'max_depth': [3,6,9,12,15]
}

param_dt = {
    'criterion': ['entropy','gini'],
    'max_features': ['sqrt','log2'],
    'max_depth': [3,6,9,12,15]
}
```

Now you set up tracking using MLFlow while training the model. This will track the models for their best configuration, as derived by the GridSearchCV.

To make this dynamic, you can loop the model trainings for the models from an array of models. Let's set up these arrays, which will help you iterate through the models.

```
models = [rfc,dt]
model_names = ['Random Forest Classifier','Decision Tree']
params = [param_rfc,param_dt]
```

Now you can begin the MLFlow journey... Finally!!

Although MLFlow is used in production, each model training to be tracked by MLFlow is considered an experiment.

MLFlow requires an experiment name, so let's give it to them by using the following line of code:

```
experiment_name = f"Iris_experiment_{datetime.datetime.now().st
rftime('%m_%d_%Y_%H_%M_%S')}"
```

You have probably been wondering why you need the `datetime` library. You will need it to format your MLFlow experiment name in production so that you can identify your good run days and bad run days later.

In principle, you need a way to log your runs; your experiment name format will help you do this.

Prepare a function for the training module just like you did for data gathering and data preparation:

```
def best_fit_models():
```

Before including your MLFlow tracking techniques, MLFlow gives you a ready-made dashboard and UI to visualize your runs. But to use that, you have to launch the built-in MLFlow server to expose the dashboard. This is optional and many data scientists choose to prepare their own visualizations by either custom-built UIs of their own or by leveraging third-party dashboarding tools such as Prometheus or Grafana.

Add the following line of code inside the `best_fit_models()` function to switch on the MLFlow visualization server:

```
mlflow.set_tracking_uri(uri="http://mlflow:5000")
```

Don't forget to add indentation as a part of your `best_fit_model` function definition in Python.

You also need to set the experiment name in the format prepared, as given here:

```
mlflow.set_experiment(experiment_name)
```

You have to tell MLFlow to start tracking by running the MLFlow tracker. You have to encapsulate everything you track inside the MLFlow tracker as follows.

```
with mlflow.start_run():
```

Now you have to iterate your model trainings for each of the models inside `mlflow.start_run()`.

```
for idx in range(len(models)):
        X,Y = get_data()
        X_train, X_test, y_train, y_test = prepare_data(X,Y)
        gs = GridSearchCV(models[idx],params[idx],scoring="a
        ccuracy",cv=5,n_jobs=-1)
        gs_fit = gs.fit(X_train,y_train)
```

The code is pretty much self-explanatory, as we have already discussed this for a single model during the experimentation phase. This code does the same thing for each model in the loop.

But within this loop, you also need to tell the MLFlowservice to track certain metrics. The following line of code allows MLFlow to log the train and test accuracy metrics using the `log_metrics` function of `mlflow`.

```
mlflow.log_metrics({
        "Train_Accuracy": gs_fit.best_score_,
        "Test_Accuracy": gs_fit.score(X_test,y_test)
    })
```

MLFlow has its own model repository, which you can use later to refer to a certain model. This technique is used when the model is retrained again and again, maybe with new incoming data. Every retrain brings a new version of the model and MLFlow allows versioning of the model that can later help you bring out a certain version of model if need be.

Hence, you also have to log your model in MLFlow along with its metrics using the following lines of code:

```
# Log the model
    model_info = mlflow.sklearn.log_model(
            sk_model=models[idx],
            artifact_path="iris_model",
            registered_model_name=model_names[idx],
    )
```

This allows the model to register into the repository with a name to keep track of.

In case you missed something, the complete best_fit_models() function definition is presented here:

```
def best_fit_models():
    mlflow.set_tracking_uri(uri="http://mlflow:5000")
    mlflow.set_experiment(experiment_name)
    with mlflow.start_run():
    for idx in range(len(models)):
        X,Y = get_data()
        X_train, X_test, y_train, y_test = prepare_data(X,Y)
```

```
        gs = GridSearchCV(models[idx],params[idx],scoring="ac
        curacy",cv=5,n_jobs=-1)
        gs_fit = gs.fit(X_train,y_train)
        mlflow.log_metrics({
            "Train_Accuracy": gs_fit.best_score_,
            "Test_Accuracy": gs_fit.score(X_test,y_test)
        })
        # Log the model
        model_info = mlflow.sklearn.log_model(
            sk_model=models[idx],
            artifact_path="iris_model",
            registered_model_name=model_names[idx],
        )
```

This concludes the `train.py` file.

Now that all your functions and modules are ready and since I promised you that this is going to be a complete production grade application, I now guide you to prepare the web-based entry point for training the data using Flask as well as the Docker files for deployment.

First, you need to prepare the Flask application to train it in a server.

index.py

```
from flask import Flask, render_template
from train import best_fit_models

app = Flask(__name__)

@app.route('/train')
def train():
    best_fit_models()
    return render_template("run_model.html")
```

```python
@app.route('/')
def index():
    return render_template("index.html")

# main driver function
if __name__ == '__main__':
    app.run(host='0.0.0.0', port=7000)
```

The application has two routes serving two services—the root (/) as an entry point and the /train route to initiate model training from train.py.

Now that you have a backend web server, you also need a UI. This UI is the interface you need to initiate training with. Don't confuse it with the MLFlow UI, which runs on a different port and shows the visuals of your model runs.

To create the UIs, create a folder called templates in your root working directory and add two HTML files from the backend services—index.html and run_model.html.

index.html

```html
<html>
    <head>
        <title>MLFlow SkLearn</title>
    </head>
    <body>
    <p>
        <h4>Click on the Submit Button Below to Train your
        Model</h4>
    </p>
    <p>
        <form action="/train" method="GET">
            <input type="submit" value="submit" />
        </form>
```

```
        </p>
    </body>
</html>
```

The `index.py` file is simple and only contains a form to initiate training. It invokes the other service—train—using the `/train` route defined in the Flask application.

Finally, you need the `run_model.html` file to show that the training has completed successfully.

run_model.html

```
<html>
    <body>
        <h2>Success!!</h2>
        <p>Check MLFlow UI</p>
    </body>
</html>
```

Now that you have the application codebase ready, you can add the pieces to deploy the application using Docker.

For that, you need a Docker file and the `requirements.txt` file.

requirements.txt

Prepare the `requirements.txt` file as shown here:

```
scikit-learn
Flask
mlflow
```

Before proceeding, there is something I want to mention.

If you are aware of containerization using Docker, you know that each Docker file is used to containerize a single application to be deployed. But in this case, you have two applications—one application renders your AI app and the other one serves the MLFlow server that you will use for visualization (i.e., the one MLFlow comes with). This is why you exposed two ports—the port 7000 exposed in `index.py` will render your AI application and the port you mentioned as your MLFlow tracker UI is 5000, which will be used for MLFLow visualizations. Hence, you need two Docker files.

You can run both Docker files separately, or you can create a single `docker-compose` file to maintain, run, and orchestrate both your containers.

You have probably worked with or heard of Kubernetes; it's one of the most popular container orchestration tools used in the current market.

For the purposes of demonstration, this example uses Docker Compose, which is a similar container orchestrator but with minimal features as compared to Kubernetes. You will run the Docker Compose file to start the application, which in turn will containerize and run the MLFlow server and the custom backend Flask server, which can trigger your model training.

Next are the Docker files and the Docker Compose files.

Dockerfiles

```
FROM python:3.11
WORKDIR /app
COPY requirements.txt /app/
RUN pip install -r requirements.txt
COPY . /app
EXPOSE 7000 8080
CMD ["mkdir","iris_model"]
CMD ["python", "index.py"]
```

This Docker file will containerize the Flask server and all the model building components along with it.

Dockerfile_mlflow

```
FROM python:3.11
RUN pip install mlflow
EXPOSE 5000
```

This Docker file will install `mlflow` and expose the other port for its internal server to allow visualization.

Finally, add the Docker Compose file with the following contents and name the file `docker-compose.yml`. (This is the default Docker Compose filename. If you call it something else, you will have to provide the Docker Compose filename with the `-f` parameter when you run the `docker-compose` command.)

docker-compose.yml

```
version: "3.3"
services:
  application:
    build:
    context: .
    dockerfile: ./Dockerfile
    ports:
    - '7000:7000'
    image: scanner_application
    container_name: scanner_application
    networks:
    - net
  mlflow:                        # create a MLFlow container
    build:
    context: .
    dockerfile: ./Dockerfile
    container_name: mlflow_container
```

```
    ports:
    - "5000:5000"                              # expose port
    command: 'mlflow server --backend-store-uri ./mlflow
    --host 0.0.0.0 --port 5000'
    networks:
    - net
networks:
  net:
    driver: bridge  #external: true
```

As you can see, the compose file runs and exposes two ports as two applications.

Your codebase is ready!

All that is left to do is to run the complete application using the following command:

```
docker-compose run –build
```

This will build and run the application using your Docker Compose file.

Once the build and run is complete, you can open your browser and navigate to 127.0.0.1:7000. You should see a web page that asks you to train your model by clicking a Submit button, as shown in Figure 6-4.

Figure 6-4. *Home page of the application*

You should know that in your backend, your MLFlow is also running and since you already have made a provision to run your MLFlow server as well, you can check the MLFlow UI by navigating to 127.0.0.1:5000.

Now train your model by clicking the Submit button on the application home web page. Monitor what's going on in the MLFlow UI.

Once your model has been trained successfully, you should see a success message on your application's web page, as shown in Figure 6-5.

Figure 6-5. *Successful training run*

Now let's look at the MLFlow UI and see what it has captured. (You might need to refresh your MLFlow UI.)

You will find a training run in the left-most sidebar attributed as an experiment since MLFlow tracks every model run as an experiment. You already set the name format for the experiment using the current timestamp. See Figure 6-6.

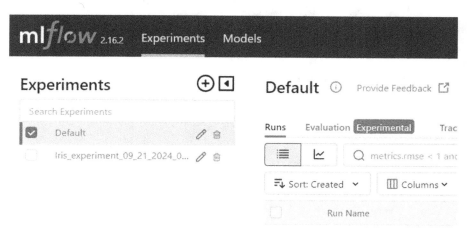

Figure 6-6. *MLFlow experiment*

Click the experiment that it logged to see the run details in the tab in the middle.

It will show a random name under Run Name, but it will show other details such as the duration of the run and the model it has used for training (see Figure 6-7).

Figure 6-7. *Run details*

Click the name of the run to get a more detailed view. You should see all the details, such as time it took, the run ID, and the model that is registered in the end. See Figure 6-8.

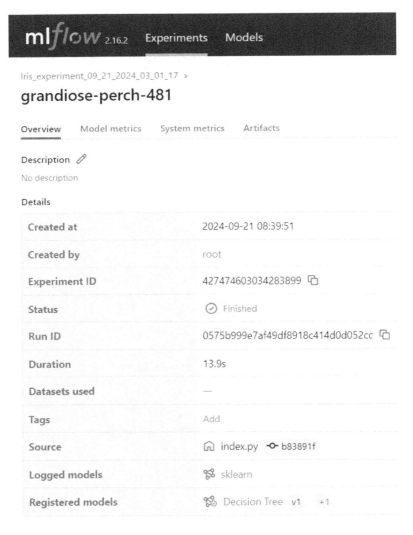

Figure 6-8. *Run details overview*

Right now you are on the Overview tab. Click the Model Metrics tab to see a graphical representation of the train and test accuracy. This is shown in Figure 6-9.

Figure 6-9. *Model metrics*

At the top menu, you are on the Experiments tab. Click the Models tab to see the logged model details. You should see the models that are registered (Decision Tree and Random Forest Classifier in this case).

These are the registered or logged models that can be used for predictions from the model registry. See Figure 6-10.

Figure 6-10. *MLFlow registered models*

Run the training again from the application home page (127.0.0.1:7000) by clicking the Submit button. Once this second run is successful, you can navigate to MLFlow UI to see another run in the same experiment. Since you preserved the timestamp for each day and formatted the name of the experiment, each run on the same day will be placed under the same experiment for that day. This is one of the methods used in the real world to categorize multiple model runs. You can also categorize by month, year, and more.

From your MLFlow UI, select both runs and click the Compare button at the top to compare the model runs. See Figure 6-11.

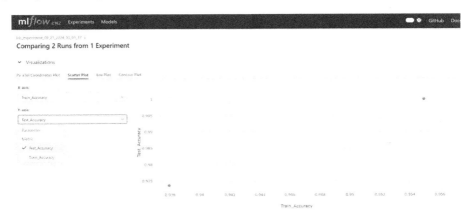

	Run Name	Created ≡↓	Dataset	Duration	Source	Models
☑	● ambitious-snipe-292	⊘ 6 minutes ago	-	8.9s	🏠 index.py	🌳 Decision Tree v2
☑	● grandiose-perch-481	⊘ 30 minutes ago	-	13.9s	🏠 index.py	🌳 Decision Tree v1

Figure 6-11. *Multiple model runs*

Once you click Compare, MLFlow will take you to the visual comparisons of the model runs. Since you have tracked training and test runs, you will be able to compare various runs graphically by selecting your preferred graphical representation format, as shown in Figure 6-12.

Figure 6-12. *Scatterplot*

In this case, I chose the scatterplot. If you have multiple tracked metrics, you can set various X and Y axis to compare your runs from the left tab, as shown in Figure 6-12.

I urge you to perform multiple runs and add metrics to play around with the MLFlow UI. You will quickly realize the power of this tool.

Now that you have seen how to use MLFlow to track traditional machine learning applications, I keep it to you as an exercise to try MLFlow to track deep learning applications. This exercise will ensure that you are well versed with tracking machine learning models of any kind using MLFlow. The method and metric for deep learning models (including the Transformer models) are the same.

But using MLFlow for tracking Generative AI applications is not that similar since the genre is different and the paradigm demands new ways of measuring performance.

Tracking LLM and Generative AI Applications

In this era of Generative AI, it's important to learn more about LLMs than deep learning or traditional machine learning models. But make no mistake, the older machine learning paradigms are never going to fade out and it is almost inevitable that you will have to conjugate traditional models with Generative AI models when you are building an end-to-end intelligent application. Sometimes it will be overkill to use Generative AI when you need simple classifiers or tasks such as sentiment analysis. You will encounter such instances when you move to building enterprise applications in this book.

But since the main focus of this chapter is tracking AI models, and you have already explored tracking traditional AI models, you'll now see how to track LLMs.

While building LLM applications, you will mostly use frameworks like LangChain instead of handling all the complexities yourself. So let's see how to use MLFlow with LangChain.

MLFlow contains a range of prebuilt evaluation metrics that you can leverage to track LLMs, similar to traditional AI models. Most of the time you will likely configure your own evaluation metrics and use them to gauge your LLM application.

Start by pulling up a Jupyter Notebook and building a RAG pipeline, which you will evaluate using MLFlow.

Install the packages mentioned in the first notebook cell:

```
! pip install langchain chromadb pypdf langchain-community
langchain-openai
```

You have seen these libraries when previously building RAG applications.

The PDF I used while preparing the application is a research paper that surveys various activation functions used in neural networks in deep learning models.

Since you have installed PyPDF and LangChain, use the PyPDF loader of LangChain, which leverages the PyPDF library to load and read your PDF file.

```
from langchain_community.document_loaders import import PyPDFLoader

loader = PyPDFLoader("Activation_Functions.pdf")
pages = loader.load_and_split()
```

Before proceeding, since you are using OpenAI in this example, set your environment variable for the OpenAI key and initialize your OpenAI model such as GPT3.5 Turbo.

```
import os

os.environ["OPENAI_API_KEY"] = '<Your OpenAI key>'

from langchain_openai import ChatOpenAI

model = ChatOpenAI(model="gpt-3.5-turbo")
```

You also installed chromadb to be used as your vector DB, so initialize and load your vector DB with your PDF pages.

```
from langchain_openai import OpenAIEmbeddings
from langchain_community.vectorstores import Chroma

vectore_store = Chroma.from_documents(documents=pages,embedding
=OpenAIEmbeddings())
```

Prepare the retriever, prompt template, and output parsers:

```
retriever = vectore_store.as_retriever()
template = """Answer the question based only on the following
context:
{context}

Question: {question}
"""
from langchain_core.output_parsers import StrOutputParser
from langchain_core.prompts import ChatPromptTemplate

prompt = ChatPromptTemplate.from_template(template)
output_parser = StrOutputParser()

from langchain_core.runnables import RunnableParallel,
RunnablePassthrough

sr = RunnableParallel({"context":retriever, "question":Runnable
Passthrough()})
```

Finally, build your LangChain pipeline (aka chain) for your RAG, as you did earlier using LCEL:

```
chain = sr | prompt | model | output_parser
```

I will let you in on a small trick, where you can also analyze and see the source documents retrieved by the vector database and used by the LLM for answering. To do this, you have to modify the chain so that you can pass a runnable (use a RunnablePassthrough) as the text retrieved from all the document pages from the context retrieved by your vector database.

Use the following code to create your chain to output the document pages as well:

```
docs_chain = (RunnablePassthrough.assign(context=(lambda x:
"\n\n".join([d.page_content for d in x["context"]]))))|prompt|mo
del|output_parser
```

You can assign this chain as your output when you receive inputs from your runnables as follows:

```
chain_1 = sr.assign(answer=docs_chain)
```

Now invoke your chain:

```
chain_1.invoke("What is Activation Function?")
```

You should see a JSON field named context, which contains the array of source documents (document pages from the PDF ingested by the vector database) used by the LLM to answer your queries.

```
{'context': [Document(metadata={'page': 3, 'source':
'Activation_Functions.pdf'}, page_content='4\nrecognition …
...
)]
'question': 'What is Activation Function?',
 'answer': 'An activation function is a function used in neural
```

networks to compute the weighted sum of inputs and biases, ..
...
the outputs of neural networks in various domains.'}

You need this to evaluate the document retrieval when using MLFlow.
It's time to prepare the evaluations using MLFlow.
First install MLFlow.

```
! pip install mlflow
```

As mentioned, MLFlow comes with some predefined Generative AI
evaluation metrics and some encapsulations to allow you to define your
own metrics. You will use the LLM as a judge strategy to evaluate your LLM
outputs, as you did when using LangGraph. In fact, what you did using
LangGraph can be achieved by MLFlow as well. Let's see how.

You need to import the Generative AI evaluation metrics from MLFlow
to start.

```
from mlflow.metrics.genai import faithfulness,
EvaluationExample
```

MLFlow uses the `faithfulness` class to assess the accuracy of an
answer using some sample inputs and outputs that you can encapsulate.
You do this using `EvaluationExample` as follows:

```
faithfulness_examples = [
    EvaluationExample(
        input="Can we solve dead neuron problem ReLU?",
        output="Yes, we can solve dead neuron problem
        in ReLU.",
        score=2,
        justification="The context says that dead neuron
        problem can be solved in ReLU.",
        grading_context={
```

```
        "context":"The ReLU has a significant limitation
        that it is sometimes fragile during training
        thereby causing some of the gradients to die.
        This leads to some neurons being dead as well,
        thereby causing the weight updates not to activate
        in future data points, thereby hindering learning
        as dead neurons gives zero activation [5]. To
        resolve the dead neuron issues, the leaky ReLU was
        proposed."
    }
),
EvaluationExample(
    input="Can we solve dead neuron problem ReLU?",
    output="Yes, Leaky ReLU can solve dead neuron problem
    for simple ReLU.",
    score=2,
    justification="The context says that dead neuron
    problem can be solved in ReLU by Leaky ReLU.",
    grading_context={
        "context":"The ReLU has a significant limitation
        that it is sometimes fragile during training
        thereby causing some of the gradients to die.
        This leads to some neurons being dead as well,
        thereby causing the weight updates not to activate
        in future data points, thereby hindering learning
        as dead neurons gives zero activation [5]. To
        resolve the dead neuron issues, the leaky ReLU was
        proposed."
    }
)
]
```

This code shows that the faithfulness metric is given two examples with justification of the scores to let MLFlow know how to measure factual correctness of the answer.

Since MLFlow uses LLM as a judge, you have to assign an LLM for MLFlow to use to evaluate faithfulness:

```
faithfulness_metric  = faithfulness(model="openai:/gpt-3.5-turbo", examples=faithfulness_examples)
```

The examples you provide will ensure higher alignment of the metrics with your data as well as your intent. If you want, you can tune your examples so that they can measure faithfulness according to your thought process by providing comprehensible justification and examples.

If you intend to be easy going, you can let MLFlow take the controls and omit evaluation examples.

Let's allow MLFlow to take the driver's seat with another metric, called relevance. Relevance measures appropriateness, significance, and applicability of the output with respect to the input and the context.

```
from mlflow.metrics.genai import relevance,EvaluationExample

relevance_metric = relevance(model="openai:/gpt-3.5-turbo")
```

Let's prepare a few queries to run the evaluation metrics:

```
import pandas as pd

eval_df = pd.DataFrame({
    "questions":[
        "Which Activation function does not have any dead
        neuron problem?",
        "Which Activation function is most faster?",
```

```
        "What are the types of ReLU activation function
        variants?",
        "What are Activation Functions?"
    ]
})
```

You can also set up a function to loop through the queries, RAG using LLM, and evaluate using the metrics.

```
def run_model(df):
  answers = []
  for idx,row in df.iterrows():
    answers.append(chain_1.invoke(row['questions']))
  return answers
```

Finally, you have to call the MLFlow evaluate function to evaluate the answers by assigning appropriate parameters, as given here:

```
import mlflow

res = mlflow.evaluate(
    run_model,
    eval_df,
    model_type="question-answering",
    predictions="answer",
    extra_metrics=[relevance_metric,faithfulness_metric],
    evaluator_config={
        "col_mapping":{
            "inputs":"questions",
            "context":"context"
        }
    }
)
print(res.metrics)
```

The `model_type` indicates how your model is tuned or how you are using it (question answering, summarization, etc.) and the `predictions` parameter tells MLFlow to watch the incoming fields and map the answer to a certain field ("answer" in this case). Similarly, `evaluator_config` gives away the column mappings to watch for input query and the context (the reason for the trick to output the context document pages as well). Finally, you have to pass your evaluation metrics to the `extra_metrics` parameter as an array. Then you are all set to go.

Sample output might look like the following after a successful run:

```
{'relevance/v1/mean': 4.25, 'relevance/v1/variance': 0.6875,
'relevance/v1/p90': 5.0, 'faithfulness/v1/mean': 5.0,
'faithfulness/v1/variance': 0.0, 'faithfulness/v1/p90': 5.0}
```

You can also check the output in tabular format, as shown in Figure 6-13, which will also give you the justifications along with the scores and the inputs and outputs using `res.tables["eval_results_table"]`.

	questions	outputs	context	token_count	relevance/v1/ score	relevance/v1/justification	faithfulness/v1/ score	faithfulness/v1/ justification
0	Which Activation function does not have any de...	Rectified Linear Unit (ReLU) Function	[{'id': None, 'ic_attributes' {}, 'ic_secrets...	8	4	The output directly addresses the question by ...	5	The output directly discusses the Rectified Li...
1	Which Activation function is most faster?	The Rectified Linear Unit (ReLU) Function is t...	[{'id': None, 'ic_attributes' {}, 'ic_secrets...	16	3	The output correctly identifies the Rectified ...	5	The output directly reflects the information p...
2	What are the types of ReLU activation function...	The types of ReLU activation function variants...	[{'id': None, 'ic_attributes' {}, 'ic_secrets...	22	5	The output provides a comprehensive answer to ...	5	The output directly mentions the types of ReLU...
3	What are Activation Functions?	Activation functions are functions used in neu...	[{'id': None, 'ic_attributes' {}, 'ic_secrets...	68	5	The output provides a comprehensive and detail...	5	The output directly reflects and expands upon ...

Figure 6-13. *Tabular representation of MLFlow evaluations*

Preparing Custom Generative AI Evaluation Metrics Using MLFlow

Up until now, the metrics that you used in MLFlow have been served to you with predefined strategies. The `relevance` metric is already programmed by MLFlow to check the appropriateness and significance of the answer with respect to the context. MLFlow knows the output fields to watch and capture to gauge relevance of the answer. The same is the case with faithfulness. MLFlow has already told the metric to use a certain strategy. All you did was provide tuned examples to score and justify. They will not budge from the basic definitions embedded within them by MLFlow.

MLFlow also allows you to create metrics that are new to the world of MLFlow and whose strategies are unknown or unheard of by MLFlow.

For example, you can define a custom metric called Resolution, which will evaluate if the answer provided by the LLM answers the user's query.

To achieve this, you have to set your examples with using EvaluationExample of MLFlow.

```
resolution_ex_1 = EvaluationExample(
    input="I have to tackle a problem with that expects large
    dataset in production environment. Which activation
    function should I choose for making the application run as
    fast as possible?",
    output="ELU's has been highlighted as a faster learning AF
    but the most notable observation on the use of AFs for DL
    applications is that the newer activation functions seem
    to outperform the older AFs like the ReLU, yet even the
    latest DL architectures rely on the ReLU function. However,
    current practices does not use the newly developed state-
    of-the-art AFs but depends on the tested and proven AFs,
    thereby underlining the fact that the newer activation
    functions are rarely used in practice.",
    score=2,
    justification="The response is formal but does not suggest
    exactly which AF to use as asked. It is confusing to
    the user."
)

resolution_ex_2 = EvaluationExample(
    input="I have to tackle a problem with that expects
```

large dataset in production environment. Which activation
function should I choose for making the application run as
fast as possible?",
output="Although current practices does not use the newly
developed state-of-the-art AFs and depends on the tested
and proven AFs, The ELU's has been highlighted as a faster
learning AF compared to their ReLU counterpart. Hence, you
should go ahead and use ELU.",
score=4,
justification="The response formal, relevant and suggests
the user with the proper AF as asked."
)

Now you have to define your custom metric using the make_genai_
metric function of MLFlow, as shown here:

```
resolution_metrics = mlflow.metrics.genai.make_genai_
metric(name="resolution",
    definition=(
        "Resolution refers to formal, relevant and pointed
        answers that"
        "should be concise and do not confuse the user."
    ),
    grading_prompt=(
        "Resolution: If the answer is pointed and not
        confusing then below are the details for different
        scores."
        "- Score 0: Language is very casual and does not lead
        to one relevant answer."
        "- Score 1: Language is formal but is not relevant and
        is also confusing."
        "- Score 2: Answer is formal and relevant but is very
        confusing."
```

```
    "- Score 3: Answer is formal, relevant and pointed but
    is not correct."
    "- Score 4: The response formal, relevant and suggests
    the user with the proper pointed answer."
),
examples=[resolution_ex_1, resolution_ex_2],
model="openai:/gpt-3.5-turbo", parameters=
{"temperature": 0.0})
```

The function should have a definition of the metric using the definition parameter, which will be used by the LLM to define its base strategy. The grading_prompt parameter should explain how the metric will score along with the justification of each score. Finally, you have to provide the evaluation examples you prepared earlier and the model to be used.

You can now run the same loop. This time, use the custom metric to evaluate your LLM generations.

```
res = mlflow.evaluate(
    run_model,
    eval_df,
    model_type="question-answering",
    predictions="answer",
    extra_metrics=[resolution_metrics],
    evaluator_config={
        "col_mapping":{
            "inputs":"questions",
            "context":"context"
        }
    }
)
```

The results you get for this new evaluation metric are similar to the previous run.

Now that you know how to prepare evaluation metrics in MLFlow, you can use the code in the notebook to prepare an end-to-end application just like you did in the beginning. I leave it to you as an exercise to bulk up and flex your MLFlow muscles!

You should now be confident enough to use MLFlow and monitor your ML runs to stay one step ahead of your data scientists and know how to use MLOps pipeline to deploy your models into production.

Although MLFlow is a powerful tool and contains necessary and relevant aids, such as model tracking and evaluations, to help you keep your modeling and developments in check, MLFlow falls short when it comes to features relevant to optimizing the consumption and processing of inferences from LLMs. The following section discusses a tool that enables you to enhance the capability of maximum throughput with optimal consumption.

Portkey

Portkey offers a unified platform to manage any LLM with a wide range of capabilities, such as caching and routing apart from features similar to tools like MLFlow such as model tracking.

Portkey integrates seamlessly with most major LLM providers. In this section, you start using Portkey and get to know the tool better.

Creating an Account

Just like any other tool provider, start by creating an account to portkey.ai.

Head over to https://app.portkey.ai/login and create an account to access portkey.ai.

When you log in for the first time, Portkey might ask you to name an organization. You can add a demo name and get started. See Figure 6-14.

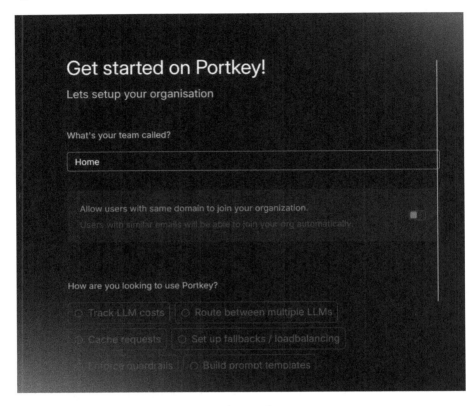

Figure 6-14. *Getting started with Portkey*

You should be sent to the dashboard. The dashboard will reveal an API Key and a space below it where it asks you to integrate your LLM provider. See Figure 6-15.

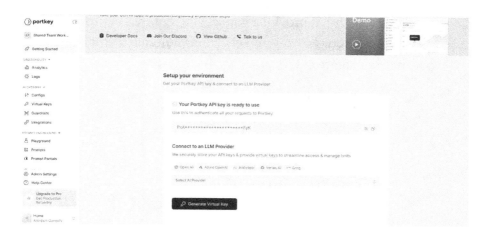

Figure 6-15.   *The Portkey dashboard*

Copy the API key and select the LLM provider (for example, OpenAI, Cohere, Anthropic, etc.) from the drop-down. See Figure 6-16.

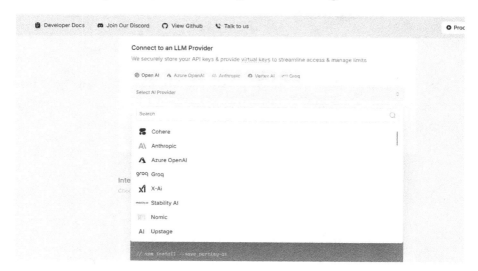

Figure 6-16.   *Select the LLM provider*

Once you select the AI provider, you will be required to provide your LLM API key. Paste your API key and click the Generate Virtual Key button at the bottom. See Figure 6-17.

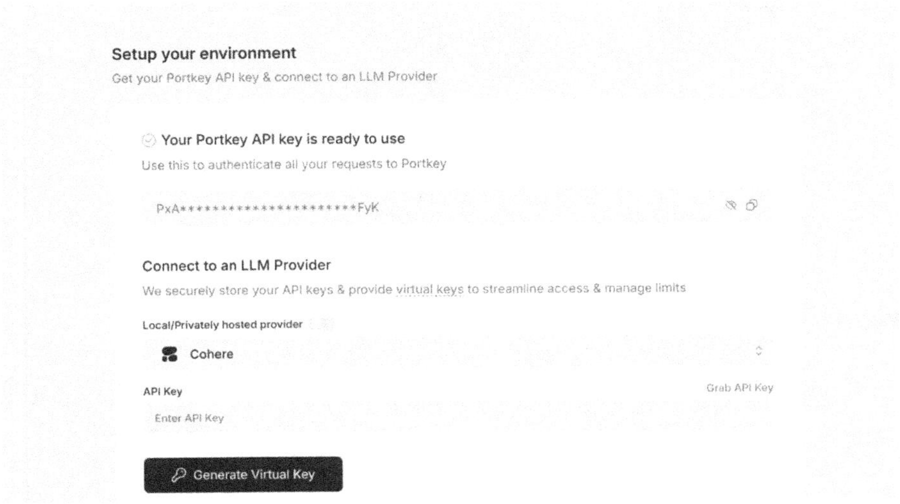

Setup your environment
Get your Portkey API key & connect to an LLM Provider

⊙ **Your Portkey API key is ready to use**
Use this to authenticate all your requests to Portkey

PxA＊＊＊＊＊＊＊＊＊＊＊＊＊＊＊＊＊＊＊＊＊＊FyK   ⊗ ⟲

Connect to an LLM Provider
We securely store your API keys & provide virtual keys to streamline access & manage limits

Local/Privately hosted provider

🐝 Cohere   ⌄

API Key   Grab API Key
Enter API Key

🔑 Generate Virtual Key

Figure 6-17. *Generate the Portkey virtual key*

As soon as you do this, you will see a code snippet that shows you how you can use the Portkey virtual key in Node.js, Python, or CuRL. Copy the integration code so you can use it in your code. See Figure 6-18.

Figure 6-18. *Portkey integration code*

Using Portkey in Your Code

At the time of writing this book, Portkey is fully compatible with OpenAI and OpenAI with LangChain, but Portkey doesn't know how to work with LangChain when the LLM is anything other than OpenAI and Together AI (even though LangChain has full compatibility with almost all LLM providers). Hence, using anything other than OpenAI when working with Portkey is a bit tricky. The trick when working with Portkey, LangChain, and other LLM provider, is that you have to wrap everything with `langchain-openai` library.

In this exercise, you use Cohere. To start, create your account with `https://cohere.com` and log in to your dashboard to get your API key. See Figure 6-19.

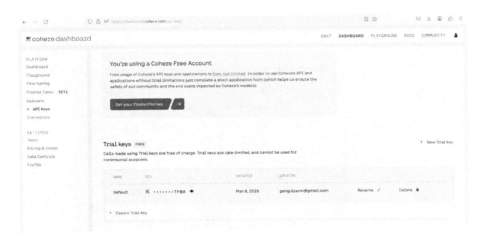

Figure 6-19. *Cohere*

To reiterate, when using LangChain, you can use the `langchain-cohere` library, which wraps your Cohere LLM with the LangChain format. But this will not be recognized with Portkey and hence you need to install the same `langchain-openai` and use it to wrap your Cohere model. You do this by providing Portkey and Cohere credentials to the `langchain-openai` wrapper so that Portkey understands the format.

Now open up a notebook so you can start implementing a RAG application with Portkey, LangChain, and Cohere.

This example uses the PDF prepared for the IT assistant (i.e., the `computer_troubleshoot.pdf` file).

Start by installing the necessary libraries:

```
! pip install langchain chromadb pypdf langchain-community
langchain-openai
```

Now load the PDF.

```
from langchain_community.document_loaders import PyPDFLoader

loader = PyPDFLoader("computer_troubleshoot.pdf")
pages = loader.load_and_split()
```

Load your Cohere API key in the environment, similar to how you did it in OpenAI.

```
import os

os.environ["COHERE_API_KEY"] = 'Your API Key from Cohere
Dashboard'
```

Apart from the libraries you have already been using, you need to install only one additional library to add your Portkey credentials:

```
!pip install -qU portkey-ai
```

Now you are ready to add the Portkey credentials, as follows:

```
from portkey_ai import createHeaders, PORTKEY_GATEWAY_URL

portkey_headers = createHeaders(api_key= "Your Portkey API
Key", ## Grab from https://app.portkey.ai/

                                provider="cohere"

                                )
```

Creating a header is essential for Portkey to piggy back your requests with the authentication and other configurations, as shown previously.

This example uses Cohere instead of OpenAI and so it provides the provider parameter called cohere.

The first parameter is the Portkey API key that you created from the Portkey portal.

You can test how Portkey tracks the LLM using this code:

```
from langchain_openai import ChatOpenAI

llm = ChatOpenAI(model = "command",

                 api_key= 'Your Cohere API Key', ## Replace it
                 with your provider key
```

```
                base_url=PORTKEY_GATEWAY_URL,

                default_headers=portkey_headers)

llm.invoke("What is the meaning of life, universe and
everything?")
```

You should receive a response and can track this call from your Portkey dashboard.

To see how Portkey is tracking your LLM, log in to `https://app.portkey.ai` and click Logs in the left menu. See Figure 6-20.

Figure 6-20. *Portkey logs*

Now let's go back to building the RAG.

Although this example uses Cohere, you can use any other LLM here. My intention of getting you used to Cohere instead of OpenAI is so that you are comfortable using any LLM provider.

Although you will be using `langchain-openai` to wrap up the Cohere LLM, the PDF text embeddings must be created using LangChain's Cohere wrapper. Hence, install the `langchain-cohere` library:

```
! pip install langchain-cohere
```

Now create the embeddings using the Cohere LLM:

```
from langchain_cohere import CohereEmbeddings
from langchain_community.vectorstores import Chroma

vectore_store = Chroma.from_documents(documents=pages,embedding
=CohereEmbeddings(model="embed-english-v3.0"))
```

The embedding model you are using here is one of the widely used embedding models when it comes to Cohere.

Now create the vector store:

```
retriever = vectore_store.as_retriever()
```

Also create your LLM template:

```
template = """You are an IT Assistant to assist in
troubleshooting of computer systems. Please answer the question
based only on the following context:
{context}

Question: {question}
"""
```

You also need to create your output parser, as you did previously.

```
from langchain_core.output_parsers import StrOutputParser
from langchain_core.prompts import ChatPromptTemplate

prompt = ChatPromptTemplate.from_template(template)
output_parser = StrOutputParser()
```

Finally, create the RunnableParallel for your LangChain chain:

```
from langchain_core.runnables import RunnableParallel,
RunnablePassthrough

sr = RunnableParallel({"context":retriever, "question":Runnable
Passthrough()})
```

Now build the chain and run your RAG application:

```
chain = sr | prompt | llm | output_parser
```

```
chain.invoke("My computer is not booting. What do I do?")
```

Similar to how you checked the Portkey logs earlier, head over to
`https://app.portkey.ai` and log in to view your dashboard. Once you
select the Log menu, you should see your logs as you did previously. Focus
on the log referring to the recent most timestamp and click the right-most
side arrow (>) to view the details of the logs. This is shown in Figure 6-21.

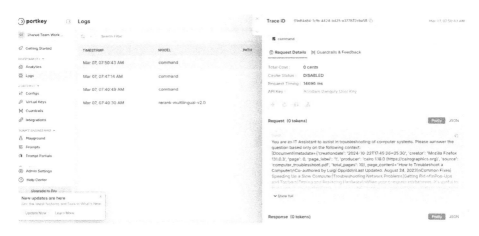

Figure 6-21. *Log details*

It shows the cost, API key, and the complete request and response.

But this is not why this example uses Portkey. As mentioned, Portkey
is a unified space that offers a lot of other useful features. The next section
explores some of them.

Load Balancing

If you are working with your LLM in a manner that you feel is too much for one LLM to handle, you can distribute the LLM requests to multiple LLMs according to some assigned weights.

To achieve load balancing, create a `config` variable, as shown here:

```
config = {
    "strategy": {
        "mode": "loadbalance"
    },
    "targets":
        [
            {
                "provider": "openai",
                "api_key": "Your-openai-key",
                "weight": 0.3
            },
            {
                "provider": "cohere",
                "api_key": "Your-cohere-key",
                "weight": 0.7
            }
        ]
}
```

As you may have already realized from the configuration, 70 percent of your requests will go to Cohere and the rest will be targeted to your OpenAI model. In such a way, you can load-balance your LLM requests considering factors such as the capacity of the LLM and the cost of the LLM (you can check your cost from the dashboard as mentioned already), and so on.

279

Finally, you need to make a small change in your code where you are creating the Portkey header to pass the `config` variable as well.

```
portkey_headers = createHeaders(api_key= "Your Portkey API
Key", ## Grab from https://app.portkey.ai/

                                provider="cohere",
                                config=config

                                )
```

Now you can fire some example requests and check your dashboard logs to see how the load-balancing is working.

Caching

Finally, this chapter introduces another useful feature that Portkey allows you to leverage—caching. You can let Portkey cache the prompts from the incoming requests and queries so that the next time you fire a request similar to the previous ones, Portkey can use cached responses and save time.

To use caching, you have to add another configuration, as shown here:

```
{
    "cache":
    {
        "mode": "semantic",
        "max_age": 1000
    }
}
```

There are only two parameters—max_age and mode. The max_age parameter defines the number of milliseconds the cache will persist. The mode parameter can be one of two values—semantic or simple. The semantic value lets Portkey match the incoming requests semantically using cosine similarity and the `simple` value matches the incoming requests character by character. Decide which to use by the criticality of the business. Your critical application should have a simple match and the less critical ones should have a sematic match.

You should be able to view all the features at work by viewing your dashboard logs and analytics. To view analytics, click Analytics in the left menu and you should be able to see something like Figure 6-22.

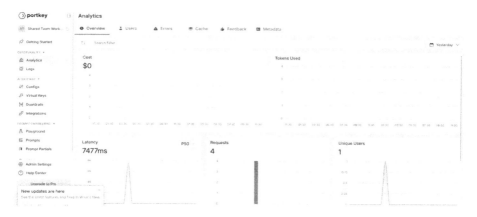

Figure 6-22. *Analytics dashboard*

This should give you some confidence on how you can leverage various situations to optimize your LLM usage.

There is one last way to optimize your LLMs. You can deploy your LLMs locally on your server.

vLLM

There are a number of platforms that allow you to deploy your LLMs locally on your server and one of the best ones among them is vLLM (virtual LLM). This section shows how to use vLLM to locally deploy a model and use it.

For this exercise, you will use an open-source model developed by IBM called Granite. You can check out its documentation at `https://www.ibm.com/granite`.

This section walks you through deploying and using Granite by vLLM step by step.

Prerequisites

Docker installed in your system

Nvidia GPU

Steps to Install

1. Pull the Docker container that supports OpenAI deployment in vLLM using the following command in CLI.

   ```
   docker pull vllm/vllm-openai:latest
   ```

2. To download the model, I suggest you download `huggingface-cli`. It will allow you to download the model from HuggingFace, which is one of the best repositories for open-source models. You can read more about `huggingface-cli` at `https://huggingface.co/docs/huggingface_hub/en/guides/cli`.

   You can download `huggingface-cli` using `pip` as follows:

   ```
   pip install "huggingface_hub[cli]"
   ```

3. Now download the model into `~/.cache/huggingface` using this command:

```
huggingface-cli download ibm-granite/
granite-3.1-8b-instruct
```

4. Now run your downloaded Granite model inside your Docker container using this command:

```
docker run --runtime nvidia --gpus all \
    -v ~/.cache/huggingface:/root/.cache/huggingface \
    -p 8000:8000 \
    vllm/vllm-openai:latest \
    --model ibm-granite/granite-3.1-8b-instruct
```

Congratulations! You have deployed your model locally.

To infer using the model, use this example cURL command:

```
curl -H "Content-Type: application/json" http://
localhost:8000/v1/chat/completions -d '{
  "model": "ibm-granite/granite-3.1-2b-instruct",
  "messages": [
    {"role": "users", "content": "How are you today?"}
  ]
}'
```

You should be able to get a response from your locally deployed model. That way, you are saved from billing costs.

You still need to know and understand some of the practical concepts and make yourself aware and recognize some guidelines while preparing and maintaining models in production, as you are not an individual player in the industry and you need to fit your application in the world.

Some concepts such as ethics, reliability, and responsibility should also be embedded into AI. The next chapter covers some of these governance concepts.

Summary

- Generative AI models are essential to maintain and RAG applications should have multiple checks to determine whether the answers generated are factual and solve the user queries.

- Corrective RAG (or C-RAG) techniques employ the LLM as a judge strategy to use LLMs in order to evaluate hallucinations and resolutions.

- You can use LangGraph, which is a LangChain derivative to prepare workflows so that you can set up C-RAG in your RAG application.

- You should also keep in mind the benchmarks that many data scientists have set to gauge your models.

- MLFlow is a tool that is a compilation of various monitoring capabilities that ML applications can use to maintain your application.

- You can also track Generative AI applications using either preconfigured MLFlow metrics or by building your own MLFlow custom metrics.

- You can use Portkey as a unified platform to optimize your Generative AI applications by load balancing and caching.

- You can minimize your LLM provider costs by deploying an open-source model locally using vLLM.

CHAPTER 7

AI Governance and Responsible AI

Responsible artificial intelligence (AI) deals with preventing and mitigating serious risks caused by AI outputs. To stay a step ahead, you need to understand the appropriate strategies that come with Generative AI. To do that, you need to monitor AI fairness. The first step to AI fairness is to carefully monitor and remediate any imbalance in the dataset you provide to your AI to train on. With the advent of LLMs, it has become very difficult to peek into the black box. You can use techniques such as SHAP and LIME to carve out explainability from traditional AI as much as possible.

You have to rely upon LLM as a judge to do the same. Drift detection is another important concept, whereby data scientists need to monitor and check for data drift and model (or concept) drift and have proper remediation techniques. When you are ready to implement AI applications at a scale, you should keep in mind various AI regulations and policies that various nations have agreed upon. These policies can safeguard you against unforeseen repercussions. Along with tracking LLMs, you should also have proper prompt governance for a long-term AI application, using Langfuse as an Ops tool.

This chapter explains some of these fundamental concepts, which go beyond the technicalities of model building, deployment, and maintenance.

© Arindam Ganguly 2025
A. Ganguly, *Scaling Enterprise Solutions with Large Language Models*,
https://doi.org/10.1007/979-8-8688-1154-8_7

AI Fairness

The first concept you need to grasp is the idea of model fairness. It might sound counterintuitive if you have always heard that automation is the key to removing human intervention and hence reducing bias among processes. However, AI systems are often black boxes.

Fairness of a machine learning model determines that it is true and fair to its requirement or purpose.

In artificial intelligence, AI Fairness is often distinguished as follows:

> **Demographic parity**: The likelihood of a positive outcome (e.g., being hired, receiving a loan) should be the same across different groups.

> **Equal opportunity**: The true positive rate (e.g., the probability of being correctly identified as qualified for a job) should be equal across groups.

> **Equalized odds**: Both the true positive rate and the false positive rate should be equal across groups.

As you learned in previous chapters, the deep learning model is built on top of weights and biases. In the real world, bias is a term used to imply an inclination to a particular factor so much so that it can lead to biased decisions. Human biases are some of the major causes of indifference and conflicts in society Machine learning models are trained on data curated by human beings, which means bias can seep into data. These factors can lead a machine learning model to adopt the same kind of bias as humans when formulating its decisions.

By no fault of the data curator or the machine learning model, the data gathered can very well contain more elements of a certain class than the others (as it may so have occurred in the real world). For example, if you are asked to create a classifier to make a primary selection in the defense division of a country, your dataset will probably be skewed gender-wise, as it is a fact that not many women choose a career in defense as compared to men and this may lead to a wrongful assessment of a female candidate. As a data scientist, it is the job of the developer to include code to debias such a dataset. One way to debias a dataset is to balance out an imbalanced class. See Figure 7-1.

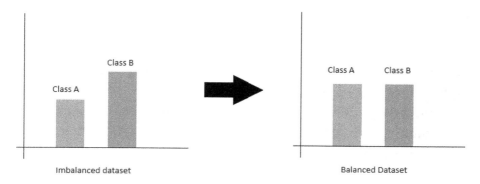

Figure 7-1. *Balance the imbalanced*

To balance out an imbalanced class, you can use Python packages such as the `imblearn` library and `Fairlearn`.

There are various techniques that libraries such as `imblearn` use for balancing datasets. For instance, one technique that you can use is to oversample the class having fewer samples to be at par with the one having more samples. You can use `RandomOverSampler` and `RandomUnderSampler` to balance the class distribution, using `imblearn` in Python with this code snippet:

```
from imblearn.over_sampling import RandomOverSampler
from imblearn.under_sampling import RandomUnderSampler

# Assuming X_train and y_train are your features and target
variable
```

```
# Oversampling the minority class
ros = RandomOverSampler(random_state=42)
X_resampled, y_resampled = ros.fit_resample(X_train, y_train)

# Undersampling the majority class
rus = RandomUnderSampler(random_state=42)
X_resampled, y_resampled = rus.fit_resample(X_train, y_train)
```

I urge you to check out various techniques for balancing out imbalanced datasets. Techniques include oversampling minor classes and undersample major classes.

Apart from this technique, you can use unstructured similar methods depending on your business requirements to see if your predictions are fair or biased. These methods generally depend on your domain and you will have to come up with custom algorithms to check them.

You can also check out Fairlearn, which solely uses techniques specializing in AI fairness.

Explainable AI

Machine learning models have been inspired from the workings of the brain, which itself is a matter of research. No one can map a thought or interpret how a certain person thinks (except maybe Sherlock Holmes!). Similar to this, the more complex your machine learning model is, the more inexplicable it is. With the evolution of machine learning and data science, machine learning models have become more and more difficult to understand.

You can make out how some of the models, such as a decision tree, work. But as you move to more complex models, such as deep learning models like CNN or RNN, the models turns out to be a black box. Finally with Generative AI, you have to try various prompting techniques, similar to talking to a human, and you cannot go even one level inside the model. This is considered a complete black box.

You have already read about some of the primary explainability parameters that can help you understand model performance.

Two explainable AI tools that attempt to interpret machine learning models, such as decision tree or random forest, are SHAP and LIME. They are discussed next.

SHAP

SHAP has been around for quite some time and it has been widely used in traditional machine learning applications to keep a eye on the model outcome by understanding what is going on underneath. SHAP (SHapely Addditive exPlanations) is used to explain the outcomes of a machine learning model. SHAP values attempt to assign importance to each feature based on game theory and other mathematical calculations. These values can help you deduce how each of the features in the feature set contributes to the model.

A simple library in Python can help you get started with SHAP.

```
! pip install shap
```

This chapter uses the iris database and a simple decision tree classifier to explain the outcomes of the model calculations.

```
from sklearn import datasets

iris = datasets.load_iris()
```

You can try listing the feature names.

```
iris.feature_names
```

As you might be working in a Jupyter Notebook environment to try SHAP, you can initialize internal JavaScript libraries of SHAP for interactive plots.

```
import shap
shap.initjs()
```

You'll build your model by following the same procedure you did earlier.

1. Split your data into training and test sets.

    ```
    from sklearn.model_selection import train_test_split
    X_train, X_test, y_train, y_test = train_test_
    split(iris.data, iris.target, test_size=0.3, random_
    state=1)
    ```

2. Initialize your model and fit it to your training set.

    ```
    from sklearn.tree import DecisionTreeClassifier

    dt = DecisionTreeClassifier()
    dt.fit(X_train,y_train)
    ```

3. Watch how your model performs.

    ```
    from sklearn.metrics import classification_report

    y_pred = dt.predict(X_test)

    print(classification_report(y_pred, y_test))
     ]
    from sklearn.metrics import classification_report
    y_pred = dt.predict(X_test)
    print(classification_report(y_pred, y_test))
        Output:
    ```

	precision	recall	f1-score	support
0	1.00	1.00	1.00	14
1	0.94	0.94	0.94	18
2	0.92	0.92	0.92	13

accuracy			0.96	45
macro avg	0.96	0.96	0.96	45
weighted avg	0.96	0.96	0.96	45

This model is now finalized and you can use SHAP to explain your model's outcome.

```
explainer = shap.Explainer(dt)
shap_values = explainer.shap_values(X_test)
shap_values
```

These values have an array of elements containing the importance of each feature for each test data row. As users might find a bit difficult to discern these values, the makers of the library provide options for you to see visual representations through various graphs and plots.

For example, you can create a summary plot using the following line of code:

```
shap.summary_plot(shap_values, X_test)
```

You might get output similar to Figure 7-2.

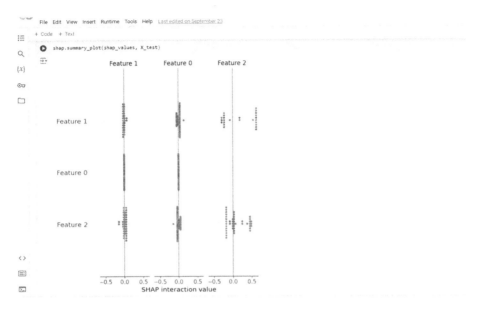

Figure 7-2. *SHAP summary plot*

LIME

SHAP calculates feature importance by looking at the overall model outcomes. If you want your explainability system to calculate feature importance for each instance of your dataset, you can limit your feature importance calculation to be localized to each dataset using Local Interpretable Model-Agnostic Explanations (LIME).

To use LIME in Python, use the same notebook you have been using to implement SHAP and install the Python package called `lime`:

```
!pip install lime
```

Once this is installed, use `LimeTabularExplainer` to initialize explainability features using LIME. As the name of the interface suggests, LIME is specific to specific types of datasets. Currently, LIME supports tabular data, image data, and text-related datasets.

```
from lime import lime_tabular

explainer_lime = lime_tabular.LimeTabularExplainer(X_train,
                          feature_names=iris.feature_names,
                          verbose=True,
                          mode='classification')
```

iris.feature_names will return the feature names of the dataset and use the mode as classification.

Now use explain_instance of LimeTabularExplainer to visualize how the feature importance comes out based on a sample test instance (say the tenth test_X row). Make sure to import matplotlib.

```
import matplotlib.pyplot as plt

exp_lime = explainer_lime.explain_instance(
    X_test[10], dt.predict_proba, num_features=len(iris.
    feature_names))

exp_lime.show_in_notebook()
```

As you can see in this code, you have to use the predict_proba function of the model, which returns the probability score instead of the predicted class for a classification model instead of the predict method. Otherwise, you will get the following error: "LIME does not currently support classifier models without probability scores". If you are using a regression model, you can simply pass the predict method as the second parameter. Also, make sure to pass the correct value of num_features, which expects the number of features used to train the dataset. show_in_notebook allows Jupyter Notebook to render visual representations of the exp_lime value using MatplotLib.

You might see output similar to Figure 7-3, which visually points out the importance of each feature through color encoding.

Figure 7-3. *LIME*

Drift

Machine Learning has been so widespread that almost all industries today are adopting AI in their landscapes. Sometimes the nature of the data leads to unnatural outcomes that scare off potential customers. To track such unusual outcomes, you need to understand the concept of drift in various premises.

Drift in machine learning implies the amount of degradation of quality in model prediction as compared to ground truth over time. Drift can be caused due to the model (model drift) or the data (data drift).

Model Drift

Model Drift, also known as Concept Drift, occurs when the type of model training was based on the kind of predictions it has to do and when the procedure or coefficients used to perform the predictions don't hold correct after the system has been running for a while. It is quite possible that the data patterns the model has adjusted to doesn't hold true for the current landscape.

For example, say you prepared a recommendation model for a retail industry some time ago. It is quite possible that customer preferences have changed over time and this leads to unsatisfactory recommendations to potential recurring customers. This signals that your model drift should be checked and acted upon.

You can think of your machine learning model as an employee who you hired to do your accounting during the past decade. This accountant has shown immense accuracy and precision in performing the kind of job you gave them in the past. After almost a decade, the employee, although loyal to the methods you set up, fails to evolve with time. They still use paper and pen to perform all of the calculations, which can lead to delay and human errors in the era of automation.

Data Drift

Data drift occurs when the environment around your data collection, processing, and so on has changed. In terms of the machine learning model, the model has stopped adapting to the current machine states with new modifications.

You may have prepared the model to predict certain feature sets and you might have updated the data integration and flows to capture more signals than it previously did. It is possible that the system now receives more data signals, which can lead to better precision based on the current data pattern. It is also possible that the nature or format of some of the data has been changed by the source input system. It is quite obvious then that your model should adapt to those changes. You can trigger such checks and modifications using data drift.

Here are some examples of data drift:

- **Seasonality**: In retail, customer purchasing patterns change throughout the year (e.g., increased spending during the holidays). A model trained on data from one season might not perform well in another.

- **Changing demographics**: The demographic makeup of a customer base can shift over time. For instance, a new marketing campaign might attract a younger audience with different preferences.

- **New trends**: Social media trends, emerging technologies, or economic shifts can alter user behavior and the data. A sentiment model trained on old data might not accurately capture new slang or evolving opinions.

- **Sensor degradation/changes**: If your model relies on data from physical sensors, changes in the sensors themselves (e.g., degradation, recalibration) can introduce data drift.

- **Adversarial drift**: In security applications, adversaries may intentionally try to manipulate the input data to cause harm to your system.

One way to remediate drift is constant maintenance and monitoring of your model using the techniques you learned in the previous chapter. But you can only do this when you can see the drift in your system.

Drift Detection

If you went through the previous chapter, you have already pulled your IDE up and used LLM to detect drift using the LLM as a judge technique. I urge you to integrate that with a complete end-to-end intelligent system as an exercise.

Another way to detect drift involves statistical tests. Explaining the mathematical intricacies behind these statistical tests is out of the scope of this book. Here are two statistical tests used to perform drift detection:

1. **Kolmogorov-Smirnof Test (or KS test)**

   A KS test is used to measure how a statistical distribution differs from the other. It leverages the Cumulative Distribution Function and checks whether the data comes from the same distribution. You can use a KS test to measure data drift.

2. **Page-Hinkley method**

The Page-Hinkley method detects changes in the means of a distribution by monitoring cumulative sums of deviations from the mean. The Page-Hinkley method is used to detect concept drift.

Nothing is worthy until you can implement and use it in real life. To detect drift in Python, you can leverage Evidently AI (`https://www.evidentlyai.com/`), which provides a wonderful platform and Python SDK to detect drift in Python.

Open the Jupyter Notebook and start installing the Evidently SDK.

```
pip install evidently
```

You'll use the same iris dataset from `sklearn` but this time you need to prepare a dataframe for later use in Evidently.

```
from sklearn import datasets
import pandas as pd

iris = datasets.load_iris()
dataset_df = pd.DataFrame(data=iris.data, columns=iris.
feature_names)
```

As before, you can prepare a training and test set and use decision tree to model it. But since the focus here is on drift detection, you'll use the training features to see how drift can be detected:

```
reference = dataset_df.sample(n=50, replace=False)
current = dataset_df.sample(n=50, replace=False)
```

In practice, you have a reference and a current dataset to see if your current dataset has drifted with respect to the reference dataset, which you may have used previously while model building.

You are ready to let Evidently generate a report on data drift using the following line of code:

```
from evidently.report import Report
from evidently.metric_preset import DataDriftPreset

report = Report(metrics=[
    DataDriftPreset()
])
report.run(reference_data=reference, current_data=current)
```

The code is self-explanatory; it leverages a Report interface to generate a report while calculating data drift using the DataDriftPreset interface. Finally, the report is generated using reference and current datasets that you set aside.

You can view the report in a Jupyter Notebook cell inline by running the following line of code:

```
report.show(mode='inline')
```

You should see something like Figure 7-4.

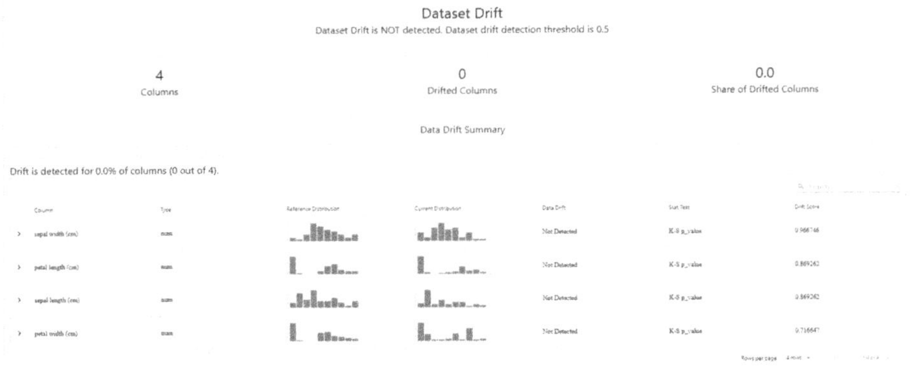

Figure 7-4. *Data drift detection using Evidently AI*

As you may have already figured out, AI governance is based on complex statistical calculations. In recent years, almost all hyperscalers have come up with their own proprietary algorithms for features like drift and fairness detection.

Azure uses AzureML, which provides its users with data drift mechanisms using their own interfaces in the AzureML library. This is also the case with IBM Watson, which released WatsonX Governance as a platform on top of their proprietary AI building platform known as Cloud Pak for data. This platform lets you build models using their own Jupyter Notebook compatible platform, deploy them, and have WatsonX governance monitor parameters such as drift and fairness while it is in production.

If you are restricted to open-source, you are at the mercy of Python libraries and packages such as Evidently AI, which nowadays is tough competition to licensed and closed platforms.

AI Regulations

All of the previous methods can help you monitor the model performance. Methods like LIME and SHAP tell you that whatever your model outputs should be fair so much so that you can let your new system loose in the world to the larger audience. With AI spreading like wildfire and having the power of Generative AI in your hands, you can almost think of conquering the world.

But if that is the case, why do many major market players still face significant challenges when deploying their AI systems into production and releasing them to the wider public? Despite efforts to ensure fairness and mitigate bias, many organizations are hesitant to fully embrace AI, due to concerns about potential risks and unintended consequences.

The answer to this question is more macro than micro when you look at the problems at 30,000 feet above sea level. With advent of Generative AI, nations have taken a step back to think about the consequences of these systems on matters outside the technical expertise. If you are about to build an intelligent system, there are several regulations to keep in mind before releasing them into the wild.

Different nations have different perspectives, and this has led to nations implementing policies and regulations on AI. In the United States, the National Institute of Standards and Technology (NIST), in collaboration with various private and public sector stakeholders, has developed a framework for managing risks and biases caused by AI. This is known as the AI Risk Management Framework (AI RMF). This framework, initially released in January 2023, serves as a voluntary guideline for the design, development, use, and evaluation of AI products, services, and systems.

Core components of the NIST AI RMF are as follows:

> **Govern**: Establish and maintain a culture of risk management within the organization.

> **Map**: Identify and understand the context in which AI systems are deployed, including potential risks and impacts.

> **Measure**: Track and evaluate identified risks using quantitative, qualitative, or mixed-method approaches.

> **Manage**: Allocate resources and implement strategies to mitigate identified risks.

The AI RMF emphasizes an iterative approach to risk management, encouraging organizations to continuously monitor and adapt their practices as AI technologies evolve. It also provides various resources, such as roadmaps and crosswalks, to help organizations implement the framework. You can access these resources at the official NIST website: `https://www.nist.gov/itl/ai-risk-management-framework`.

These frameworks ensure proper acceptance of systems released to the larger audience for use and reuse.

Beyond the NIST AI RMF, organizations developing AI systems in the United States should also be aware of existing and proposed legislation related to algorithmic accountability. For instance, the Algorithmic Accountability Act, which was initially proposed in 2019 and reintroduced in 2022, aims to require companies to conduct impact assessments for automated decision systems, evaluating them for accuracy, fairness, bias, discrimination, privacy, and security. Although not yet enacted into law, it reflects a growing trend toward increased scrutiny of AI systems' societal impact.

You should also abide by the data privacy and protection acts by ensuring that your AI doesn't leak data in any way. Your system should be air tight and secured so it's not prone to bad intentions.

When your system is attending to other geographies, you should make sure that it abides by the policies in effect in those areas. For example, European Unions have the General Data Protection Regulation (GDPR), which ensures data privacy and protection. GDPR is considered the benchmark regulation for data privacy and protection and every nation has their own regulations for data privacy and protection similar to GDPR. For example, if your system is running in Asian countries like India, they adopted the DPDPA (Digital Personal Data Protection) act in 2023 after the advent of Generative AI. Similarly, the UK has the UK Data Protection Act and Singapore has the Personal Data Protection Act, which are regulations for data privacy and protection in the UK and Singapore, respectively.

After the advent of Generative AI, governments started intervening to ensure safe, responsible, and trustworthy releases of intelligent systems. They did this by appending sections pertaining to AI outputs so they do cause any collateral damage.

You should make sure to include fairness, bias, and avoid damaging outputs containing hate, profanity, or derogatory text in your AI pipeline. For this, you should take into account all the knowledge you have acquired from this and the previous chapters and make good use of the toolkits you have learned so far.

Before closing the chapter, I cover another toolkit for governing your system.

LLM and Prompt Governance

You were introduced to LLM governance in the previous chapter, where you learned how to maintain an LLM and a model using MLFlow. MLFlow gives you the capability to track and monitor machine learning models built using either Scikit-Learn (such as decision tree) or deep learning models (built using PyTorch or TensorFlow). The current market scenario is much more interested in evaluating LLMs. You got an idea of maintaining and evaluating LLMs using MLFlow by using another LLM to judge the performance of the primary LLM in the system. MLFlow makes it a bit easier by providing interfaces to add your judgment model and a subjective instruction on the qualitative metric you want to judge it on. You have a ready-to-use method with just a few lines of code. You also used LLM to judge the faithfulness and relevance of a RAG application using MLFlow. Model governance techniques like these are one of the most important pillars to safeguarding your intelligent applications.

In the case of LLMs, it's almost impossible to fine-tune the models due to various factors, such as budget, server, and so on. An LLM works through prompts and prompts also need to be maintained and monitored. This section introduces prompt governance.

To use MLFlow, you need to localize MLFlow by installing it in your server and exposing it in a server. Using the tracking server, you can monitor and govern your ML models or LLMs.

MLFlow has the capability to govern your LLM generation through the LLM as a judge technique, but has limited capability when it comes to prompt governance. At the time of writing this book, MLFlow has recently released a beta version of a prompt governance platform.

Langfuse

This section explains another toolkit, called Langfuse (`https://langfuse.com/`), which is built by leveraging LangChain, which has similar capabilities to LangGraph (such as workflows) and has a platform to govern prompts. Unlike MLFlow, you can use it online and it is open-source at the time of writing this book. You can also host it on your own server, but this example shows how to use it online.

You'll start by creating a Langfuse account.

Go to `https://cloud.langfuse.com/auth/sign-up` and sign up with your region (cloud location), name, email. and password. Or you can sign up with your Google or GitHub account.

Once you are logged in, you have to create an organization by clicking the New Organization button at the top right. You should be prompted to enter an organization name. You can name it a dummy name, such as `my-org` for demo purposes. See Figure 7-5.

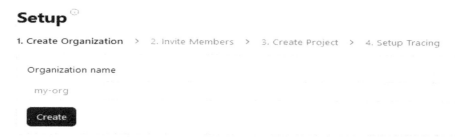

Figure 7-5. *Create organization in Langfuse*

On the next page, you will be asked to confirm and add members. This part is essential when you are working on a team and need to restrict access to your development team. For now, you can keep it as it is. After this, finally, you will be prompted to enter the name of the project. You can use a demo name such as rag-bot.

Once you have set up the project, Langfuse will show you the project details in the Project Settings page, as shown in Figure 7-6.

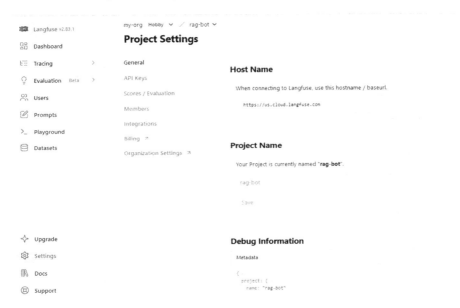

Figure 7-6. *Langfuse project settings*

You need to create an API key next. Click API Keys in the menu tab just below Project Settings header to see the API keys created for this project. If you are navigating to the API Keys section for the first time, you should already have one. I recommend you create a new API key by clicking Create New API Keys below the list of API keys. See Figure 7-7.

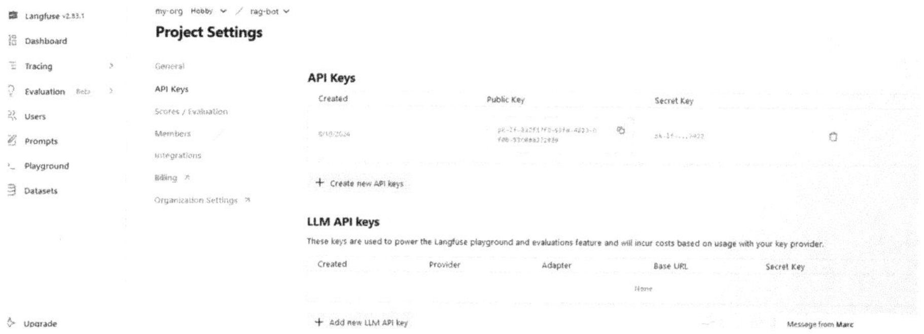

Figure 7-7. *Langfuse API keys*

Once you create an API key, Langfuse will display the details of the key. Make sure to save the secret key and public key and note the host. See Figure 7-8.

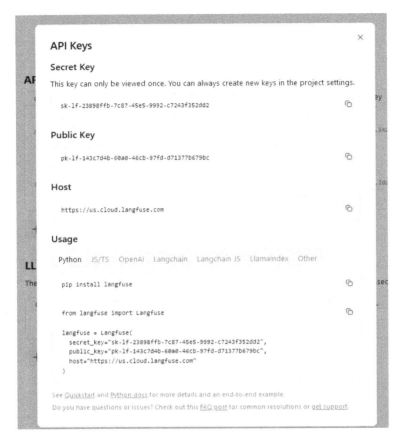

Figure 7-8. *Langfuse API key details*

You'll start by infusing Langfuse in the code. The first step you need to take is to check out how you can make Langfuse work in the simplest terms, such as via an LLM call using the prompt.

You learned how to call an LLM through a prompt in Python using LangChain in Chapter 5. This example uses the same code with Langfuse in it.

Open your Jupyter Notebook and start by installing the libraries:

```
! pip install langchain langchain-openai langfuse
```

The last library, as you might have guessed, is the Python SDK for Langfuse.

You now need to set your OpenAI key as the environment variable and identify the LLM to use in the ChatOpenAI interface:

```
import os

os.environ["OPENAI_API_KEY"] = "<Your Open AI API Key here>"

from langchain_openai import ChatOpenAI

model = ChatOpenAI(model="gpt-3.5-turbo")
```

You can set up your prompt template exactly like you did in Chapter 5.

```
from langchain_core.prompts import ChatPromptTemplate
prompt = ChatPromptTemplate.from_messages([
    ("system", "You are a computer science trainer. You will
    be asked to provide some technical documentation and your
    task is to explain those technical concepts in layman's
    terms."),
    ("user", "{input}")
])
```

Now that the basics are complete, you need to integrate Langfuse. To use Langfuse in LangChain, you have to create a callback. A *callback* is a method that LangChain can call while invoking an LLM.

```
from langfuse.callback import CallbackHandler
#Get project ID from the project setting page in langfure
project_id = "<your-project-id>"
langfuse_handler = CallbackHandler(
    secret_key="sk-lf-23898ffb-7c87-45e5-9992-c7243f352dd2",
    public_key="pk-lf-143c7d4b-60a0-46cb-97fd-d71377b679bc",
```

```
        host="https://us.cloud.langfuse.com",
        project_id=project_id
)
callbacks = [langfuse_handler]
```

As you can see from this code, the public and secret keys are the ones you generated when you created the new API key. The host was also mentioned in the API key details in Figure 7-8.

Langfuse is ready to be integrated into your LangChain chain:

```
chain = prompt | model
chain = chain.with_config(callbacks=callbacks)
```

with_congif allows LangChain to add extra handlers, such as callbacks, which it will use while invoking the chain.

You can invoke your LangChain pipeline and you should see your code working.

```
chain.invoke({"input": "What is deep learning?"})
```

But what about the Langfuse callback you added?

Go to your Langfuse dashboard (on right-most menu, under the Langfuse banner) to see if your LLM call has been tracked.

In the first row, you should see KPIs such as the number of traces, the model cost incurred for the LLM calls, and any scores that you might have traced. This is shown in Figure 7-9.

Figure 7-9. *Langfuse dashboard 1*

The second row should show a graphical representation of the traces and model costs that you saw in the previous row, as shown in Figure 7-10.

Figure 7-10. *Langfuse dashboard 2*

Finally, toward the end, you should see other details related to user consumption and latencies. These are shown in Figures 7-11 and 7-12.

Figure 7-11. *Langfuse dashboard 3*

Figure 7-12. *Langfuse dashboard 4*

You should now be familiar with the objective Langfuse is built for. But along with LLM user consumption and tracing, one of the pillars that drives any LLM application is a prompt. Langfuse can help you govern prompts by prompt versioning and maintaining a repository of prompts. The next section explains how to implement prompt governance using Langfuse.

Prompt Governance Using Langfuse

To see how Langfuse helps in prompt governance, you will revisit the same code for building a RAG application that was implemented in Chapter 5 and see how prompt governance with Langfuse can fit in the context of a RAG application.

Pull up your Jupyter Notebook and start by installing the essential packages:

```
! pip install langchain chromadb pypdf langchain-community
langchain-openai
langfuse
```

I think you are already familiar with the Python packages. If you have any doubts, revisit Chapter 5.

Now load the PDF in PYPDF for OCR. You can use the same PDF used in Chapter 5. Otherwise, you can use a new PDF like the one I used while implementing the code. This PDF is a paper on concept drift, which you can download from https://arxiv.org/abs/2004.05785.

```
from langchain_community.document_loaders import PyPDFLoader

loader = PyPDFLoader("Concept_Drift_Paper.pdf")
pages = loader.load_and_split()
```

add the credentials for Langfuse and OpenAI in the environment variables:

```
import os

os.environ["OPENAI_API_KEY"] = '<OpenAI API Key here>'
os.environ["LANGFUSE_PUBLIC_KEY"] = 'pk-
lf-143c7d4b-60a0-46cb-97fd-d71377b679bc'
os.environ["LANGFUSE_SECRET_KEY"] = 'sk-
lf-23898ffb-7c87-45e5-9992-c7243f352dd2'
os.environ["LANGFUSE_HOST"] = "https://us.cloud.langfuse.com"
```

You should also select your LLM:

```
from langchain_openai import ChatOpenAI

model = ChatOpenAI(model="gpt-3.5-turbo")
```

To use Langfuse, just as you did in the previous code, you have to initialize the Langfuse client and create a callback handler for LangChain to use.

```
from langfuse import Langfuse
from langfuse.callback import CallbackHandler

langfuse = Langfuse()

langfuse_callback_handler = CallbackHandler()
```

Now you can get back to building the rest of the parts of RAG, as you did in Chapter 5. Prepare the vector store for vectorizing using OpenAI Embeddings to be consumed in the vector store (ChromaDB in this case) and then prepare a retriever from the vector store.

```
from langchain_openai import OpenAIEmbeddings
from langchain_community.vectorstores import Chroma

vectore_store = Chroma.from_documents(documents=pages,embedding
=OpenAIEmbeddings())

retriever = vectore_store.as_retriever()
```

Once this is done, you have your gears set up for RAG.

It's time to move on to the part of RAG you have likely been waiting for—creating a prompt and using the Langfuse to version, maintain, and govern it.

Start by creating a prompt template in a string variable:

```
template = """Answer the question based only on the following
context:
{context}

Question: {question}
"""
```

Now it's time to use this as a prompt and let Langfuse version and govern it. You use the create_prompt function of the Langfuse client for this, as shown in the following code:

```
langfuse.create_prompt(
    name="simple-rag",
    prompt=template,
    config={
        "model":"gpt-3.5-turbo",
        "temperature": 0,
```

```
},
labels=["rag_prod"]
);
```

As you can see in this code, you need to pass a name and a label that will be utilized by you and Langfuse when you need to access the prompt. You can also pass some metadata for the kind of LLM to use while using this prompt. You do this in the `config` parameter as an object. I show you how to leverage this later in this chapter.

Go to the Langfuse dashboard and click the Prompts menu from the left-most menu. You should see your prompts been tracked by Langfuse along with the versions. Click the version and it will display the details, as shown in Figure 7-13.

Figure 7-13. *Langfuse prompt versioning*

Now use the prompt you just versioned in Langfuse using `get_prompt`. You have to use the name and label to access and use the prompt as follows:

```
prompt_template = langfuse.get_prompt("simple-rag",
label="rag_prod")
```

313

This will return a Langfuse object to access the prompt template in your RAG application, just like any other prompt. To get the prompt from this template, use the get_langchain_prompt function, as shown in this code:

```
from langchain_core.prompts import ChatPromptTemplate
prompt = ChatPromptTemplate.from_template(prompt_template.get_
langchain_prompt())
```

The rest of the code is a usual RAG application using the previous prompt:

```
from langchain_core.output_parsers import StrOutputParser
output_parser = StrOutputParser()
```

```
from langchain_core.runnables import RunnableParallel,
RunnablePassthrough
```

```
sr = RunnableParallel({"context":retriever, "question":Runnable
Passthrough()})
```

Now that you have everything ready, you can finally create the LangChain pipeline and invoke your chain:

```
chain = sr | prompt | model | output_parser
```

```
chain.invoke("What is Concept Drift?")
```

Once you have invoked the prompt, Langfuse traces it. You can see the traces in the Langfuse dashboard under the Tracing menu, as shown in Figure 7-14.

Figure 7-14. *Langfuse traces*

You can also check out the details of the traces by clicking it, as shown in Figure 7-15.

Figure 7-15. *Langfuse trace details*

The metadata that you recorded in the Langfuse as prompt metadata (i.e., the model ID and the temperature) can be used to call an LLM and add parameters while calling the LLM. Try this code:

```
model = prompt_template.config["model"]
temperature = str(prompt_template.config["temperature"])
model = ChatOpenAI(model=model, temperature=temperature)
chain = sr | prompt | model | output_parser

chain.invoke("What is Concept Drift?")
```

315

As you can see, the model and the temperature of the model are gathered from the metadata that you stored in the prompt trace in Langfuse. They are used in the LangChain pipeline just like any other LLM.

Now that you have a fairly good idea of how Langfuse works, you can now try to fiddle with various metrics in the dashboard for analytics. Refer to the Langfuse documentation and try to come up with various use cases that you may be able to implement in your current environment. Prompt governance and tracing is an extremely important toolkit in your machine learning toolbox and large industries cannot do without AI governance in the current market.

The remaining chapters look at the big picture and stitch everything together to show you how you can make a large enterprise work with machine intelligence.

Summary

- Proper governance is needed to prevent AI from generating refuting outputs. For that, you need AI fairness, which involves carefully monitoring and remediating any imbalance in the dataset that AI is training on.

- Techniques such as SHAP and LIME can be used to eliminate explainability from traditional AI.

- Drift detection is used to monitor and check for data drift and model (or concept) drift.

- It's important to understand international AI regulations and policies, which can safeguard you against unforeseen repercussions.

- Use the Langfuse as a ops tool for prompt governance.

## CHAPTER 8

Adding Intelligence to Large Enterprise Applications

With AI and Generative AI as frontrunners of the technical landscape and driving a complete application with multiple complex workflows, it is almost necessary now to design a proper AI architecture to get a clear picture before proceeding to develop.

AI development lifecycles should have an experimentation environment, where you can use Jupyter Notebooks to try your architecture using sample data. Currently there are a lot of applications that serve large enterprises (enterprise applications), but there is a need to add intelligence to these applications. You need to properly understand the REST APIs that almost all of the large enterprise applications provide as interfaces.

The next step to adding intelligence to these large enterprise applications is to understand the concept of AI agents. Agents act as directors that drive an intelligent application.

Agents use prompts to make decisions based on tools. Tools are modular functions that perform individual tasks. These tools should have docstrings that describe the functionality of the task. These docstrings are

© Arindam Ganguly 2025
A. Ganguly, *Scaling Enterprise Solutions with Large Language Models*,
https://doi.org/10.1007/979-8-8688-1154-8_8

used by the agents to make decisions about which tool to invoke when a query hits the agent. You can develop a complete application and the agents using LangChain.

A Typical Chatbot

This book has discussed various models and several problems that pertain to real life. Many of the solutions have almost been solved by large enterprises and industry leaders. We looked at Generative AI and how it can be used as a chatbot in the modern world. However, back in the days of traditional AI, chatbots had two main designs—entity and intent extraction. Whenever a chatbot encounters text from a user, the system deciphers the text to gather the intent and the list of entities from the text. A dialogue flow determines what the chatbot will respond or do based on a predesigned flow, which branches based on entities and intent. Intents are the summary of the text the user provides.

For example, the intent of "How do I do a restaurant booking?" is restaurant booking. The list of intents and entities are predefined and each intent and entity can be considered a class or category. The intent recognition system leverages a pretrained classification model to determine the class that the text falls in. Similarly, entities are predetermined categories that certain words fall into. For example, the word "Samsung" represents a company name and hence falls into a predetermined category that represents company names. Entity extraction systems extract entities from text. For example, the statement "Is Samsung headquartered in South Korea and popular with electronic items?" contains several entities, including the following:

- "Samsung" is a company name

- "South Korea" is a geographical location

- "Electronic items" are product types

Although company name and geographical location might be obvious entities, product type is not so obvious. Hence, you need predetermined categories and data to train the model on. Thus, your dataset for entities will be a set of words and their corresponding entity classes. Your system will tokenize each text and pass it to your model, which will determine the entity class for each token. Once you have the intent and entity recognition models, you can prepare your dialogue flow, and you have a chatbot ready. Figure 8-1 shows this process.

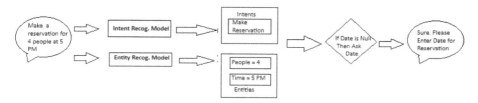

Figure 8-1. *The Chatbot workflow*

Although the main components that build a chatbot are few, the complete detailed architecture to deploy such a simple chatbot into an enterprise application is highly complex.

Let's look closer at the chatbot workflow shown in Figure 8-1.

A typical chatbot workflow has an intent recognition model and an entity recognition model. The intent recognition model understands the intent of the user's statement. For example, the intent of, "Can you make a reservation for four people at 5 PM" is to create a reservation to a restaurant. The chatbot should therefore redirect to a system that takes reservations to that restaurant. Similarly, as another example, the intent of "Hi! Good Morning" is a greeting. Your chatbot respond could by saying something like, "Hello, Good Morning to you too. I am your restaurant assistant to help you with reservations."

Entities are particular values that the intent points to and holds. For example, the first example—"Can you make a reservation for four people at 5 PM"—may have an intent as reserving a restaurant, but the entities here

319

is the number of people, i.e., four (People = 4) and time, i.e., 5PM (Time = 5PM). Intent and entity recognition models are primary requirements for building any kind of chatbot.

Finally, the chatbot should be able to come back with any necessary clarification queries. as shown in the chatbot workflow diagram in Figure 8-1, the chatbot should evaluate whether all the inputs are received or not. According to the example in the diagram and the statement in the first example, the customer didn't mention a date. Hence, the chatbot responds by asking for the date of the reservation.

This is one of the goals you will try to achieve by the end of the book. This chapter starts with baby steps so you comprehend the components and the complete architecture.

The Need for AI Architecture

Let's look at a simple architecture showing a proof of concept (POC). A POC is designed to show the feasibility of a technical concept and is often considered the initiation of a development lifecycle. The chatbot discussed in the previous section consists of multiple wheels and gears in action. Let's start with a simple project for a POC and move to an enterprise chatbot toward the end of the book.

The project requirements consist of only one model and you will see how to productionize such a model. You will incrementally add components to this project to make it stronger and to fit the business requirements.

The final goal is to build an enterprise chatbot. However, you will use an interesting dataset first—the Stanford QUestion and Answering Dataset (SQUAD) dataset. This dataset can be found at `https://rajpurkar.github.io/SQuAD-explorer/`. It consists of 100,000 sets of questions, the context, and the answers to the questions from 536 articles from Wikipedia. If you train a model on this dataset, the model will be able to tackle basic questions about some topics based on Wikipedia articles.

The task boils down to creating a question-answering model. Since you have tools like BERT at your disposal, it might seem like a walk in the park. But here are a few questions to ponder:

1. What is the data source for the training data? What if the training data resides in a database or an enterprise application?

2. What if you want the model to improve with every wrong answer, so that once the wrong answer is identified, the model is retrained with the new data?

3. What if the test or final user data using the model is real time?

4. Where does the model reside and what if the application needs to be containerized?

5. How do you monitor the performance of the model?

6. How do you use the model in a final product to be used by a website?

These are the struggles you will face once you dive into the real world. To tackle these problems and requirements, you need to understand the components that make up such a system.

To understand how to come up with a production-level architecture for an intelligent application, you have to understand the two phases of production—the training phase and the prediction phase. The training phase is what we have been concerned with up until now and the one most aspiring data scientists focus on. But once you have the trained model, you have to embed it into your production system and monitor it. The next section focuses on this part of the intelligent system building process.

Experimentation Environment

Once you have the requirements sorted, you need sample data for data analysis and model building. Until now you have been doing these things in a Jupyter Notebook or a simple Python file. This is your experimentation environment, where you play around with your data and model until you have the final plan.

Once your experimentation environment is ready, you have to think about designing a production environment. As mentioned previously, the production environment has a lot going and a number of factors to be considered. I show you all the bits and pieces eventually as you proceed with the applications that you will build in this chapter through the end of the book.

From this chapter onwards, you will start using all the knowledge you acquired in the previous chapters and implement full-fledged applications to be run in production environments. You do not do anything all at once, but will take one step at a time to reach the ultimate goal of building a wonderful, state-of-the-art, end-to-end intelligent application. You will:

- Learn to add intelligence to large enterprise applications to improve and enhance upon the needs and demands of the current market (in this chapter).

- Add data pipelines to support big data and variations of data sources (in the next chapter).

- Build an end-to-end enterprise application (in the last chapter).

Start by imagining how you can add intelligence to an existing large enterprise application. You will take small steps and get introduced to concepts here.

The next section goes through the application building process step by step, starting with understanding the business requirements.

The Intelligent IT Assistant

The application you attempt to configure is the intelligent IT assistant, which is an improvement on the IT assistant application you built in Chapter 4. This application can assist associates in troubleshooting IT infrastructure problems. For example, say an associate is working on their computer and suddenly the screen goes blank. The next step that the associate can take is log in to the Intelligent ITSM UI and type the issue that they are facing on the chat engine of the application. This system is connected to the same knowledge resource (through RAG) that you used in Chapter 4, which contains resolutions about keyboard, monitor, and printer issues and tries to determine a solution from the available resources. But if the issue that the associate is facing is related to something other than those three components, the bot will automatically log a ticket in the built-in enterprise CRM (Customer Resource Management) tool with the proper content and a description so that a "human in the loop" can intervene.

As promised, this application is mainly aimed at showing you how to embed Generative AI into an existing large enterprise application. Before proceeding, let's check the components of the application.

As you might have realized, there are three main components of the application—the chatbot, the knowledge resource (or repository), and the enterprise CRM application that handles the ticketing. See Figure 8-2a,b.

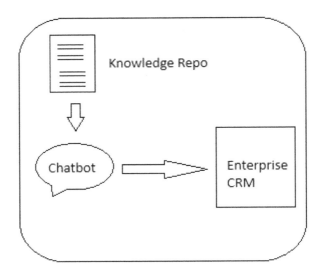

Figure 8-2a. *The intelligent ITSM*

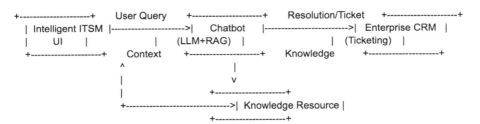

Figure 8-2b. *The intelligent ITSM (with arrow labels)*

The interesting part is when you put everything together, especially adding the intelligent chatbot to the Enterprise CRM. Once you are confident about adding an intelligent component to an enterprise application, you should be proficient in appending intelligence to any other enterprise CRM applications.

The next section covers building the application.

The Enterprise CRM

To begin, bring in the Enterprise CRM. For the purpose of this application, you need a CRM that provides users with a platform to raise incident tickets. There are a number of Enterprise CRMs that are the industry leaders, including ServiceNow, JIRA, and so on. You may be acquainted with one or more of these CRMs. The used here is HubSpot (`https://www.hubspot.com/products/crm`). For the purpose of building this application, there is no cost associated with acquiring HubSpot CRM. If you have a license to use any other CRM, you can go through the following steps and using your preference and still learn the concepts.

If you are new to HubSpot, check out the following section about setting it up.

Setting Up HubSpot

Start by registering your account from the HubSpot homepage (`https://www.hubspot.com/products/crm`).

When you start setting up your HubSpot account, you will be asked some basic questions to set up for profile information.

HubSpot will ask the industry you are in, your role, your company's name (you can provide a demo name if you don't want to specify your company name), the number of people who work at the company, the company's website (you can provide a demo website name such as `ww.abc.com`), and your reason for using HubSpot.

During the account setup process, it will set up the preferred UI template for you by asking for the starting template. For this example, select Customer Service and Track Support Tickets as the service template, as shown in Figure 8-3.

Step 1 of 3

RECOMMENDED FOR YOUR BUSINESS

We recommend starting with a Customer Service template

We'll give you a head start by setting up your Smart CRM with basics like pipelines, report dashboards, custom views, and more.

Decide what to set up first:

Sales   Marketing   Customer Service

Choose a Service template: ⓘ
You can edit any of these changes later.

Track support tickets   Manage customers   Manage renewals

Tickets pipeline

NEW   WAITING ON CONTACT   WAITING ON US   IN PROGRESS   CLOSED

Apply template

Set up manually instead

Figure 8-3. *Add the template to HubSpot*

It will then ask you to add contacts for any associates (you can keep it blank) and your email address.

Once your HubSpot Service template is set up, you should see a ticketing portal, as shown in Figure 8-4.

Figure 8-4. *HubSpot Service template for incident management*

You can also visit this portal in HubSpot at any time by clicking the CRM menu from the sidebar on the left and choosing Tickets.

Try to create a new ticket or play around in the portal. You might also see a dummy ticket created for you by HubSpot.

Setting Up HubSpot Private App for REST API integration

This section focuses on the integration of HubSpot with your code (that you have yet to build).

If you are an experienced industry associate, you should already be well versed with using REST APIs to integrate enterprise applications into a custom application. Nowadays, there are various tools that allow you to integrate APIs with your own application, such as App Connect. HubSpot also allows you to use its REST APIs to connect to your application.

To use the HubSpot APIs, you need to create a private app. A HubSpot private app will allow you to generate authentication tokens which will be tagged to your private apps and you can use them to invoke REST APIs exposed by HubSpot.

To create a private app, go to the Settings page by clicking the Settings menu from the top bar (a gear icon). In the Settings, go to the Account Management menu section on the left sidebar menu and click Integrations, where you will find the Private Apps menu. If you are creating a private app for the first time or navigating to the Settings page for the first time, you should see something like Figure 8-5. If the account already has a private app, it will show in the same Settings page with the Create a Private App button.

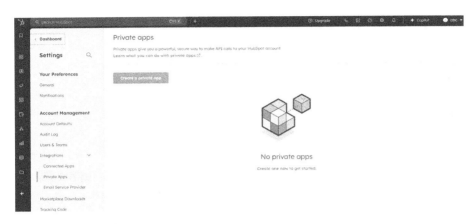

Figure 8-5. *HubSpot settings*

To create a private app now, click the Create a Private App button. It will then start creating a private app for you, which you will be using to generate specific authentication tokens to use the HubSpot REST API.

It will ask for a name and a description in the first step (you can provide a dummy name and description if you want) and then take you to add the scope. Make sure to check the Tickets scope in the Scopes page, as you will be using their features in the CRM through REST APIs, as shown in Figure 8-6.

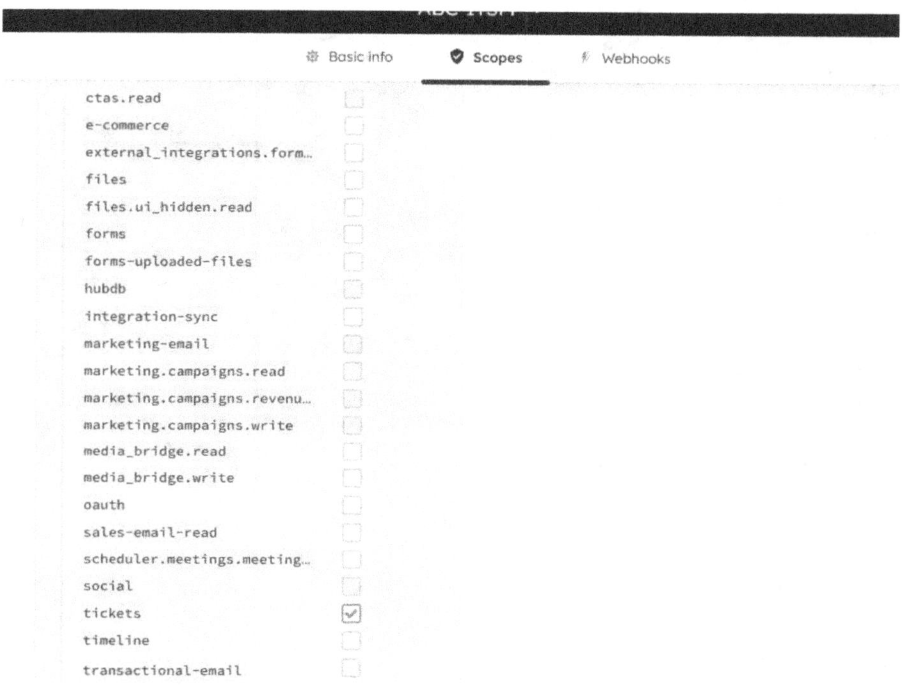

Figure 8-6. *Scopes for creating private apps*

You can ignore the Webhooks and continue creating the private app.
Finally, HubSpot will generate the authentication token, as shown in
Figure 8-7, which you need to copy and save in a secure place. You'll use
this token to connect to HubSpot from your code.

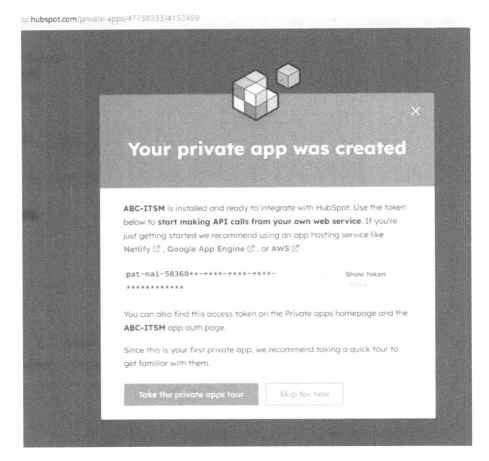

Figure 8-7. HubSpot API authentication token for private apps

Now that you have your authentication token ready with you, check out the HubSpot REST API documentation page at `https://legacydocs.hubspot.com/docs/overview`.

Although this is legacy documentation, as of writing this book, these APIs seem to work just fine. At least the tickets APIs, which you can check out (as you will be using them).

Specifically, take a look at these two API documentations that you will use for this application:

1. You will need a REST API to fetch all the tickets in
    your dashboard. You can check this link for the
    documentation: `https://legacydocs.hubspot.`
    `com/docs/methods/tickets/get-all-tickets`.
    This one describes a GET request of the format
    `https://api.hubapi.com/crm-objects/v1/`
    `objects/tickets/paged`.

    This API needs an authorization header with a
    bearer token, which is the authentication token you
    got during the creation of the private app. It will
    return a list of tickets in the format of an array of
    JSON as objects. For example:

    ```
    {
        "objects":[....]
    }
    ```

    Your tickets will be inside the array as a single ticket
    object in this format:

    ```
    {
        "objectType": "TICKET",
        "portalId": ID of the portal (you dont need to
        worry about this now),
        "objectId":(an unique ID),
        "properties": {}(any property),
        "version": 2 (the version),
        "isDeleted": false (is deleted or not)
    }
    ```

2. The other API is a POST request, which you will
    need when you want to create a ticket. You can
    check this link for the documentation: `https://`
    `legacydocs.hubspot.com/docs/methods/tickets/`
    `create-ticket`.

    You have to post to the following endpoint:
    `https://api.hubapi.com/crm-objects/v1/`
    `objects/tickets`

    The data is the payload containing your ticket details
    that you want to raise. The payload should be in the
    following format:

```
[
  {
    "name": "subject",
    "value": "A subject line for the ticket"
  },
  {
    "name": "content",
    "value": "A description containing the details"
  },
  {
    "name": "hs_pipeline",
    "value": "0" (you can keep this as is)
  },
  {
    "name": "hs_pipeline_stage",
    "value": "1" (you can keep this as is)
  }
]
```

    Once you push a POST request, you will get a detailed
    response showing the ticket.

Now that you know how to raise and check tickets in HubSpot through REST APIs, try them out once. If you comfortable using a console, you can use the powerful cURL command to run them.

For example, to try the API to see the list of tickets, you can run the following cURL command:

```
curl --location --request GET 'https://api.hubapi.com/
crm-objects/v1/objects/tickets/paged' \
--header 'Authorization: Bearer Your_Authorization_Token'
```

Similarly, to test the POST request for creating a ticket, you can use the following cURL command:

```
curl --location --request POST 'https://api.hubapi.com/
crm-objects/v1/objects/tickets' \
--header 'Authorization: Bearer Your_Authorization_Token' \
--header 'Content-Type: application/json' \
--data-raw '[.. Your Payload JSON data as shown previously..]'
```

Otherwise, you can use Postman to see how the REST APIs perform.

Once you create a ticket, you should be able to see it in the tickets dashboard in HubSpot.

Now that you have the Enterprise CRM ready, the next section moves on to the next step of gathering knowledge articles to set up the knowledge repository.

Setting Up the Knowledge Repository

Data in intelligent applications are the foundations on top of which the entire application works. Your data can be either the training set upon which your model is trained, or it can be the data that your model refers to while performing RAG. It can also be data that your application uses to manipulate while processing certain functions or features. In short, data is the cornerstone of your application.

Your data should be routed and processed properly before it arrives at the destination where your application will use it. Data engineering is a skill that needs to be mastered to understand how to route your data. With the rising need of intelligent applications, data engineering has emerged as a separate expertise that industries desire to keep their data and applications in good shape.

This example uses simple PDF documents as the data for this application. A separate chapter tackles the various data engineering concerns when building an end-to-end intelligent application for enterprise architects.

This example uses two PDFs from the same set of PDFs used in Chapter 4:

1. `monitor.pdf`

2. `printer.pdf`

See Chapter 4 to learn how you can gather these PDFs.

Now that the data repository is ready, you can proceed with the final part of building the bot.

Agents

Consider the pharmacy business as an example. Assuming that the pharmacy has one attendant who deals with customers and a backend employee who finds the medicines or bandages and places orders to the warehouse.

A regular day assumes the following business:

- A customer visits the store and asks for one of the following—medicine, non-medical products such as bandages, or some kind of diagnostic tool such as a glucometer.

- If they ask for medicine and if the medicine is in stock, the attendant asks the backend employee to get it from the self. The attendant then provides the customer with the medicine. Once the medicine is provided, the medicine ID is entered into the database to stock up. Since medicines are specific, they need to specifically enter the product details, unlike other products such as non-medical products, which might be filled monthly or quarterly at specific intervals in bulk.

- If the customer asks for a non-medical product, the item is provided right away as there is a regular stock up.

- If the customer asks for a diagnostic product, the attendant asks the backend employee to place an order and provide a tentative delivery date.

Consider for a moment only the medicines and the diagnostic tools. The sequence flow is visually represented in Figure 8-8.

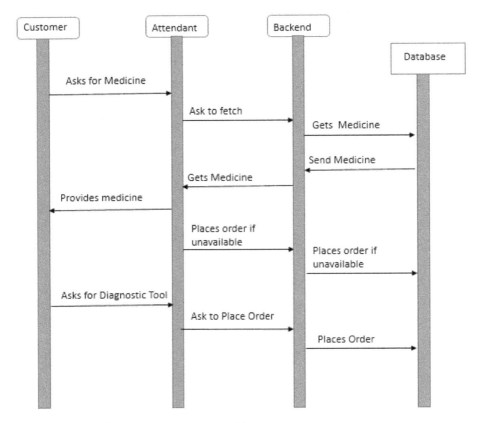

Figure 8-8. *Pharmacy sequence diagram*

If you think about the workflow, you should have realized that it's the attendant who is the decision maker. They discern between medical, non-medical, and diagnostic tool and direct the backend worker to perform accordingly.

In the digital era, where everything is attempted through automated apps, if you are asked to automate the pharmacy attendant role, you might imagine that there needs to be a chatbot that will interact with the user, a backend that can access the catalog database, and a system to place orders for unavailable medicines.

If you attempt to prepare a flowchart to build your workflow, there needs to be a decision-making mechanism, as shown in Figure 8-9.

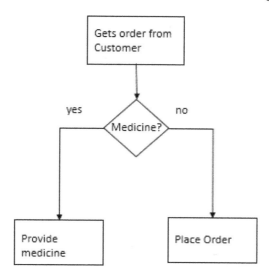

Figure 8-9. *Pharmacy flowchart*

Now let's get a bit more technical and think about modularizing the applications in terms of Generative AI. A very brief overview of the architecture of the application might look like Figure 8-10.

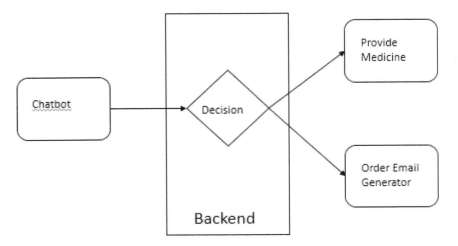

Figure 8-10. *Technical architecture*

As you can see in Figure 8-10, there is a chatbot that you can build using LangChain. Then you need a backend, possibly using Python. This backend should be able to access and interact with the database and decide whether the request is a medicine or a diagnostic tool. If it's a medicine, the backend can also trigger delivery of the medicine to the customer. In that case, the chatbot can leverage the database and send the details of the medicine. The bot backend can use RAG to get the details about the medicine. Otherwise, it places an order if the ask is a diagnostic tool.

Unfortunately, although the LangChain chatbot can connect to the database through RAG, it can't make the decision to perform either of the jobs—get the medicine details or place an order.

But what if I tell you that it can! Generative AI can!

Using LangChain, you can build tools for each task that you want your application to work on. In this case, the tools include an order tool for ordering a diagnostic tool by generating an email to the supplier or the warehouse, and another tool that provides the name and details of the medicine using RAG.

Your agent will be able to choose either of the paths, leveraging a carefully designed prompt.

Agents are now a go-to procedure to create powerful intelligent applications; they provide an easy way to divide and conquer. You understand the business requirements, plan and prepare the tools, as each module is supposed to perform a specific task. These set of tools will then be directed by agents driven by predefined prompts.

With the rising demand of intelligent applications, defining AI processes becomes more and more complex with every passing month. This has led to designing agentic patterns for Generative AI systems. Some of these patterns rely on a single agent driving multiple tools. Some of these patterns are multi-agent patterns, where either a single agent drives multiple agents which in turn drive their tools, or various agents working in a mesh network form a workflow. See Figure 8-11.

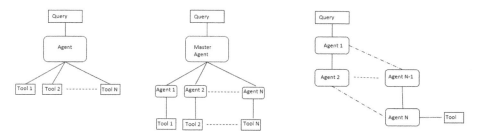

Figure 8-11. *Some agentic patterns*

Building the Bot

Now that you have a good idea about agents pertaining to Generative AI, this section returns to building the intelligent IT assistant. As of now, the Enterprise CRM Application (HubSpot) and the knowledgebase are ready. You now have to start building the bot that connects the CRM and knowledgebase so that your CRM has an automated way of understanding and raising a ticket.

Keep in mind that the bot will interact with the customer, use the knowledgebase from the PDFs using RAG, and connect to the enterprise CRM to raise a ticket. Let's use the agentic AI to drive this Python bot.

Pull up your Jupyter Notebook and start by setting up the vector database for the RAG.

Setting Up the Vector Database

To start, install the libraries:

```
! pip install -U langchain_community langchain-openai
langchainhub chromadb langchain langgraph pypdf
```

I don't think any of these libraries are new to you if you have been following along in the previous chapters.

The next step is to set your OpenAI API key to the environment and decide which LLM to use:

```
import os
from langchain_openai import ChatOpenAI

os.environ["OPENAI_API_KEY"] = 'Your API Key'

model = ChatOpenAI(model="gpt-3.5-turbo")
```

Follow these steps to ingest the `monitor.pdf` file into Vector DB:

- Use PyPDF to OCR the PDF text and split it into chunks (pages).

  ```
  from langchain_community.document_loaders import
  PyPDFLoader

  loader = PyPDFLoader("monitor.pdf")
  monitor_pages = loader.load_and_split()
  ```

- Now store this ingested text as embeddings into the ChromaDB vector store and prepare a LangChain retriever to be used later.

```
from langchain_openai import OpenAIEmbeddings

from langchain_community.vectorstores
import Chroma

vectore_store_monitor = Chroma.from_
documents(documents=monitor_pages,embedding=Open
AIEmbeddings())

retriever_monitor = vectore_store_monitor
.as_retriever()
```

- Use the steps you followed previously for processing printer.pdf:

```
loader = PyPDFLoader("printer.pdf")
printer_pages = loader.load_and_split()
vectore_store_printer = Chroma.from_
documents(documents=printer_pages,embedding=Open
AIEmbeddings())
retriever_printer = vectore_store_printer
.as_retriever()
```

The next step is to plan and prepare the agents.

Developing Agents in LangChain

As mentioned, you will use an agent to drive the bot. But before diving into developing this agentic AI pattern, you need to understand the purpose and workflow of the bot.

This bot will interact with the customer, whereby the customer will enter the issue or problem they are facing. The bot serves as the first line of defense in receiving the query and passing it on to the intelligent system to see whether a resolution can be derived out of the knowledgebases. If it can't, then it passes the mantle to the enterprise CRM by raising a ticket with the proper description of the issue.

One might think of this system as a chatbot system that uses an enterprise CRM to raise issues. That is one way to look at it. But the objective here is the other way round. You have an enhanced enterprise CRM that can raise a ticket by itself after understanding the issues. This is as opposed to having a human in the loop do the heavy lifting of searching through all the documents in the knowledgebase to find a resolution and filling in all the necessary information in the fields to raise a proper ticket in the CRM.

Let's plan the agent you are going to use.

As mentioned, agents use tools that are specific functionalities that perform certain tasks. Hence, this agent has to make a decision among the following:

- Decision: The query is about a monitor.

  Activity: Use the monitor RAG tool to RAG on the contents of `monitor.pdf`.

- Decision: The query is about a printer.

  Activity: Use the printer RAG tool to RAG on the contents of `printer.pdf`.

- Decision: The query is not about a monitor or a printer.

  Activity: Raise a ticket in the enterprise CRM (HubSpot in this case).

The agent should work something like Figure 8-12.

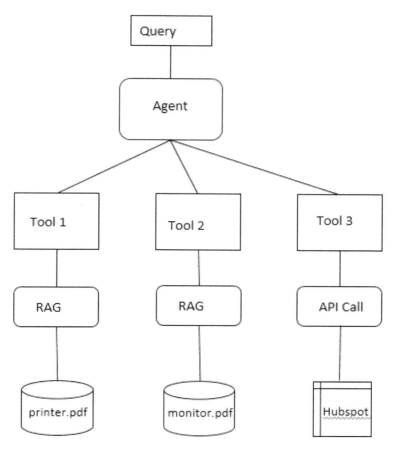

Figure 8-12. *IT assistant application architecture*

Now let's hit the keyboard and start developing the agent.

To begin, you have to create the tools, which are the functionalities that define the tasks the agents need to route to.

LangChain provides all kinds of wrappers to develop a fully functional agent. Use the @tool decorator of LangChain to create the tool that raises a ticket in HubSpot:

```
import requests
import json
```

```python
from langchain.agents import tool

# Get project id and api key
project_id = "<your-project-id>"
api_key = "<your-api-key>"

@tool
def raise_ticket(content_obj):
    """Creates ticket in ITSM portal with proper subject and
    description"""
    hs_pipeline = '0'
    hs_pipeline_stage = '1'
    obj = content_obj
    subject = obj['subject']
    content = obj['content']
    headers = {
        'Authorization': f'Bearer {api_key}',
        'Content-Type': 'application/json',
    }

    data = {
        "properties": {
            "subject": subject,
            "content": content,
            "hs_pipeline": hs_pipeline,
            "hs_pipeline_stage": hs_pipeline_stage,
            "hs_ticket_category": "IT_SUPPORT" # Example
            category - adjust as needed
        },
        "associations": [
            {
                "to": {
```

```
            "id": get_contact_id_by_email(obj['user_email'],
            api_key) # Assumes you have the user's email
            },
            "types": [
                {
                "associationCategory": "HUBSPOT_DEFINED",
                "associationTypeId": 4
                }
            ]
        }
    ]
}
url = f"https://api.hubapi.com/crm/v3/objects/tickets?
project={project_id}"
response = requests.post(url, headers=headers, json=data)

if response.status_code >= 200 and response.status_code
< 300:
    return f"Ticket created successfully with ID:
    {response.json().get('id')}"
else:
    return f"Error creating ticket: {response.status_code}
    - {response.text}"
```

If you go through this code, you will see that it is quite simply. It is a simple function that uses the argument passed in the function to derive the ticket contents and the description to send a POST request to the HubSpot REST API, as you saw previously, to raise a ticket. Two things worth mentioning: Note the use of the decorator @tool to use this function as a tool. This decorator is imported from the langchain.agents module. Since it will now act as a tool, you can invoke this function using invoke() as raise_ticket.invoke().

Another point worth mentioning is the docstring used after the first line of the function in """". This docstring should mention the purpose of the tool that will be used by agents while finding the appropriate tool for the task.

Now that this tool is ready, look at preparing the tool for calling the RAG pipeline. This tool is easier to develop—thanks to LangChain for coming up with `create_retriever_tool`. This function instantly derives a tool out of a retriever especially designed to perform RAG agents. The following code should make this clear:

```
from langchain.tools.retriever import create_retriever_tool

monitor_retriever_tool = create_retriever_tool(
    retriever_monitor,
    "vectordb_search_monitor",
    "Search for information about Computer Monitor
    troubleshooting. For any questions about troubleshooting
    computer monitors use this tool.",
)
```

As you can see, `create_retriever_tool` expects the retriever, a name for the tool, and a description to show the purpose of the tool, as was done previously using a docstring when using @tool.

The previous code showed how to create a tool out of the retriever that was derived from the ChromaDB vector database for the `monitor.pdf` text. You can develop a similar tool for the `printer.pdf` contents, as shown here:

```
printer_retriever_tool = create_retriever_tool(
    retriever_printer,
    "vectordb_search_printer",
    "Search for information about Printer troubleshooting.
    For any questions about troubleshooting printers use
    this tool.",
)
```

Now that the tools are ready, the next step is to create the agent.

The first step to creating the heart of the agent is to carefully design the prompt. This prompt will tell the agent where to route when a query arrives. To create this prompt, use ChatPromptTemplate as you did earlier. One additional system you need to add to the prompt is an agent scratchpad. This is memory that will be used by the agent to load and look at the tools you are associating your agent with. It will load and look into the purpose and description of the tools that you provided, either in a docstring or in a parameter, and it will make a decision to route to a particular agent based on these tools. The agent scratchpad should reside in a message placeholder within the prompt in order to make the prompt in the following format.,

Prompt for describing how to arrive at a decision and the output format.

> Description of tool 1 (residing in MessagePlaceholder)
>
> Description of tool 2 (residing in MessagePlaceholder).... so on..

The MessagePlaceholder allows LangChain to add certain text to the prompt at that particular position.

Similarly, if you also want to make the system conversational, you can add a memory to store the chat history. This can also reside in the message placeholder in your prompt:

```
from langchain_core.prompts import ChatPromptTemplate,
MessagesPlaceholder

ticket_prompt = ChatPromptTemplate.from_messages(
    [
        (
            "system",
```

```
        """You are a IT Support Assistant. If the input
        is a query regarding monitor then use the monitor
        retriever tool vectordb_search_monitor.
        If the input is a query regarding printer then use
        the printer retriever tool vectordb_search_printer.
        Otherwise use the raise ticket tool.
        If you are using the monitor or printer retriever
        tool then output should be the resolution text.
        If you are using the raise ticket tool then
        you have to create a proper subject line and
        description to be used to raise a ticket in the
        ITSM portal.
        Output should be of the format {{"subject":
        "Subject line generated","content":"Description
        content"}}""",
    ),
    MessagesPlaceholder(variable_name='chat_history',
    optional=True),
    ("user", "{input}"),
    MessagesPlaceholder(variable_name="agent_scratchpad"),
  ]
)
```

Now that the prompt for the agent is ready, you have to put these together—that is, the prompt, the tools, and the LLM—and create an agent. Use the create_tool_calling_agent function of langchain.agents to prepare a tool, as shown here:

```
from langchain.agents import create_tool_calling_agent

ticket_agent = create_tool_calling_agent(model, [monitor_
retriever_tool, printer_retriever_tool,raise_ticket],
ticket_prompt)
```

Your agent is ready!

But wait! How do you call the agent?

You can use an agent executor from `langchain.agents` that lets you stream the outputs in the format of its decision making.

```
from langchain.agents import AgentExecutor
ticket_agent_executor = AgentExecutor(agent=ticket_agent,
tools=[monitor_retriever_tool, printer_retriever_tool,raise_
ticket], verbose=True)
```

To stream the output while you call the agent with an input, use the following code:

```
list(ticket_agent_executor.stream({"input":"My monitor is
suddenly blank. What do I do?"}))
```

As you can see, the query is regarding a monitor, which should route the system to RAG from `monitor.pdf`.

The output I received was similar to this:

> **Entering new None chain...**

Invoking: `vectordb_search_monitor` with `{'query': 'monitor is blank'}`

Use the following steps to scan for corrupt files and fix them:
- **Click the Windows Start menu.**
- **Type "CMD."**
- **Right-click the Command Prompt and click Run as Administrator.**
- **Type sfc /scannow and press Enter.**
Advertisement[3]
Run a virus scan.
Check your computer for malware. Viruses or malware could be causing
... The full monitor.pdf content..

If the issue persists after trying these steps, it could indicate a faulty monitor or power supply. In that case, you may need to take it to a repair shop or consider purchasing a new one.

> **Finished chain.**

[{'actions': [ToolAgentAction(tool='vectordb_search_monitor', tool_input={'query': 'monitor is blank'}, log="\nInvoking: `vectordb_search_monitor` with `{'query': 'monitor is blank'}`\n\n\n", message_log=[AIMessageChunk(content='', additional_kwargs={'tool_calls': [{'index': 0, 'id': 'call_nJzEJjRrKtFTpDIHo68FruJA', 'function': {'arguments': '{"query":"monitor is blank"}', 'name': 'vectordb_search_monitor'}, 'type': 'function'}]}, response_metadata={'finish_reason': 'tool_calls', 'model_name': 'gpt-3.5-turbo-0125'}, id='run-48bd6fd5-51ce-463e-960a-f405dfbd601d',

..several tool calls to make a decision, done by the agent...

, tool_calls=[{'name': 'vectordb_search_monitor', 'args': {'query': 'monitor is blank'}, 'id': 'call_nJzEJjRrKtFTpDIHo68FruJA', 'type': 'tool_call'}], tool_call_chunks=[{'name': 'vectordb_search_monitor', 'args': '{"query":"monitor is blank"}', 'id': 'call_nJzEJjRrKtFTpDIHo68FruJA', 'index': 0, 'type': 'tool_call_chunk'}])], tool_call_id='call_nJzEJjRrKtFTpDIHo68FruJA'), observation='Advertisementgraphics driver. Use the following steps to scan for corrupt files and fix them:\n• Click the Windows Start menu.\n• Type "CMD."\n• Right-click the Command Prompt and click Run as Administrator.\n• Type sfc / scannow and press Enter.\nAdvertisement[3]\nRun a virus scan.\nCheck your computer for malware. Viruses or malware could be causing\nhardware problems on your computer that interfere with your monitor

```
...... the monitor.pdf page content that is relevant to the
query ....
```

```
teps, it could indicate a faulty monitor or power supply. In
that case, you may need to take it to a repair shop or consider
purchasing a new one.', additional_kwargs={}, response_
metadata={})]}]
```

You can try to query the agent about a printer as well. You should get
similar output, but from the printer.pdf.

But the moment of confidence will arrive once you query about
something else, such as a mouse:

```
list(ticket_agent_executor.stream({"input":"My mouse is not
working. I have tried restarting also but it doesnt work."}))
```

The output should call the raise_ticket tool and raise a ticket in the
HubSpot portal with the generated description and subject line.

Here is the output I received:

> **Entering new None chain...**

Invoking: `raise_ticket` with `{'content_obj': {'subject':
'Mouse Not Working', 'content': 'The user reported that the
mouse is not working despite restarting the system. Further
investigation is needed to troubleshoot the issue.'}}`

```
{'subject': 'Mouse Not Working', 'content': 'The user reported
that the mouse is not working despite restarting the system.
Further investigation is needed to troubleshoot the issue.'}
<class 'dict'>
[{'name': 'subject', 'value': 'Mouse Not Working'}, {'name':
'content', 'value': 'The user reported that the mouse is not
working despite restarting the system. Further investigation is
needed to troubleshoot the issue.'}, {'name': 'hs_pipeline',
'value': '0'}, {'name': 'hs_pipeline_stage', 'value': '1'}]
```

<Response [200]>A ticket has been raised for the issue regarding the mouse not working. Further investigation is needed to troubleshoot the problem.

> Finished chain.

```
[{'actions': [ToolAgentAction(tool='raise_ticket', tool_
input={'content_obj': {'subject': 'Mouse Not Working',
'content': 'The user reported
....
....
the problem.',
  'messages': [AIMessage(content='A ticket has been raised
for the issue regarding the mouse not working. Further
investigation is needed to troubleshoot the problem.',
additional_kwargs={}, response_metadata={})]}]
```

This output should convince you of the performance of your agent. Note the subject line and the content generated by the LLM that's passed to the agent in the form of a JSON object. Check your HubSpot portal for any ticket that is created. See Figure 8-13.

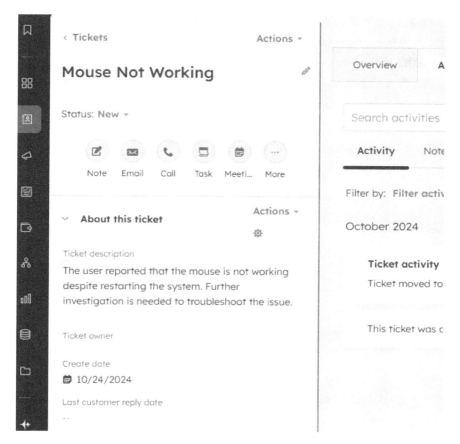

Figure 8-13. *HubSpot Ticket created by the AI agent*

Now that your enterprise CRM automation is ready and you are confident on enterprise integration using the agentic pattern, I suggest you try this technique with other enterprise applications. You'll be amazed by the power that agents can bring into the world of AI.

I also urge you to take this notebook and prepare a full-fledged application out of it, containing a Docker container to keep it environmentally agnostic. You can have an additional index.py file, which can serve as your entry point. You can have two routes—a loader route to load the PDFs for RAG and another route to receive the chatbot query.

You can also modularize your file structure so that it can have separate Python files as modules to act as tools and other ones to use in an agent. I leave the rest up to you as an exercise.

But don't be content just yet! Your data still resides in the project folder and you are still not handling databases or large data structures such as big data. The next chapter discusses handling such complicated data mesh in your AI application and explains how you can use various data formats and structures to aid your AI's workflow.

Summary

- Generative AI is the frontrunner in the current market, but a complete end-to-end system has a lot of tasks and workflows going underneath it. For example, a simple chatbot application has an intent recognition model, an entity recognition model, and a model to provide clarification queries or responses.

- To understand how to build end-to-end intelligent systems, an architect must adhere to the best practices of building a scalable architecture. This includes preparing an experimentation environment, a development environment, and the production pipelines.

- An AI engineer/developer should also master the concepts of web development, including mastering REST API integrations.

- Using Generative AI agents gives you the power to break your system into various systems and allows you to drive various systems with the power of Generative AI.

- LangChain and LangGraph allow you to develop agentic AI patterns easily.

CHAPTER 9

Data Pipelines in Generative AI

Data is a fundamental block of all applications. Data is to a molecule as an application is to an object. Data pipelines are necessary to engineer data coming from various sources in various formats, as data powers the intelligence in an intelligent application. This chapter discusses data. Covering all the aspects of data is difficult to do in one chapter. In fact, it is difficult to do in a single book. This chapter attempts to cover some of the aspects of data engineering that explain how data engineering pipelines fit into an intelligent Generative AI application.

Some common data formats, such as JSON, CSV, and XML are traditional. Some other formats, such as Avro and Parquet, are used for unconventional data formats and Big Data. Some data models, such as the relational data model, is used in everyday SQL. NoSQL bases its data structure on nonrelational data models.

You have to think about data storage issues when you deal with output and input. For example, data files for RAG can be gathered not only from local and on-premise file systems, but also from the cloud, such as in S3 buckets. AWS provides S3 buckets where you can store files in the cloud. If you don't have easy access to AWS or other clouds, you can use MinIO, which spins up S3-compatible clusters, and you can also use S3 bucket like services.

© Arindam Ganguly 2025
A. Ganguly, *Scaling Enterprise Solutions with Large Language Models*,
https://doi.org/10.1007/979-8-8688-1154-8_9

You can use boto3 to read file contents from S3 buckets and ingest data into vectorDB for RAG applications.

Apache Kafka is another component that you can add to your data pipelines if you want distributed data streaming. Kafka has Python SDK, which you can use in Flask applications. It uses the publish-subscribe concept, where you spin up a Kafka server and publish a data stream using a producer and subscribe using a consumer.

A Closer Look at Data

All system inputs and outputs are ultimately a forms of data. What varies is the format or the representation of the data.

For example, consider a system that generates video out of a prompt. The prompt you provide is text that represents the data format and so is the video that you get to see.

Now if you go deeper, everything is a string of bits (i.e., ones and zeros). So does data equate to a bit?

Data is a representation of information. For example, say the age of the customer is 23. This information can be translated to data as an input to a system (or algorithm) as follows:

```
{
    "Age":23
}
```

We all know that this format is a JSON and this in turn is a representation of the information. The JSON file is further broken down into binary so the computer can process it. Just like you can't talk in binary, a computer can't talk in words. Hence, a computer needs preprocessors to convert formats such as JSON to binary. But wait! Before that, you need to convert your information into JSON. Hence, humans need to know the various formats of data that a computer can take in and convert into binary.

File Formats

Previous chapters dealt with PDFs and other document files. This section looks at some of the formats that a large enterprise system can accept as input data.

JSON

One of the most popular data formats is JSON. JSON stands for JavaScript Object Notation and it represents data in the form of an object similar to how you do when you are defining a JavaScript object. Nonrelational databases such as MongoDB store data in this format. Most of the REST APIs use JSON as payload data and send responses in JSON format.

Although JSON format is used by MongoDB to store data, when you try to store images, MongoDB uses BSON (Binary JSON) to store the contents of the file.

CSV

CSV (or comma separated value) is probably the most intuitive data format and can be used to store structured data. By structured data, I mean that if there is a set of data, all the data has the same set of fields and subfields. You may relate CSV to tables. If you can imagine the data in the form of a table, you can use the CSV format of that data. CSV is also widely used when you want to import or export tabular data into databases or algorithms.

XML

XML data formats are similar to JSON except that you need tags like HTML (for example, `<id>123</id>`) instead of braces (`{ "id":123 }`). JSON is faster than XML when it comes to processing data due to its widely used format in several coding languages to represent objects.

The file formats mentioned here are traditional file formats often used in applications to store or transfer data. When the data is large and huge, developers turn to new technologies that can handle Big Data.

Avro and Parquet

Today's age is driven by large volumes of data. With each passing day, the overall volume of data increases and the entire world is consuming huge amounts of data. This might provoke you to ponder about the processing power needed to handle simple applications. For example, consider that your favorite search engine tries to find the appropriate link from the list of all the links in the whole world; this requires immense processing power. But apart from processing power, what you would also need is an appropriate way to represent and format your data for big data algorithms to accept, process, and output. One such format is Avro. The schema of Avro is out of the scope of this book, but it reformats JSON so as to allow faster processing of Big Data applications for search and retrieval. In brief, it tries to prepare a columnar representation for easy retrieval of large systems.

A similar data format is Parquet, which uses row-based representation and converts to a binary representation of the same.

Although these file formats are some of the most popular file representation formats used in the industry, always keep an open mind when visiting an application's data structure, as you might be introduced to some unknown data representation format. Sometimes some applications maintain their own file formats and schemas to maintain security and consistency.

Data Models and Data Storage

Data formats ensure data transfer and storage in a certain representation. You also need a data model to adapts your algorithm and system so that it can work seamlessly. Your data model should respect your database. There are generally two ways you can model your data—relational and nonrelational. Relational data models are used in SQL databases and nonrelational databases work with NoSQL databases. These databases serve as data storage formats and systems and they are used widely in almost all applications.

The other worth mentioning data storage system is the file storage system. In the current market scenario, files are either stored in on-premise folders or on cloud in containers such as buckets (for example, you will use S3 buckets of AWS later in this chapter).

With the advancement in technologies, graph-like data models have also become very popular. At the time of writing this book, vector databases are sometimes altered with knowledge graphs using Neo4j. Knowledge graphs allow data to be stored in the form of graphs, which allows better relational representation of data. This in turn allows easy retrieval of data leveraging semantic relations between data.

It might also interest you to know the internal data structures used by various databases to store the data such as B-Tree and hash tables. Although that is out of the scope of this book, do take some time to check them out on the Internet.

Data Processing Systems

Data processing systems define how your data will flow when you are deriving data from external systems. When deriving data from external systems you can either process it in batches or stream the data and process it. Batch processes take chunks of data broken into batches and process them independently. The other way is to set up message queues.

These message queues consume data in bits and pieces. The consumer system gathers the pieces and sends them together for the entire stream to process.

You will now stitch these together and learn to plan and build a data-intensive intelligent application to get an idea of how various data pipelines work in tandem with a Generative AI application. The responsibility of building efficient data pipelines lies with data engineers who work with AI engineers and data scientists to deliver the best results. This book is targeted mainly toward AI Architects, though, and as an AI architect, you need to understand all of the parts of an application or at least have an idea of how data pipelines work with AI. Also, you will never find a range of data files or PDFs being handed over to you to be processed directly. Your system will always expect a pipeline of input data sources. The application you are going to build now illustrates how to ingest data from various complex and standard data pipelines used in the current industry.

The Data-Intensive AI Assistant

The application that you are going to build now is a simple RAG application that answers users' queries based on PDF documents. The real challenge I want you to learn here is building real-life production grade data pipelines.

A simple RAG application should look like Figure 9-1.

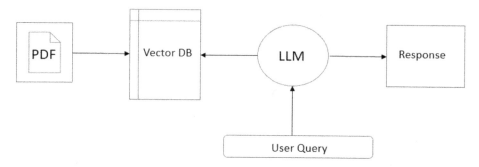

Figure 9-1. *Simple retrieval augmented generation*

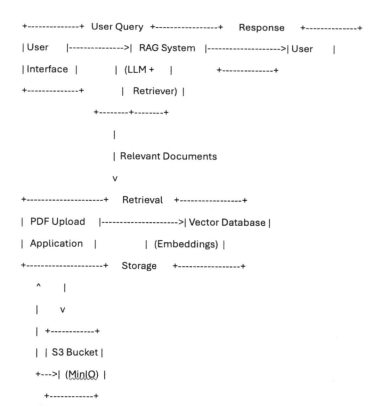

You have been building a RAG application like this since Chapter 5. But if you think about this carefully, the PDF document (or any other data source) is in the same working directory for the application to access it. But in the real world, these data sources are going to come from pipelines. You will try to set up a similar data pipeline for your document to be used in the RAG. You will also add other data pipelines for chat/query input as and try to prepare this as production grade as possible.

You will not do this in Jupyter Notebook this time. Pull up your favorite Python IDE or development studio and start by building a simple RAG application.

Start by creating a folder inside your working directory with the name of the app as /minio_app.

The first thing you are going to do is prepare the data pipeline to upload, store, and receive the data source of the RAG application.

In today's world, personal hardware storage is becoming near obsolete with the rise of cloud-based storage, which maintains all our personal artifacts such as photos and videos. You must have a smartphone with a cloud drive space to store all your artifacts; this is the same mechanism being adapted by large industries. Realize also that one of the main reasons large industries are adapting to this pattern is due to maintainability. Big enterprises spend a lot on on-premise storage hardware. Although the cost of hardware is declining, if you let popular cloud storage devices keep your data, these large cloud players also take the responsibility of maintaining your data which would otherwise be your infrastructure team's job. These large cloud players offer such reasonable prices for storing and maintaining your storage that it feels like pennies on a dollar when you compare it with maintaining your own devices with your own hardware and infrastructure team.

Most of the cloud players use the concept of buckets when storing your artifacts. AWS was one of the first cloud providers that introduced the concept of S3 (Simple Storage Service) buckets. These buckets act as individual storage providers that store artifacts.

You are going to use MinIO, which allows you to spin up storage service providers that resemble S3 buckets. You can visit MinIO official website at `https://min.io/`.

MinIO is suggested as a S3 provider, as an alternative to AWS or other S3 buckets in the cloud. If you have S3 bucket access or access to AWS or another cloud provider, feel free to skip the next section on setting up MinIO and use your S3 provider instead. I point out the place to add your credentials for S3 in the upcoming sections.

Setting up MinIO

To begin, set up MinIO in a Docker Container using the following Docker Compose file (`docker-compose.yml`):

```
version: '3'

services:

 minio:
    image: docker.io/bitnami/minio:2023.12.21-debian-11-r1
    ports:
      - '9000:9000'
      - '9001:9001'
    volumes:
      - 'minio_data:/data'
    environment:
      - MINIO_ROOT_USER=userid
      - MINIO_ROOT_PASSWORD=password
      - MINIO_DEFAULT_BUCKETS=mybucket1
    container_name: minio_application
    networks:
      - net

networks:
```

```
net:
  driver: bridge
```

```
volumes:
 minio_data:
  driver: local
```

This Docker Compose file, when it runs, spins up a MinIO service at ports 9000 and 9001. These are the default ports used when MinIO is set up. Port 9001 allows you to access a MinIO interface and Port 9000 accesses the MinIO APIs.

A user ID, password, and bucket ID are provided in the environment section.

Once you run the Docker Compose file (you should be familiar with running Docker Container since Chapter 4), you can open `127.0.0.1:9001` in your browser and you will be greeted with MinIO login page. See Figure 9-2.

Figure 9-2. *MinIO login page*

Log in using the user ID and password you added to your Docker Compose file; you should be able to see a page with a section mentioning your bucket ID, as you provided in your Docker Compose file as your default bucket. See Figure 9-3.

Figure 9-3. *MinIO buckets*

You can click it and you will land on a page that allows you to upload or remove files in the bucket. You can try adding a random file and removing it just to test the system.

A point worth mentioning is that all the artifacts that you store will reside inside the volume that you asked your Docker Compose file to mount, as `minio_data` in the last three lines of your `docker_compose.yml` file.

Upload File Application

Now that the S3 bucket is ready, this section shows you how to prepare a small application to upload a file in MinIO. It is easier to upload your file manually, but you need to have an interface for the users to upload files and you will use a Flask web application to do this.

367

Go to the application folder (/minio_app) and pull up your Python IDE. Start with a Python file to contain all your functions to upload files in S3. This example uses boto3 to interact with the S3 bucket. Boto3 was developed as an AWS SDK and is widely used to interact with S3 buckets. There is also a MinIO SDK, but it restricts users to only MinIO users.

Since you have Docker Compose to set up MinIO, keep your containerization ready as well. Create a requirement.txt file to add all the Python packages that you will need.

Add the following packages to requirement.txt as of now. You will continue adding more as you progress.

```
python-dotenv
boto3
Flask
```

Also add an .env file to keep your credentials safe with the following contents:

```
S3_ROOT_USER=user_id
S3_ROOT_PASSWORD=password
S3_DEFAULT_BUCKETS=mybucket1
```

The credentials should match the ones you provided in your docker-compose.yml file if you are using MinIO and running it using Docker Compose. If you are using cloud providers, such as AWS for your S3 bucket, add your AWS S3 credentials here.

You need to add a mechanism to trigger the ingestion of the uploaded PDF into the vector database. There are several ways to do this:

- **Option 1: Poll the S3 Bucket:** Create a separate script or service that periodically polls the S3 bucket for new files. When a new file is detected, download it, extract the text, generate the embeddings, and add them to the vector database.

- **Option 2: S3 Event Notifications (for AWS S3):** If you're using AWS S3, configure S3 event notifications to trigger a Lambda function whenever a new file is uploaded. The Lambda function can then download the file, process it, and update the vector database.

- **Option 3: Webhook from the Upload Application:** Modify the /upload route in your Flask application, in addition to uploading to S3. Also send a message to a message queue (e.g., Kafka) or trigger a separate service responsible for RAG ingestion.

- **Option 4: Direct Ingestion after Upload:** Modify the upload_file function to directly ingest the PDF into the vector database after uploading it to the S3 bucket. This is the simplest approach for might not be ideal for large files or high-volume uploads.

For this example, you'll implement Option 4 (direct ingestion). You will modify the s3_functions.py and index.py files to incorporate the vector database ingestion logic.

First, create the Python file called s3_functions.py to keep your Python function and upload a file using boto3 APIs. Later, you also need to add function to fetch the file and ingest it into your vector database.

Start by importing these packages:

```
from dotenv import load_dotenv
import os
#from io import BytesIO
#from PyPDF2 import PdfReader
import boto3
```

BytesIO and PDFReader read and ingest the file that's uploaded into the bucket (that's why they are commented out for now).

Load your S3 bucket credentials next:

```
load_dotenv()

s3_access_key = os.getenv("S3_ROOT_USER")
s3_secret_key = os.getenv("S3_ROOT_PASSWORD")
s3_bucket = os.getenv("S3_DEFAULT_BUCKETS")
```

Now you will need to create a S3 client using boto3.

```
s3 = boto3.client('s3',
                  endpoint_url='http://minio:9000',
                  aws_access_key_id=s3_access_key,
                  aws_secret_access_key=s3_secret_key)
```

The endpoint_url needs to be same as the endpoint URL you need to access your S3 APIs. Readers setting up MinIO on their machines using Docker Compose need to add the URL mentioned in the code. Readers who are not using containerization should use the localhost instead of MinIO (i.e., http://localhost:9000). Note port 9000 that I mentioned previously. Docker Compose uses the service name as the hostname. For other cloud providers, you need to check the endpoint URL of your S3 provider.

Now you are ready to create your upload function as follows:

```
def upload_file(filename):
    print(filename)
    s3.upload_file(os.path.join('/tmp', filename), s3_bucket,
    filename)
    return True
```

Boto3 makes it easy by providing easy SDKs for S3 APIs.

Now you need to create the index.py file that will use Flask to run. It will have a route /upload that will upload a file and put it into the S3 bucket.

Create the index.py file and add the code shown here to create a simple Flask application with an upload route:

```
from flask import Flask, request, render_template,jsonify
from s3_functions import upload_file

app = Flask(__name__)

@app.route("/upload",methods=['GET', 'POST'])
def upload():
    f = request.files["resource"]
    filename = f.filename
    f.save(os.path.join('/tmp', filename))
    upload_file(filename)

    return render_template("success.html")

@app.route("/home")
def home():
    return render_template("index.html")

@app.route("/")
def root():
    return render_template("index.html")

if __name__ == '__main__':

    app.run(host="0.0.0.0",port="5000")
```

Note the upload() function that serves the route (/upload). It takes in the file object from the request and saves it in a temporary location (/tmp) and then calls the upload_file function of the s3_functions Python file that you imported in the beginning. You reviewed this function earlier. After all this, it loads a success page.

There are also two routes (/home and /) that render the same index. html web page for the root and home page, respectively.

Now let's look at the HTML Jinja templates needed in the Flask application.

Create a folder called /templates inside the application folder in your workspace. Create the index.html file, which should contain the upload button to upload file.

```
<html>
    <head>
        <title>Upload Resource PDF</title>
    </head>
    <body>

        <form action="/upload" method=post enctype=multipart/
        form-data>
            <label for="resource">Upload PDF</label>
            <input type="file" id="resource" name="resource">
            <input type="submit">
        </form>
    </body>
```

This form posts the file data to the /upload route, which in turn calls the upload_file function in the route defined in the index.py file. Be sure to add enctype as multipart/form-data to let your form send the file data in proper format.

You also need to create a success.html file, which the /upload route should render after you successfully upload a file. This should be a simple HTML file as follows:

```
<html>
    <head>
        <title>File Upload Success</title>
    </head>
    <body>
```

```
<h3>File Upload Successful</h3>
    </body>
</html>
```

The last step is to add your containerization configurations. So, add a dockerfile for the Flask application as follows:

Dockerfile

```
FROM python:3.11

WORKDIR /app
COPY /minio_app/requirements.txt /app/
RUN pip install -r requirements.txt
COPY /minio_app/. /app
EXPOSE 5000

CMD ["python","index.py"]
```

This dockerfile is quite self-explanatory. Since the application is inside the minio_app folder in the workspace, you need to add the relative folder path as well.

Finally, use this dockerfile to spin up a service for the application in docker-compose.yml.

```
u_application:
   build:
     context: .
     dockerfile: ./minio_upload_app/Dockerfile
   ports:
     - '5000:5000'
   image: u_application
   container_name: u_application
   networks:
     - net
```

Be sure to add this to the `service.yml` element, like your MinIO service.

Now run Docker Compose and navigate to `localhost:5000`. You should be able to see a page with a form to upload a file. Browse and add a file. Once you add it, you can navigate to `localhost:9001` to your MinIO console. You should see the file you uploaded inside the bucket, as shown in Figure 9-4.

Figure 9-4.   *Uploaded file in S3 bucket*

Now that you the file upload application is ready, it's time to use the file being uploaded to RAG.

RAG from an S3 Bucket

In the workflow's first step, the users open the home page and can upload a document. Once their document is uploaded, they can then move to the chat page and ask questions based on the document.

Internally, once the document is uploaded, it should be ingested in a vector database. Now when the user types a query, an LLM should use the same vector database to retrieve context and the LLM in turn will generate an answer.

The first step is to add the following Python packages needed for RAG in the requirement.txt file:

```
langchain_community
langchain-openai
langchainhub
langchain-chroma
chromadb
langchain
pypdf2
openai
```

As you may have noticed, the vector database is ChromaDB and LangChain helps build the RAG using OpenAI LLMs. Pypdf2 is needed to OCR into the document you intend to ingest.

Next, you need to add the OpenAI API key to the .env file, as OPENAI_API_KEY.

Next, add the function to ingest the file from the bucket in s3_functions.py.

```
def get_file(filename):
    pdf_file = s3.get_object(Bucket=s3_bucket, Key=filename)[
        "Body"
    ].read()
    reader = PdfReader(BytesIO(pdf_file))
    page_texts = [page.extract_text() for page in reader.pages]
    return page_texts
```

Boto3 can fetch you objects inside your s3 bucket, but they come in a streaming object format. The get_object function of boto3 returns a dictionary, where the body element of the dictionary contains the streaming object. You can use the read() function to stream the object contents, but you have to wrap it with BytesIO from the io Python package to make the object readable as a Python bytes (or binary) object. Once you have the binary object, you can let PyPDF2 OCR it using PdfReader, as you did in the earlier chapters.

Now that you have a way to get the document contents from the S3 bucket, you'll add the other functionalities needed for a RAG.

Create a file called langchain_func.py in the application folder. It will contain the functions for data ingestion and generation.

You will use the official Python SDK from ChromaDB to create the client instead of using LangChain, but you will use LangChain to integrate it into the LLM and query it on the ingested data.

Start by importing the necessary Python packages:

```python
import os
from langchain_openai import ChatOpenAI
from langchain_community.document_loaders import PyPDFLoader
from langchain.docstore.document import Document
from langchain_openai import OpenAIEmbeddings
import chromadb
import chromadb.utils.embedding_functions as embedding_functions
from langchain_chroma import Chroma
from langchain_core.output_parsers import StrOutputParser
from langchain_core.prompts import ChatPromptTemplate
from langchain_core.runnables import RunnableParallel,
RunnablePassthrough
from dotenv import load_dotenv
```

The LangChain packages should be well known to you from the previous chapters. This code also imports the ChromaDB Python package from the ChromaDB Python SDK. It uses embedding_functions from chromadb.utils so that you can directly use this in the ChromaDB client from the ChromaDB Python SDK.

Next, you need to add your OpenAI credential from the `.env` file using `dotenv()`. Just add `dotenv()` and you are done.

You can now load your LLM and the embedding function from OpenAI using the following lines of code:

```
load_dotenv()

model = ChatOpenAI(model="gpt-3.5-turbo")

embeddings = embedding_functions.OpenAIEmbeddingFunction(
            api_key=os.getenv("OPENAI_API_KEY"),
            model_name="text-embedding-3-small"
        )
```

`Text-embedding-3-small` is one of the recommended embedding models that you can use from OpenAI when you are using models like `gpt-3.5-turbo`.

Now add the function to ingest and load your vector database:

```
# load document text into vectordb
def load_into_vectordb(texts):
    docs = []
    for text in texts:
        docs.append(Document(page_content=text.encode('utf-8'),
        metadata={}))
    client = chromadb.PersistentClient(path="/chroma")
    collection = client.get_or_create_collection("resources",
    embedding_function=embeddings)
    uids = ['uid'+str(i) for i in range(len(docs))]
    collection.add(documents=texts, ids=uids)
    return True
```

The `texts` parameter you see is the same array of page texts that you get from `get_file`, from `s3_functions.py`. The text content of a page is then encoded to UTF-8, a persistent ChromaDB collection is created, and the embedding function is configured. These page texts are added as documents to the collection. Note that you will need to add IDs to index each document (or page contents). You can generate IDs like in the function using a simple loop, generating uid1,uid2, and so on, or you can also generate random numbers.

Go to index.py and add this function to load the vector database as soon you upload the file in the bucket. Hence add the import statement as follows:

```
from langchain_func import load_into_vectordb
```

Then add the load_into_vectordb function call in the upload route function as follows:

```
@app.route("/upload",methods=['GET', 'POST'])
def upload():
    f = request.files["resource"]
    filename = f.filename
    #f.save("/tmp/tmp.pdf")
    f.save(os.path.join('/tmp', filename))
    upload_file(filename)
    load_into_vectordb(get_file(filename))
    return render_template("success.html")
```

Note that once the file is uploaded successfully, you use get_file to get the file contents and load it into vector database, using the load_into_vectordb function.

One other function you need to add to the langchian_func.py Python file is the one for querying the vector database:

```
def send_query(query):
    client = chromadb.PersistentClient(path="/chroma")
    vector_store = Chroma(
```

```
    client=client,
    collection_name="resources",
    embedding_function=OpenAIEmbeddings(model="text-
    embedding-3-small"),
)
retriever = vector_store.as_retriever()
template = """Answer the question based only on the
following context:
{context}

Question: {question}
"""

prompt = ChatPromptTemplate.from_template(template)
output_parser = StrOutputParser()
sr = RunnableParallel({"context":retriever, "question":Runna
blePassthrough()})
chain = sr | prompt | model | output_parser
return chain.invoke(query)
```

Here you use the same persistent client from the persistent storage
(/chroma), initiate the vector store using the Chroma client from
LangChain here (unlike the one you created in the previous function
from the ChromaDB package), and combine the other functionalities of
LangChain.

Similarly, you initiate the embedding function and retriever from
LangChain. In short, this function uses LangChain functionalities to make
life easier.

Finally, create the prompt, he output parser, and the chain so that you
can call the chain for the query that is passed as a parameter.

Come back to the index.py file and add some routes for the query
and RAG.

Add the following routes:

```python
@app.route("/chat")
def chat():
    return render_template("chat.html",res="")

@app.route("/send_message")
def send_message():
    query = request.args.get("message")

    res = send_query(query)

    return render_template("chat.html",res=res)
```

The /chat route will render the chat page for you to enter the query and send_message processes the query entered in the /chat route.

The chat.html template is the single HTML frontend that serves as the frontend for query processing. Create a chat.html file in the template folder as follows:

```html
<html>
    <head>
        <title>Chat</title>
    </head>
    <body>
        <hr/>
        <a href="/home">Home</a>    

        <hr/>
        <p>
            {{res}}
        </p>
        <hr/>
        <form action="/send_message" method="GET">
            Type your query</br>
```

```
        <input type="text" id="message" name="message" />
        <input type="submit" value="submit" id="submit" />
    </form>
  </body>
</html>
```

As you can see, the res variable is either blank (for the first launch of the page) or is the generated answer to the query based on RAG. The page also contains a form for the next query. Don't be vexed by the name chat, because you can easily convert this one-on-one Q&A into a chatbot if you can maintain the history and display it through a session. Do try it!

Don't forget to add the import statement for send_query as follows:

```
from langchain_func import send_query
```

For ease of access to the users, add a chat hyperlink as a menu in the index page (index.html inside the template folder), like the following before the form:

```
<a href="/chat">Chat</a>
```

Now start running Docker Compose. If everything works, you should see all services spinning up in the console (i.e., the application and the MinIO cluster).

Navigate to the MinIO console at localhost:9001 and then open the application at localhost:5000 in another tab. See Figure 9-5.

Figure 9-5. *The index home page*

Once you upload the file in the form from the home page, your document will be added to MinIO cluster in the backend. Once this is over, you should see the File Upload Successful success message, as shown in Figure 9-6.

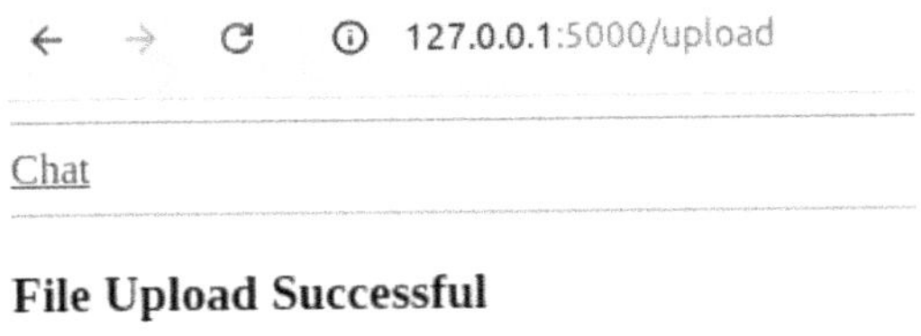

←   →   C   ⓘ   127.0.0.1:5000/upload

Chat

File Upload Successful

Figure 9-6. *The Success page*

You should see the chat menu at the top, where you need to navigate to start RAG Q&A. See Figure 9-7.

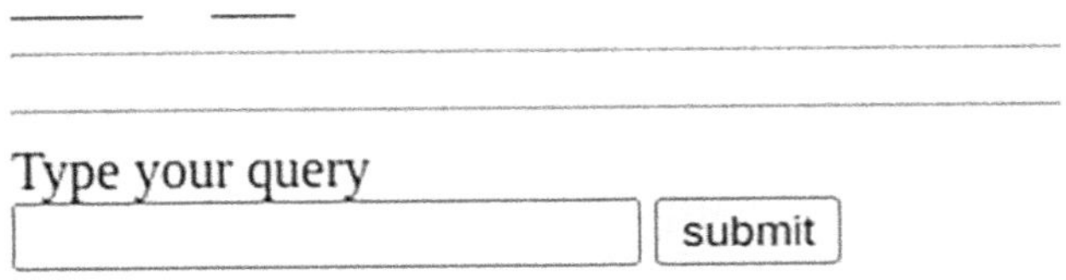

Type your query

[   ] [submit]

Figure 9-7. *The Chat page*

Now enter a query and click Submit. I uploaded a `seq2seq` model paper and asked, "What is neural network"?

If you see a conversational answer, you have successfully built a RAG application based on a document from the cloud, specifically a S3 bucket. Data source pipelines are generally used in real-life production applications in the current market scenario.

But don't be content yet! You can add another data pipeline to hone your data engineering skills for Generative AI applications.

Sometimes you have to deal with streaming data pipelines, especially when the application captures data real time. The next section introduces Apache Kafka for streaming analytics processing.

Apache Kafka for Streaming

Apache Kafka is a streaming processing platform written in Java and Scala and developed by the Apache software foundation. It helps you build a streaming pipeline and works in a pub-sub (publish-subscribe) mechanism in the form of a messaging queue. To learn more about Apache Kafka, visit `https://kafka.apache.org/`.

When you want to publish a message in Kafka, you have to push it into the producer. The producer stores it under a particular topic. Each message is published under a topic to categorize it. This message resides in the Kafka stream until you want to subscribe it. When a system is ready to subscribe, you have to call the consumer through a topic. The subscriber will yield the message as a stream. In between lies the Kafka broker, which takes care of transferring data between the producer and the consumer. Figure 9-8 visualizes this process.

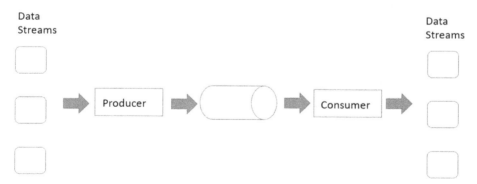

Figure 9-8. *Apache Kafka*

Apache Kafka has a Python SDK that you can use to try Kafka messaging. The next section explains this process.

Apache Kafka in Python

This section explains how to set up and use Kafka to stream a message in Python.

You will spin up Kafka in a Docker container, so the first step is to create a Docker-Compose.Yml file as follows:

```
version: '2'

services:

  zookeeper:
    container_name: zookeeper
    image: docker.io/bitnami/zookeeper:3.7
    ports:
      - "2181:2181"
    volumes:
      - "zookeeper_data:/bitnami"
    environment:
      - ALLOW_ANONYMOUS_LOGIN=yes

  kafka:
    container_name: kafka
    image: docker.io/bitnami/kafka:2
    ports:
      - "9092:9092"
      - "9093:9093"
    volumes:
      - "kafka_data:/bitnami"
    environment:
      - ALLOW_PLAINTEXT_LISTENER=yes
```

```yaml
      - KAFKA_CFG_ZOOKEEPER_CONNECT=zookeeper:2181
      - KAFKA_CFG_LISTENER_SECURITY_PROTOCOL_MAP=CLIENT:PLAINTE
    XT,EXTERNAL:PLAINTEXT
      - KAFKA_CFG_LISTENERS=CLIENT://:9092,EXTERNAL://:9093
      - KAFKA_CFG_ADVERTISED_LISTENERS=CLIENT://kafka:9092,
    EXTERNAL://localhost:9093
      - KAFKA_INTER_BROKER_LISTENER_NAME=CLIENT
    depends_on:
      - zookeeper

  kafka-ui:
    image: provectuslabs/kafka-ui
    container_name: kafka-ui
    ports:
      - "18080:8080"
    restart: always
    environment:
      - KAFKA_CLUSTERS_0_NAME=local
      - KAFKA_CLUSTERS_0_BOOTSTRAPSERVERS=kafka:9092
      - KAFKA_CLUSTERS_0_ZOOKEEPER=zookeeper:2181
    depends_on:
      - kafka
      - zookeeper

volumes:
  zookeeper_data:
    driver: local
  kafka_data:
    driver: local
```

A careful inspection of the Docker Compose file should tell you that there are three services:

- **Kafka:** This is the main service that spins a Kafka server.

- **Zookeeper:** Another Apache product that takes care of the server that Apache spinned up for Kafka and also the distributed processing that Kafka holds.

- **Kafka-UI:** Kafka-UI helps you visually check the topics, messages, and other details for the Kafka server.

Navigate to `localhost:18080` to see the Kafka UI. You can check the number of Kafka brokers, the topics, and the messages in the topics. See Figure 9-9.

Figure 9-9. *Kafka UI*

Now you'll learn how to use Python for message streaming. Open a Jupyter Notebook and start installing the Python SDK:

```
! pip install kafka-python
```

Next, start importing the Python packages:

```
import json
from kafka import KafkaProducer
```

Create a topic name and a JSON `dict` object, which you will use as a streaming message.

```
topic="mess"
data={"m":"Hi","u":"2"}
```

Now prepare a Kafka producer.

```
producer = KafkaProducer(bootstrap_servers='localhost:9093')
```

Since the Kafka server is spinned up at ports 9093 and 9092 in the Docker Compose file, you have to mention that server here as well.

You can use `KafkaProducer`, which was imported earlier, to publish it to the Kafka stream.

```
producer.send(topic,json.dumps(data).encode('utf-8'))
```

The reason for converting to a string and encoding to UTF-8 is so that you can ingest it as a string that `KafkaProducer` has no problem ingesting.

Don't forget to close the producer stream:

```
producer.close()
```

Now that the message is published, you can see how to subscribe to the message. Import `KafkaConsumer` to do this.

```
from kafka import KafkaConsumer
```

Now prepare the consumer using the following code.

```
consumer = KafkaConsumer(topic,
        bootstrap_servers=['localhost:9093'],
        consumer_timeout_ms=3000,
        auto_offset_reset='earliest',
        enable_auto_commit=True,
        value_deserializer=lambda x: json.loads(x.decode
        ('utf-8')))
```

What you see here is the server and some of the other parameters—such as `timeout` (in case you want your Kafka server to wait until it can successfully reach the server), `enable_auto_commit` (to let it save the message states), `auto_offset_reset` (for FIFO subscription), and `value_deserializer`, which is a postprocessor used to convert the string back to `dict`.

Now subscribe to the message from the consumer and check it out:

```
for msg in consumer:
    x = msg.value
    print(x)
```

You should see your dictionary that you ingested in the producer.

Now that you understand how Apache Kafka works, you can use it in your application.

Using Data Pipelines in AI Assistant

Before proceeding, you need to decide on the complete AI assistant and its data pipelines.

In production environments, data-intensive applications are designed so that they can handle multiple concurrent requests coming from various distributed sources at the same time and attain high network throughput. When you have multiple requests coming at a single moment, Kafka is one way to stream messages coming from various resources.

Kafka is also very efficient for data streams when there is a video streaming application sending data streams from multiple distributed sources at a single server.

In this application, you place a data pipeline that will take your chat as a stream and have Kafka publish it to the messaging server to put into your database. When the LLM generates a conversational answer, it will subscribe to your message stream and feed it into the database. Figure 9-10 shows the complete view of the data architecture of the data-intensive AI application.

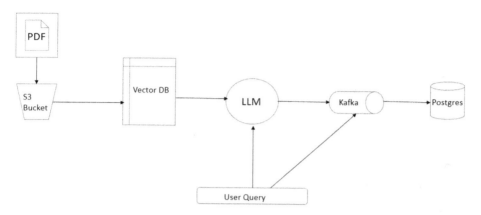

Figure 9-10. *The complete data-intensive AI application architecture*

It's time to start coding. Go back to your workspace and add the following services to the docker-compose.yml file:

```
postgres:
  image: postgres:14-alpine
  ports:
    - '5432:5432'
  volumes:
    - ~/apps/postgres:/var/lib/postgresql/data
  environment:
    - POSTGRES_PASSWORD=agpass
    - POSTGRES_USER=arindam
    - POSTGRES_DB=chat_db
  networks:
    - net

zookeeper:
  container_name: zookeeper
  image: docker.io/bitnami/zookeeper:3.7
  ports:
    - "2181:2181"
```

```
volumes:
  - "zookeeper_data:/bitnami"

environment:
 - ALLOW_ANONYMOUS_LOGIN=yes
networks:
  - net

kafka:
  container_name: kafka
  image: docker.io/bitnami/kafka:2
  ports:
    - "9092:9092"
    - "9093:9093"
  volumes:
    - "kafka_data:/bitnami"
  environment:
    - ALLOW_PLAINTEXT_LISTENER=yes
    - KAFKA_CFG_ZOOKEEPER_CONNECT=zookeeper:2181
    - KAFKA_CFG_LISTENER_SECURITY_PROTOCOL_MAP=CLIENT:PLAINTEXT,
    EXTERNAL:PLAINTEXT
    - KAFKA_CFG_LISTENERS=CLIENT://:9092,EXTERNAL://:9093
    - KAFKA_CFG_ADVERTISED_LISTENERS=CLIENT://kafka:9092,
    EXTERNAL://kafka:9093

    - KAFKA_INTER_BROKER_LISTENER_NAME=CLIENT
  networks:
    - net
  depends_on:

    - zookeeper

kafka-ui:
  image: provectuslabs/kafka-ui
```

```
container_name: kafka-ui
ports:
  - "18080:8080"
restart: always
environment:
  - KAFKA_CLUSTERS_0_NAME=local

  - KAFKA_CLUSTERS_0_BOOTSTRAPSERVERS=kafka:9092
  - KAFKA_CLUSTERS_0_ZOOKEEPER=zookeeper:2181
networks:
  - net
depends_on:
  - kafka
  - zookeeper
```

The first service runs a Postgres database. The next three services are zookeeper, kafka, and kafka UI, which you saw in the previous section. The only change is KAFKA_CFG_ADVERTISED_LISTENERS, where the localhost is replaced with the service name (i.e., Kafka:9093 for external access instead of localhost:9093). Feel free to change the credentials in the docker-compose. yml file to your needs.

Two additional things you need to add to your docker-compose.yml file are the dependencies for the Flask application and the volumes (or drives) added to the end.

Add these service names to the dependencies in your service application as follows:

```
depends_on:
    - kafka
    - postgres
    - zookeeper
```

Your final Flask application service should look like the following:

```
u_application:
  build:
    context: .
    dockerfile: ./minio_upload_app/Dockerfile
  ports:
    - '5000:5000'
  image: u_application
  container_name: u_application
  networks:
    - net
  depends_on:
    - kafka
    - postgres
    - zookeeper
```

Finally, at the very end of the docker-compose.yml file, be sure you have the following:

```
volumes:
 minio_data:
   driver: local
 zookeeper_data:
   driver: local
 kafka_data:
   driver: local
```

You should already have the minio_data driver volume. You will need to add volumes for zookeeper and kafka to allow them to store the data they are using.

When your docker-compose file is ready, start by adding the Python modules that will be needed for Apache Kafka.

Go to your application folder (/minio_app) and create a Python file for your Kafka producer module (producer.py). Then add the following code.

```python
import json
import datetime
from kafka import KafkaProducer

topic = 'message_stream'

def stream_produce(usr, msg):
    producer = KafkaProducer(bootstrap_servers='kafka:9093')
    data = {
        "message":msg,
        "user":usr,
        "time":str(datetime.datetime.now())
    }

    producer.send(topic,json.dumps(data).encode('utf-8'))
    producer.close()
```

The code is pretty straightforward; it works just as same as the producer part you wrote in the Jupyter Notebook in the previous section. The code starts by importing the required Python packages. The name of the topic should be maintained consistently in the producer and consumer modules. Finally, a function ingests a dict as a message in the KafkaProducer instance. The dictionary contains the following fields:

1.   message: The query or response text provided or generated.

2.   user: Identifies whether it is a user query (with the value user) or an LLM response (with the value bot).

3.   time: The timestamp of the provided or generated text.

The message and user ID are provided in the function as parameters from the index file and the timestamp is generated from the Python datetime package.

You need to create the consumer module next in another Python file called consumer.py and then add the following code:

```
from kafka import KafkaConsumer
import json
import psycopg2

topic = 'message_stream'
host = 'postgres'
port = '5432'
database = 'chat_db'
username = 'arindam'
password = 'agpass'

def get_connection():
    con = psycopg2.connect(database=database,user=username,password
    =password,host=host,port=port)
    cursor = con.cursor()
    return (con,cursor)

def stream_consume():
    print("Called stream_consume")
    consumer = KafkaConsumer(topic,
        bootstrap_servers=['kafka:9093'],
        consumer_timeout_ms=3000,
        auto_offset_reset='earliest',
        enable_auto_commit=True,
        value_deserializer=lambda x: json.loads(x.decode('utf-8')))

    for m in consumer:
        msg = m.value
```

```
try:
    con,cursor = get_connection()
    sql = f"insert into Chat (userid, message, timestamp)
    values ('{msg['user']}','{msg['message']}','{msg
    ['time']}')"
    cursor.execute(sql)
    con.commit()
except Exception as e:
    return repr(e)

return True
```

There are two functions here. The first one creates a database connection using psycopg2 for a Postgres connection. You used psycopg2 in Chapter 4 when working with the Postgres database in Python. Make sure to check it out if you need a refresher.

The other function—stream_consume—is the one you'll focus on here. You are doing the same thing in this function that you did in the Jupyter Notebook when you explored Apache Kafka using Python. Here, you are not passing or using any function parameters because you want to subscribe to all the messages that the stream produced. When you are subscribing and receiving the message from the Kafka consumer, you insert the dict values into a Postgres database table.

But wait! You have to create the Chat table, right?

For that, you'll create another Python file for handling database functions called tables_init.py. Add the following code:

```
import psycopg2

conn = psycopg2.connect(database='chat_db', user='arindam',
        password='agpass', host='postgres', port='5432')

def create_tables():
    sql = "Create Table IF NOT EXISTS Chat (userid varchar,
    message varchar, timestamp varchar)"
```

```
cursor = conn.cursor()
cursor.execute(sql)
conn.commit()
conn.close()

def get_values():
    con = psycopg2.connect(database='chat_db', user='arindam',
        password='agpass', host='postgres', port='5432')
    sql = "select userid,message,timestamp from Chat"

    cursor = con.cursor()
    cursor.execute(sql)
    rows = cursor.fetchall()
    print(rows)
    con.close()
    return rows
```

Before running through the code, note the database credentials that
are there, right inside the codebase, instead of in an environment file. I
leave this to you as an exercise.

Let's look at the code in consumer.py now. You should be able to
understand this if you are familiar with psycopg2 and Postgres SQL. The
create_tables(0 function creates a table called Chat with the exact
fields you used to insert into the consumer.py file—userid, message, and
timestamp.

To give your users a way to see the list of conversations that you are
storing in the database, you use the get_values() function. It lists all the
records in the database.

You will also need to build a UI and a router. This section explains how
to do that, step by step!

To create a frontend for users to view the conversations being stored
in the database, create an HTML template inside the /templates folder
called list.html and add the following lines of code to it:

```
<html>
    <head>
        <title>Messages</title>
    </head>
    <body>
        <h2>Messages</h2>
        <table border="1">
            {% for r in rows %}
            <tr>
                <td>{{r[0]}}</td>
                <td>{{r[1]}}</td>
                <td>{{r[2]}}</td>
            </tr>
            {% endfor %}
        </table>
    </body>
</html>
```

Assuming that you use a variable named rows to pass the list of records in the database from the Flask backend, the code simply displays the records in the database using a Jinja template.

Also create a route in the index.py file, as follows:

```
@app.route("/list_all", methods=['GET'])
def list_all():
    print("Called list_all")
    rows = get_values()
    return render_template("list.html",rows=rows)
```

This route uses the get_values() function you developed in the tables_init.py file. Add the following import statement to index.py:

```
from tables_init import create_tables, get_values
```

Don't forget to add the create_tables function in the main function. This will fire the function just before running the server in the application, so that the application finds the Chat table before accessing it.

```
if __name__ == '__main__':
    create_tables()
    app.run(host="0.0.0.0",port="5000")
```

Now you will add the producer and consumer functionalities in the send_message() function as follows:

```
@app.route("/send_message")
def send_message():
    query = request.args.get("message")
    stream_produce('user',query)
    res = send_query(query)
    stream_produce('bot',res)
    stream_consume()
    return render_template("chat.html",res=res)
```

The function works as follows:

- Gets the query from the user.

- Publishes the query to the Kafka message stream.

- Gets the LLM response using RAG.

- Publishes the LLM response to the Kafka message stream as well.

- Subscribes to the message stream data.

Don't forget to add the following import statements:

```
from producer import stream_produce
from consumer import stream_consume
```

Add a `list_all` route hyperlink to the `chat.html` so the users can check the message records any time:

```
<a href="/list_all">List</a>
```

Now you are ready to run your application.

Run the Docker Compose YAML; you should see a List link on your Chat page once your file upload is successful. See Figure 9-11.

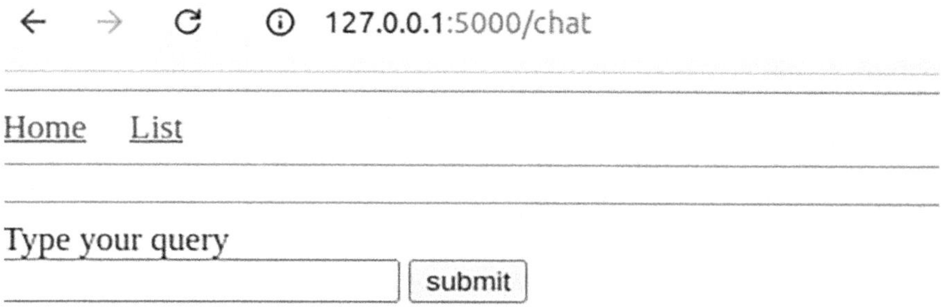

Figure 9-11. *The Query/Chat page*

Once you get a response from the query, you can click the List link to see the contents of your database. See Figure 9-12.

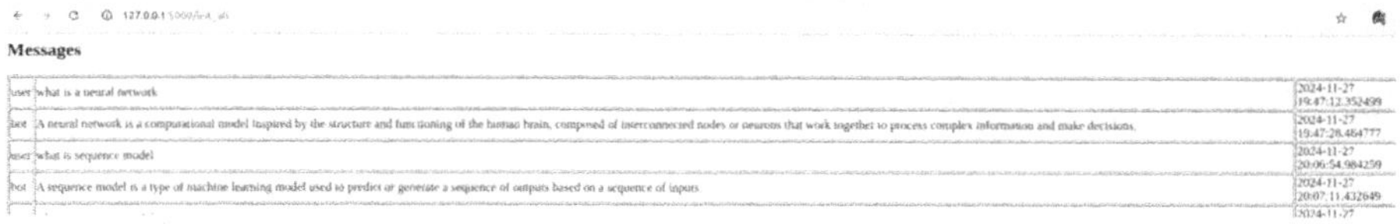

Figure 9-12. *Database records*

You can also browse to the topics in your Kafka UI and see the topic that is created. See Figure 9-13.

Figure 9-13. *Topics from Kafka UI*

To drill down further, click the topic and go to the Messages tab. You will be able to see the data messages that were sent if you expand the records, as shown in Figure 9-14.

Figure 9-14. *Message data from Kafka UI*

You have successfully implemented a data pipeline of multiple components in your application.

This chapter should instill the confidence in you to pull up a complicated data pipeline. One more thing I would like you to try is using Spark in between Kafka and the database so that you also get the hang of how Big Data can give your basket a lot of power.

Now that you have an in-depth understanding of how data pipelines work in tandem with intelligent Generated AI applications, the next chapter shows you how to bring it all together.

Summary

- Data is a fundamental building block of an intelligent system that allows your system to train and attend to the new dataset in real time. Hence, understanding the various aspects of managing data is essential in building an intelligent system.

- Although CSV, XML, and JSON are known by almost all developers, it is imperative to understand how to use these common data file formats in a large, intelligent enterprise system.

- Along with these common file formats some other data formats such as Avro and Parquet are essential when working with Big Data and streaming applications.

- Another important decision you need to address is the data modeling technique used to build the database. To cater to this, you need to understand the basic ideas of relational and nonrelational data modeling.

- Data storage on the cloud can be achieved easily using the S3 buckets that AWS pioneered. You can store any kind of data format on the cloud in S3 buckets and work with them by leveraging the boto3 Python library.

- To address real-time data requirements, you can use Apache Kafka for distributed data streaming.

- Finally, you can build a data-intensive RAG application by stitching all these technologies and concepts together.

CHAPTER 10

Putting It All Together

In the previous chapters, you saw all the gears and parts that drive an intelligent application through various perspectives. You saw the techniques that can be used to stir up intelligence and embed it in a complex, nonintelligent system. You have seen ways to containerize it and make the complete system environment-agnostic. Now that you know all the complexities, you also need to consider some of the ways to make the application as optimal and efficient as possible.

As an enterprise architect, you now know how to build an intelligent system and/or embed intelligence into a complex system. This chapter discusses some small alternatives and tricks to scale and optimize your strategies and achieve maximum effectiveness at minimal cost. To do this, the chapter reviews two approaches to getting the best out of Generative AI and machine learning:

- Minimizing your cost while maximizing efficiency.

- Maximizing system performance while incurring almost the same cost, effort, and time.

Preparing an intelligent solution for an enterprise application often requires architects to consider multiple variables such as budget, time, work hours, and so on. You have to make a tradeoff on compromising cost for efficiency or securing quality at minimal extra cost. You need to determine the optimal type of language models of the various parts of your application. You can use to small language models (SLMs) for trivial tasks.

© Arindam Ganguly 2025
A. Ganguly, *Scaling Enterprise Solutions with Large Language Models*,
https://doi.org/10.1007/979-8-8688-1154-8_10

One such SLM is Phi 3.5; it was developed by Microsoft and you can use it through HuggingFace.

On the other hand, if your budget is a bit larger, you can explore fine-tuning the LLMs. But to fine-tune LLM, you have to consider PEFT to reduce compute power and memory by using a technique known as LoRA.

At the time of writing this book, context length windows have been increasing with every new research paper and there is an ongoing debate to either fit large text into the LLM or use RAG through the LLM. You can also explore hybrid approaches through the LLM as a judge technique, using a technique known as self-route.

Option 1: Minimizing Cost while Maximum Efficiency

The first option is to analyze the ways you can minimize your cost as much as possible while receiving the same kind of efficiency. Here, you can compromise 10 percent on the quality at the expense of a 90 percent reduction in costs. To do this, you have to analyze the kind of intelligence you want your system to be assigned at the various modules. You may want to use a less intelligent model in some specific places in the system.

Determining Optimal Intelligence

When application development is in progress, the first decision is to not only plan on the intelligence and its technology, but also consider the cost implications. As an enterprise architect, your budget should always be a factor when you are considering or determining which technology to use. You'll see this with a familiar example.

Adding Further Analytics to AI Assistant Dashboard

If you have been following along in the previous chapters, you have the AI Assistant application implemented and running. In this section, you'll accommodate a minor addition where the dashboard also expresses the sentiment of the chats. A lot of industries (especially ones dealing in contact centers) try to monitor the sentiment analysis of the conversations in order to improve on the existing products or keep track of the services being rendered to their customers.

Sentiments give you insights into the overall performance of your industry through customer interactions. If you monitor most of the chats and analyze their sentiments, you can capture and point out the sections that indicate bad sentiments and the ones with good sentiments to forecast your next set of actions.

For instance, detecting negative sentiment in user interactions with the IT assistant could help identify areas where the system is failing to meet user needs, highlight potential problems with IT infrastructure or services, or even signal the need for additional training for the support team. This sentiment information could be displayed on a dashboard, providing valuable insights for IT managers and executives.

Considering the immense power that Generative AI brings, it should you can very easily employ an LLM that will be invoked every time a chat record is entered into the database and record the sentiment of the chat. See Figure 10-1.

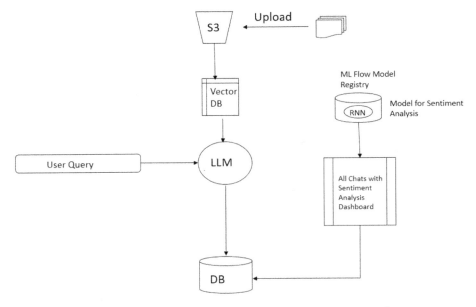

Figure 10-1. *Adding traditional RNN for sentiment analysis*

Sentiment analysis is one of the basic predictive analytics that even the smallest and least powerful model can help with. With OpenAI, you can employ even the most basic GPT3.5 Turbo to take care of it (at the time of writing the book, GPT4 is the topmost performing model in OpenAI and is also the most expensive one; see `https://openai.com/api/pricing/`).

Think about this solution carefully in terms of factors such as cost, efficiency, and work hours. You can use the same GPT model that you have been using in the application for other purposes, but that would not help with operating costs, since OpenAI (and all other LLM providers for that matter) charges you for every API call. For every LLM call for a query response, you are employing two LLM calls—one for the query and one for the answer.

Total Cost = cost(LLM call for query response) + cost(LLM for sentiment of query) + cost(LLM for sentiment of response)

Where

> `cost(LLM call for query response)`: The cost of the LLM call to generate a response to the user's query using the RAG system.
>
> `cost(LLM for sentiment of query)`: The cost of the LLM call to analyze the sentiment of the user's query.
>
> `cost(LLM for sentiment of response)`: The cost of the LLM call to analyze the sentiment of the LLM's generated response.

Thus, your cost just tripled if you use the same LLM for all purposes.

If you could instead use the least expensive model, it would bring your cost down to some extent. You can bring the cost down to double your operating cost for LLMs if the LLM you select to analyze sentiment is half the cost of the main LLM you are using for the purpose of Q&A.

Hence, if a smaller, cheaper LLM is used for sentiment analysis:

Total Cost = cost(Main LLM for query response) + cost(Smaller LLM for sentiment of query) + cost(Smaller LLM for sentiment of response)

Also, if a traditional ML model is used for sentiment analysis:

Total Cost = cost(LLM call for query response) + cost(Training and deploying traditional model)

It's worth mentioning that cost (training and deploying traditional model) is only charged during retraining.

An alternative way to go is to use a traditional ML model to do this, instead of an LLM. You can very well train a simple RNN and employ it to predict the sentiment of each chat. This will reduce your cost for sentiment analysis to zero except for a repository to keep your model. Let's analyze this route and look at the positive and negative implications this can lead to.

Training Data

Considering you are using a supervised model—be it a traditional model or a deep learning model—you need historical data. But a major concern of such a system is data collection. In this case, the best approach is to gather previous conversation logs as training data. If your system is a development from scratch and a new project, it is not possible to have historical data. In that case, you can opt for another alternative, such as a cheap LLM or a SLM (SLM is covered soon).

Although the cost is accounted for, data collection and curation requires some extra effort, so it increases your person-cost a bit.

Model-Building Capability

Although sentiment analysis is very basic and easy to implement and any kind of simple modelling can achieve it, the concern is not sentiment analysis to be specific. You are trying to establish supporting intelligence that can be achieved by traditional modeling. Building a traditional model requires significant expertise and effort. Hence, if you are trying to use traditional modelling, you should consider the effort, cost, and time required to put the model in place. You should carefully analyze the resources you have, along with the time and cost.

Model Maintenance and Retraining

Traditional models require model monitor and maintenance and also require considerable expertise as compared to using LLMs, because they are pretrained and don't require retraining that you might need when using traditional models built on curated data. On the other side of the coin, having custom curated training data and frequent retraining ensures that your models are updated with your present circumstance. If you system attracts more young adults, then you can curate your data so that you can include their phrases and casual conversations rather than having more formal conversations.

On the other hand, if you are planning to go the LLM route to analyze sentiment, you can include some prompt examples to suit the needs when required.

The debate is endless, but you should definitely have all your considerations in place before committing to a particular technique.

Instead of using large language models to accumulate large amounts of cost, you can resort to using SLMs, which will relieve your billing to some extent. You will learn about SLMs in the next section.

Small Language Models

While we are on the topic of introducing new features that augment the current capability of the application, this section introduces another alternative that can save you time and money.

You have worked with and used LLMs for Generative AI. Generative AI came into existence with the inception of the Transformers architecture. But the rise of research and development in the field has led data scientists to come up with very powerful models that can now almost replace human intellect. But these LLMs are almost impossible for small to medium industries to host. They require powerful servers and multiple GPUs.

As a counterpart, data scientists have also come up with small language models (SLMs), which can easily run on smart devices, such as wearables, watches, smartphones, and other similar firmware. They can easily reside on your device and you can cut down on the network latency.

SLMs are decoder-only models derived from Transformer architectures and they have parameters ranging from 100 million to 5 billion. These models have been widely used in daily smart devices to cut down on the cost of hosting LLMs and to reduce the latency that LLM responses cause.

The next section explains one of the SLMs devised by Microsoft—Phi 3.5.

Phi 3.5

Phi 3.5 was designed by Microsoft as a successor to the Phi model family. This model has been trained on specifics set of documents that Microsoft has used for its earlier version of Phi models. It used high-quality images and various types of text for training.

Similar to other SLMs, it is a decoder-only Transformer model and is multilingual and 128K in context length.

Phi 3.5 has been released in multiple versions; the one used in this chapter is the Phi 3.5 MOE. MOE stands for Mixture of Experts and it tries to pull up a model that performs exactly as mentioned in the name—like a mixture of experts.

In MOE models, all the feed-forward dense neural network layers are replaced by a layer that contains multiple FFNs, each having its own capability. A gated network is learned by the model to route an input to the appropriate expert (FFN).

It is also noteworthy that most of the Generative AI models are named according to the objective they were trained for. For example, Phi-3.5-MOE-Instruct is an instruct model that aims to generate responses considering the input is a set of instructions for the model to perform.

Meta introduced the Llama model family, which had variations of training objectives. You will find that Llama instruct models as well as Llama chat models are specially trained to engage in colloquial conversations.

HuggingFace hosts the SLM and you can download and use it in your system. This section explains how to use HuggingFace and the Phi 3.5 MOE instruct model in Python.

Pull up your Jupyter Notebook and start by installing the following packages:

```
flash_attn==2.5.8
torch==2.3.1
accelerate==0.31.0
transformers==4.46.0
```

This exercise uses PyTorch instead of TensorFlow, which is a similar framework for deep learning. The transformers package is provided by HuggingFace to encapsulate Transformers in a package. The accelerate package is used to run PyTorch in a distributed environment in order to divide the processing into parallel threads. The flash_attn library encapsulates the Flash Attention mechanism, which is an effective technique to parallelize the attention calculation in order to achieve the most in the least amount of computation.

Now you have to import the packages:

```
import torch
from transformers import AutoModelForCausalLM, AutoTokenizer,
pipeline
```

Now load the model in AutoModelForCausalLM so that it can be downloaded in your system:

```
model = AutoModelForCausalLM.from_pretrained(
    "microsoft/Phi-3.5-MoE-instruct",
    device_map="cuda",
    torch_dtype="auto",
    trust_remote_code=False,
)
```

You should also load a tokenizer in a similar way:

```
tokenizer = AutoTokenizer.from_pretrained("microsoft/Phi-3.5-MoE-instruct")
```

Now it's time to set up the prompt to be sent to the model. Phi 3.5 expects prompts to be entered in a certain format:

> *System: You are a helpful AI assistant.*
>
> *Query: What are tokenizers?*
>
> *Response:*

To set up the similar prompt in Python, you'll prepare an array:

```
prompt= [
    {"role": "system", "content": "You are a helpful
    AI assistant that can answer queries on NLP."},
    {"role": "user", "content": "What are tokenizers?"},
]
```

Now you can create the transformers pipeline and ask the SLM to generate text using your pipeline.

```
pipe = pipeline(
    "text-generation",
    model=model,
    tokenizer=tokenizer,
)

args = {
    "max_new_tokens": 500,
    "return_full_text": False,
    "temperature": 0.2,
    "do_sample": False,
}
```

```
output = pipe(prompt, **args)
print(output[0]['generated_text'])
```

You should see a response similar to an LLM.

Let's come back to the IT assistant application you built. You can use this model as an optimal tradeoff; it has almost all the power of an LLM, without the huge computation and charges incurred by hypervisors such as Azure, AWS, or even OpenAI.

The next section explains another alternative, where you can even have the flexibility to fine-tune and train LLMs.

Option 2: Getting the Best Performance with the Same Cost

The second option is to get the best performance possible while incurring nearly the same cost, effort, and time. Here, you compromise a 10 percent increase in expenditure at the expense of a 90 percent increase in the quality. For this, you can attempt to fine-tune your Generative AI LLM with your own data or use an expensive model in some places in the system.

Fine-Tuning Large Language Models

As mentioned, all the LLMs require a significant amount of storage and compute power to run. But you should not also forget the amount of compute power needed to train these models. Companies such as OpenAI, Amazon, IBM, and so on, are heavily invested in pulling up an infrastructure that can accommodate an immense amount of compute capability to train large models from scratch. Just so that you get an idea—for a computer with the capability to perform 10^{18} computations per second, it would take the system approximately 3.5 days to train GPT3, which is the older version of the GPT models.

You are probably not thinking about establishing a server farm to host a powerful LLM right now! It would be almost impossible to train a large language model locally. But what if you intend to fine-tune the model to suit your needs, similar to the fine-tuning exercise you performed in Chapter 3 for BERT? If you followed along in Chapter 3, you must have already felt the pain that your system endured while you tried to run your fine-tuning exercise. It must have taken an enormous amount of time and processing power to converge the training to a certain loss and accuracy just for BERT. Now consider that you try to push the same data in your LLM!

Keeping this in mind, data scientists came up with a novel approach to reduce the burden on compute power while fine-tuning LLMs (or any language model for that matter), which you see in the next section.

Parameter Efficient Fine Tuning (PEFT)

With the widespread use of LLMs and LLMs becoming the new tool for everything, it is inevitable to have a way to fine-tune and/or pretrain. But fine-tuning such a large model is not the best solution when it comes to achieving high performance at scale. It is very easy to understand the difficulties in fine-tuning such a large model that itself takes such a large amount of compute power to load and run. If you try to fine-tune the complete model with some custom data, it will demand enormous amounts of compute and processing power.

If you load a model into memory or train it with data, the heart of the model that is recalibrated and calculated is the weight matrix. The weight matrix determines the number of parameters that the model is supposed to learn and use to predict a new set of data. For instance, OpenAI's GPT4 is estimated to have around 1.76 trillion parameters. You can fairly imagine that operating such a model offline would require immense compute power and memory. Hence, fine-tuning trillions of parameters is out of question for a simple server.

But what if you could come up with techniques that could reduce the number of parameters while training? Another way to look at it is training only a certain number of parameters that are sufficient to lead to the same effect as training the complete model. Such a technique is known as PEFT (Parameter Efficient Fine Tuning).

PEFT states that instead of training the whole model, you train only a certain number of layers and keep the others frozen.

One method often associated with PEFT is LoRA (Low Rank Adaptation), which leverages a simple mathematical concept. The next section explains this method.

Low Rank Adaptation (LoRA)

LoRA had been into production since GPT3 but had not been used with such popularity until the inception of models such as GPT4 and Claude-3. You can check out the paper at https://arxiv.org/pdf/2106.09685.pdf.

LoRA is a parameter-efficient fine-tuning technique that leverages the concept of rank in matrices, since the main object you are training is the weight matrix.

A rank of a matrix is the number of linearly independent rows and columns. Rank of a matrix of dimension 3x3 can be anywhere between 1 and 3. LoRA attempts to take a lower rank version of the weight matrices. There is a very simple way to do that! Consider a weight matrix of size dxd. LoRA decomposes the matrix into a dxr matrix and a rxd matrix so that the memory needed to operate them is less than the dxd matrix. This decomposition can be done using a technique known *as singular value decomposition,* which breaks a matrix down into three matrices—U, Σ, and V where Σ is a diagonal matrix Of dimension rxr, U having dimension dxr and V having dimension rxd (see Figure 10-2). The detailed mathematics are complicated and involve core aspects of linear algebra, which is out of the scope of this book.

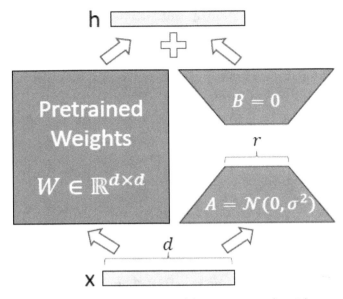

Figure 10-2. *LoRA (Credit:* $https://arxiv.org/pdf/2106.$
$09685.pdf)$

Being an enterprise architect and a developer, you should be eagerly awaiting to see how to get hold of all of these in Python. The next section covers this.

Implementing PEFT LoRA in Python

I suggest that you to try this exercise in Google Colab and enable the TPU or GPU settings. The data you are going to use is from a competition from Kaggle that closed years ago. You can use the data anyway even if you are not participating in the competition.

This competition was initiated by Alex Ellis, Julia Elliott, Paula Griffin, and William Chen, and it aims at finding questions in Quora that are insincere. That is, instead of looking for genuine knowledge, the question aims to make a statement. The dataset is a simple labeled dataset with questions and a label indicating whether they are sincere. You can visit

this link and check out the details: `https://kaggle.com/competitions/
quora-insincere-questions-classification`.

You can also implement this exercise in Kaggle if you have a login.
Otherwise, you can download the dataset and try it in Google Colabatory.

Pull up your Jupyter Notebook, either in Google Colabatory or Kaggle,
and start by loading the data:

```
import numpy as np
import pandas as pd
data = pd.read_csv("/kaggle/input/quora-insincere-questions-
classification/train.csv", nrows=500)
```

The `train.csv` file contains the training data and I only use the first
500 rows, as it would otherwise be impossible to run it in a shared hosted
environment such as Google Colabatory or Kaggle.

The next step is to install all the required packages:

```
! pip install transformers accelerate bitsandbytes peft
datasets
```

Among all the libraries being installed here, you have already seen
`transformers` and `accelerate`. The `datasets` library is used to create
data loaders compatible with neural network libraries. The `bitsandbytes`
library is a lightweight package that allows you to maintain 32-bit
performance at a small fraction of the memory. The `peft` library tells you
its significance by the name.

The next step is to convert the `pandas` dataframe to the `datasets`
format to directly use it in a training algorithm. Since there are 500 data
rows, you'll have 400 training data rows and 100 test data rows.

```
from datasets import Dataset

train_ds = Dataset.from_pandas(data[:400])
test_ds = Dataset.from_pandas(data[400:])
```

Now you invoke the model that you want to fine-tune. This exercise uses a simple model such as Google Flan T5, and use the same as a tokenizer.

```
from transformers import AutoTokenizer, AutoModelForSeq2SeqLM

tokenizer = AutoTokenizer.from_pretrained("google/flan-t5-small")
model = AutoModelForSeq2SeqLM.from_pretrained("google/flan-t5-small",load_in_8bit=True)
```

Note in the last line of this code snippet, where the model is downloaded, the parameter load_in_8bit is true. This enables the model to be downloaded into 8-bit quantized blocks for easy quantization and memory efficiency.

To start fine-tuning using PEFT, you have to prepare your model to be capable enough for LoRA to work on. For that, you have to make sure all your model matrices are stored in a 8-bit quantized format and have full precision for float numbers, have gradients ready to be calculated, and have memory checkpointing enabled so your system memory is efficient. The following code does this:

```
from peft import prepare_model_for_int8_training

model = prepare_model_for_int8_training(model)
```

Now you have to set up the configurations for LoRA as follows:

```
from peft import LoraConfig, get_peft_model

loraconfig =LoraConfig(r=16, lora_alpha=32, target_modules=['q','v'], lora_dropout=0.05, bias="none", task_type="SEQ_2_SEQ_LM")
```

LoRA needs to decompose a dxd weight matrix to dxr and rxd, so you have to mention the parameter r for LoRA to decompose it into. This parameter is mentioned as the first parameter value r. `lora_alpha` is a hyperparameter for scaling. The `target_modules` parameter names which parameter LoRA should be applied to. In this case, you are applying it to query and value, and not the key. Finally, `task_type` defines the task you want your data to be fine-tuned for.

Finally, add this configuration to the model instance prepared for fine-tuning using PEFT:

```
model = get_peft_model(model,loraconfig)
```

The next step is to prepare the data for training. If you are training using a text dataset, you need a function to convert each statement into numerical vectors. This step takes care of that process:

```
def tokenize_function(examples):
    return tokenizer(examples["question_text"], padding="max_
    length", truncation=True)

text_column = "question_text"
label_column = "target"
max_length = 128

def preprocess_function(examples):
    inputs = examples[text_column]
    targets = [str(x) for x in examples[label_column]]
    model_inputs = tokenizer(inputs, max_length=max_length,
    padding="max_length", truncation=True, return_tensors="np")

    labels = tokenizer(targets, max_length=3, padding="max_
    length", truncation=True, return_tensors="np")
```

```
labels = labels["input_ids"]
labels[labels == tokenizer.pad_token_id] = -100
model_inputs["labels"] = labels

return model_inputs
```

This code tells you a very obvious story. The tokenize_function is used to tokenize a statement using Flan T5. Finally in the preprocess_ function you tokenize each statement and label.

Finally, when you have the desired formatted inputs and labels, prepare your train and test dataset as follows:

```
train_dataset = train_ds.map(
    preprocess_function,
    batched=True,
    num_proc=1,
    remove_columns=data.columns.tolist(),
    load_from_cache_file=False,
    desc="Running tokenizer on dataset",
)

test_dataset = test_ds.map(
    preprocess_function,
    batched=True,
    num_proc=1,
    remove_columns=data.columns.tolist(),
    load_from_cache_file=False,
    desc="Running tokenizer on dataset",
)
```

As you can see, you map the dataset to the preprocess_function created in the previous step. Make sure to keep load_from_cache_file set to false so the system does not use repeated data and gradients. Also keep batched set to true for efficient parallel computation in memory.

You need to prepare the training arguments and the trainer as follows:

```
from transformers import TrainingArguments, Trainer

training_args = TrainingArguments(
    "temp",
    evaluation_strategy="epoch",
    learning_rate=1e-3,
    gradient_accumulation_steps=1,
    auto_find_batch_size=True,
    num_train_epochs=1,
    save_steps=100,
    save_total_limit=8,
    report_to="none"
)
trainer = Trainer(
    model=model,
    args=training_args,
    train_dataset=train_dataset,
    eval_dataset=test_dataset,
)
model.config.use_cache = False
```

The training arguments mention hyperparameters like learning rate, when to save the step results, when to release the accumulated gradients, and the number of epochs. The auto_find_batch_size if set to false; otherwise, you would have to provide the number of batches per epochs.

The trainer is an encapsulation of an executable model to start training. Hence, finally, you can start training as follows:

```
trainer.train()
```

If everything is fine, you should see your model has started training. Congratulations! You have just fine-tuned an LLM.

"With Great Power Comes Great Responsibility!"

You probably have felt how power-hungry your fine-tuning exercise was if you ran the exercise. You must be very careful to determine when you can use this technique and it must be used only when you absolutely need it. Using it everywhere will drain your compute resources and as well as budget!

Before winding up, I give you one last trick to increase your efficiency.

Long Context LLM and RAG

At the time of writing this book, there have been a lot of enhancements in the two main fields—inventing various techniques for RAG and developing various models with longer context lengths.

At the time of writing this book, Google's Gemini 1.5 has been introduced and it can process up to 1 million tokens. This is compared to its previous versions, which had a context window length of 32K tokens. Hence with time, the number of context window lengths has been increasing.

Consider an IT Assistant where the system needs to answer certain queries based on some text passages from a document. It is quite obvious that LLMs perform the best when they have the complete context passage loaded into their memory instead of using RAG to load multiple chunks of context passages, which can lead to gaps in knowledge. Unfortunately, nothing is free and using long-context LLMs is definitely more expensive, mostly because the LLM providers charge you by the token length per API call for the LLM.

The tradeoff between long-context LLMs and RAG is an ongoing debate right now. There have been multiple survey papers written on this topic. But it is best to use a hybrid approach to determine which part of the system can use long context LLMs and where you can use RAG with less expensive models.

Self-Routing

Consider a system where you have to develop a conversational assistant that can respond to queries from a document. A hybrid approach to determine and use both long context LLM and RAG is to use LLM as a judge. Let's break down this approach into two steps:

- **Step 1:** Get a retriever to retrieve text passages for RAG. Employ an LLM as a judge to respond to the following prompt, given the retrieved text passage and the query: "Write unanswerable if the query cannot be answered based on the provided text."

- **Step 2:** Based on the answer, the system can decide to either employ RAG with shorter context window length LLMs or have the long context LLM respond with the full text in its context window.

This is the self-route idea, which explores which approach is better based on the current developments—long context LLM or RAG. This paper also mentions an alternative as a hybrid instead of getting stuck in the debate. You can read the paper at https://arxiv.org/abs/2407.16833.

Figure 10-3 visualizes the self-route approach.

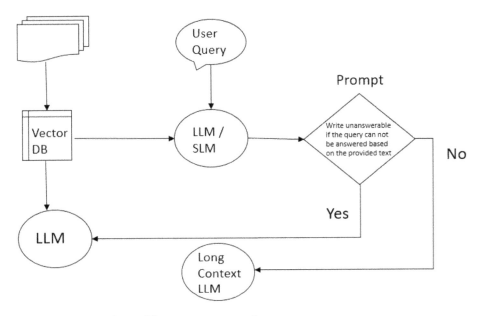

Figure 10-3. *The self-route approach*

It is difficult to ingest a complete document into a context window of an LLM if the document is fairly large. Hence, this idea usually works when the complete document you want to let your LLM hold is less than the context window length of the long context LLM.

Summary

As you reach the end of this chapter as well as the book, I suggest that you expand your horizons while architecting an intelligent enterprise application.

When you have to come up with a solution for a complicated enterprise application, analyze your business requirements carefully and note the skills and techniques you will need for this development, including various options. Certain modules might require Generative AI, but it is not necessary to use LLMs when the goal can be achieved using SLMs. In such cases, explore both the options. Note and plan all the routes, including all the options.

Try to come up with a mix and match of various options and try to develop a hybrid approach. Hybrid approaches generally constitute adversarial technologies with a decision management system taking control of the routes.

Always keep in mind that there is no perfect system and your job is to pursue perfection, knowing that it's never absolute.

With this, I leave the task to you and wish you success in your endeavors in the world of intelligent applications. Happy learning!

Index

© Arindam Ganguly 2025
A. Ganguly, *Scaling Enterprise Solutions with Large Language Models*,
https://doi.org/10.1007/979-8-8688-1154-8

M

N

P

S

GPSR Compliance
The European Union's (EU) General Product Safety Regulation (GPSR) is a set
of rules that requires consumer products to be safe and our obligations to
ensure this.

If you have any concerns about our products, you can contact us on

ProductSafety@springernature.com

In case Publisher is established outside the EU, the EU authorized
representative is:

Springer Nature Customer Service Center GmbH
Europaplatz 3
69115 Heidelberg, Germany